THREE FOR SHIP

A Swan Song To Dartmouth Beer Pong

Crispus Knight

THREE FOR SHIP
A Swan Song to Dartmouth Beer Pong
By Crispus Knight

Published by Fuzzy Plum Press, Brooklyn, NY
Please visit the website at www.threeforship.com

ISBN: 978-0-615-98632-6

Printed in the USA

First Paperback Printing April 2014
e d c b a

THREE FOR SHIP

A Swan Song To Dartmouth Beer Pong

Crispus Knight

FUZZY PLUM PRESS

Brooklyn

Contents

A Note from the Author

At many points during the arduous ten-year journey of finishing this book I have questioned both my motives for writing it and the wisdom of actually publishing it. In the end, I decided the pros outweighed the cons and that as long as I could tell my story in a truthful and responsible way then maybe this was a story worthy of being told.

In various sections throughout the text I have deliberately ignored the conventional wisdom of maintaining consistent use of tenses strictly as a narrative device to illuminate the major themes I wanted to convey. You may find it jarring at first but I implore you to bear with me as I attempt to tell my story.

The lifestyle I lived and breathed is not reflective of the vast majority of Dartmouth's CFS members or its student population in general, though events such as I describe did take place on campus during the early 2000's. I don't pretend to speak for the Greek system, nor is my intent to present a defense or condemnation of these organizations for political reasons. Mine is only one of many such tales of wasted youth unfolding behind a smoke screen of higher learning at academic institutions across the country and my primary goal has been to give these lost students hope and show them that they are not alone in their despair and misery.

Lastly, I would be remiss not to mention that the events that take place are only *mostly* true. Usual memoir rules do apply. Names have been changed and in almost all cases composite characters have been engineered from multiple real life sources. Personal characteristics of major characters are disguised or downright fabricated. Dialogue has been reconstructed. Tiny details I could in no way realistically remember have been included for narrative effect. At times, I meticulously recount personal black-outs that I have absolutely no recollection of but have confirmed through multiple sources. Stories sometimes occur out of sequence. Memory gaps have been filled. Time is compressed. Fraternity names are... accurate.

"One must be a great man indeed to be able to hold out even against common sense"
"Or else a fool."
—Fyodor Dostoevsky, Demons

Preface

The Dartmouth College Student Life Initiative (SLI) was an undertaking supported by then president of the college, James Wright, shortly after being appointed by the Board of Trustees to the presidency in 1998. President Wright's charge to the SLI was to deliver a thorough and honest assessment of the social and residential conditions of the campus and offer recommendations in a variety of areas that included improving housing on campus, expanding dining options, adding new college run social spaces, and most importantly, bringing about changes within Dartmouth's Coed, Fraternity, and Sorority (CFS) system to address the dominance of these institutions on campus and the rampant problem of alcohol abuse among members.

Prologue

A brass plaque screwed loosely into the door in front of me said "Career Services," but I wasn't exactly sure what that meant. This well-hidden office was in the basement of our main dining hall, Thayer. A pool table sat unused in the rec room directly adjacent to its entrance; the eight ball was tucked safely into one pocket.

I was wearing a black pea coat, a blue Polo shirt, and Tommy Hilfiger jeans that were rigid and mud stained from the knee down. Despite the foot of snow on the ground, my feet were tucked into bath sandals and wrapped in a pair of mismatched Cole Haan dress socks meant to protect my toes from frostbite. Although these articles of clothing seemed to fit me perfectly, I'm quite certain that I didn't actually own any of them. With one hand I was dislodging a pair of Calvin Klein boxer shorts and with the other I tightly clutched a Dartmouth Dining Services bag full of bright red whipped cream cans.

Thayer Hall was at the tail end of a string of administration buildings running up the side of our campus green. It was my fourth winter in Hanover, but I was still not quite sure why I was there at all. My jumbled mind jumped from event to event, effectively skipping the messy details that dragged along in between infecting the majority of the campus around me with a kind of zombie like zeal. Standing there, outside this deserted little office, there was only one consideration on my mind. The whippets I held must be consumed.

I retreated upstairs to the men's bathroom and set myself up in the handicap stall, which was larger, seemed cleaner, and had a higher seat. With my jeans around my ankles and my cock in one hand, I lifted the first whipped cream canister to my lips—pausing momentarily before pressing down lightly on the nozzle to intentionally project a powerful blast of nitrous oxide into my mouth.

As I suck the nitrous down, my lungs expand; my spine springs erect into a straight edge as the can continues to leak gas with a hissing sound, inflating my body like a balloon. Ten seconds later the nitrous is kicked, the cream trapped in its shiny prison and no longer holding any interest for me. I toss it aside and greedily paw at the next can.

I do a few more whippets and then feel a familiar buzzing in the back of my head. At these times I can actually feel the nitrous burning through brain cells. My vision blurs, and my eyes are suddenly swooshing around in their sockets with a bobbing for apples type buoyancy, but I'm happy, or at least this seems like happiness, even though the feeling only lasts twenty seconds or so. Crippling normalcy starts to return and I begin to panic until I notice the rest of the whippets begging to be administered beside my right leg. I lift another can to my face, and the entire sad ritual repeats three or four more times until there is but a single can left. I then start masturbating, thinking about a girl with enormous breasts I saw walking across The Green that morning, and right at the point of orgasm I do the last whippet and am so out of it that I don't even care when viscous ejaculate shoots all over one pant leg.

It was tough not to feel slightly bewildered at the pathetic nature of this display as I lifted my jeans and fastened their button. How many human beings had masturbated in that stall? I cleaned the sperm from my body and pants with toilet paper, tossed the empty canisters, and left without washing my hands.

The steps leading downstairs were a maze of dirty melted snow puddles. I passed a girl I vaguely recognized as I descended. She smiled and said hello, but I didn't even look in her direction. This was a human being with no discernible qualities. It later occurred to me that I probably met her freshmen year. Why was she still acknowledging me anyway? Didn't she know what a disgusting human being I had become?

As I approached the door a second time a fraternity brother of mine, James Halifax, was just leaving. His usual Michigan State baseball cap, glued backwards on his head at all times, pinned several clumps of hair against his forehead like a cowlick. He wore a simple white striped, baby blue, button down dress shirt, and deliberately faded, factory blue jeans. He also had on a pea coat, though his was dusted gray with ethereal particles that were dancing around him in the vivid halogen lights of the dining hall. His appearance was in fact so faded that approaching him was akin to your eyes adjusting to an optical illusion. From a distance he didn't seem to be there. The eyes beneath his strange bangs were bloodshot a morbid shade of red and the huge grin plastered across his face engaged nearly all of his facial muscles. This gave him a sort of evil puppet look. I didn't know whether to embrace him or draw back in fear. We were both genuinely shocked to see each other, chuckled, and exchanged friendly greetings.

"Brother Balls! What's up, dude?" Halifax said while shaking my hand, "What the fuck are you doing here?"

"I guess I'm a bit lost. Same as you I would imagine." I followed him upstairs and seriously considered abandoning my entire mission.

"Actually, seeing about an on-campus job, if you can believe this shit," Halifax snorted, motioning his arm towards my intended destination with some obvious dramatics. "They're fucking idiots in there. Assholes. Career Services is completely useless, Balls, trust me."

"I'm running out of options here."

We had reached the ground floor of the building and the side exit leading outside. Halifax, previously looking intent to exit immediately, actually turned back toward me at the door and smiled unnaturally.

"Fuck, Balls," he said. "Let's smoke a bowl and play some Ship."

His face brightened up to display this really inviting look. Halifax could often be so convincing about such utterly awful and wild ideas with merely a playful smile and a slight shrug. Nine times out of ten this wouldn't be a decision at all.

"Dude, I don't particularly feel like watching you scrape that bowl for twenty minutes just to self-induce a headache and it's a little early for Ship."

"Suit yourself."

He stuck a cigarette in his mouth and lit it while still in the building.

"Whelp… see ya later."

And with that he exited.

This time I was careful not to think as I headed downstairs for a third time. I allowed my feet to carry me to the door, my hand to open it, and my brain to accept the inevitable. Mentally I began planning how I would make my introductions, what questions I would ask, who I thought they wanted me to be...

The room I stepped into appeared empty. A deserted desk faced me on which a purple, bulbous shaped i-Mac was flashing one of three standard screensavers. Everywhere I looked, smiling Dartmouth students were staring back at me. Plastered across the walls were posters depicting commencement, homecoming, matriculation, and DOC trips—where there were hikers and rafters and skiers. I approached one particular collage that caught my attention. Among the photos was a snapshot of several matriculating students dancing the "salty dog" in front of our administration building. One of these freshmen looked disturbingly like me, no I realized, it was me! I was actually laughing in this photo with my arms wrapped around another beaming first year and I genuinely looked happy.

"Can I help you?"

This unpleasant voice cut in from behind as I stood there contemplating my past life. In another instant I was face to face with a Career Services Officer. Whether this person had been hiding behind the door I had just entered, or crouched under the only desk in the room, or if she had simply materialized out of thin air, I did not know.

She was identical in appearance to every admissions, financial aid, or housing officer I had ever seen. You saw these women smoking outside their respective buildings and were relieved that these were not the same women serving your food. This officer ushered me into the next room, a tastelessly decorated office, which I'm assuming, belonged to her. She took a seat across from me and for a few awkward seconds we sat there waiting for one of us to summon the initiative to begin the conversation.

"Hello. I'm a super senior and was wondering what services, specifically speaking, the Career Services office had to offer me?"

I frowned as this statement fell flat. My intended humor, sarcasm, arrogance—whatever you want to call it—seemed to have no effect on this preposterous woman. Keep in mind that I didn't know her, had never seen her before but was still unable to have anything but utter contempt for her. She was affiliated with the college, an association that immediately identified her as an enemy. Sitting there, waiting for her mouth to open, the helplessness of being trapped in the situation dawned on me. It was shameful that I had even ventured there in the first place so I prepared to stand up and walk out of her office, but at that exact moment her mouth opened and nonsense began spilling out.

"Well that really depends on you," she said, clearly oblivious to my discomfort. "After graduation you will have a wealth of options at your feet. Have you considered corporate recruiting?"

I scowled and tried to look as personally insulted as possible.

"Have you started getting your resume together?"

"Don't be ridiculous."

"Okay," she drew a slow measured breath. "Let's start at the beginning. What do you want to do when you graduate?"

Isn't she getting a little ahead of herself? Rather than continue down this path I muttered a fairly normal response: "Well, I'm thinking about law school and have started some LSAT work, but I really don't want to be a lawyer so what's the point? Though you can do almost anything with a law degree but I'm already in debt enough as it is. Honestly? I don't see myself as ever having a permanent profession or career. I want to write, to travel, and to teach; it would be interesting to be a police officer for a few years and rather than spend the rest of my life in and out of a gym I think I'll do some construction work—I guess that's sort of what I want to do, at this exact moment anyway."

She frowned and tried another line of attack.

"Where do you see yourself in ten years?"

The obvious answer (on a beach sipping a cocktail) flashed through my mind but instead I said, "In ten years I want your job." This took her slightly by surprise. "I want to be sitting right where you are now, talking to a student who may or may not be just like me."

"And you'd tell them what exactly?"

"I'd tell them something nobody had the courage to tell me. I would say, 'Stand up and march out that door right now because resumes, cover letters, term papers, case studies, admissions officers, interviews—these are all meaningless and in ten years you'll be the same unhappy little shit that you are today.'"

On the verge of defeat she gave one last feeble attempt to reach out to me.

"What do you want out of life? Don't you have a passion?"

"I'm a dipsomaniac," I told her frankly. "Dartmouth bred. I drink every single night of the week—dangerous amounts even and I routinely blackout and vomit in my own bed. You wouldn't believe how rarely I attend class and when I do I'm usually drunk or hungover. The only thing I care about at Dartmouth is Pong and I'm one of the best players on campus. If Ship were a varsity sport, I would be an All-American. You honestly believe that someone could possibly be interested in employing me?"

And with that I got up and left.

As if in a daze and clearly still feeling the after effects of the nitrous oxide, I stumbled out of the building, brushing past and bumping into several people in the process. I lowered my head to avoid potential eye contact with fellow students and began the familiar trek across campus to frat row. It was frigid that day, amplified by the fact that my coat wasn't buttoned, but it was my mind, not my body, that was numb with pain. This losing battle I had been waging had gone on too long. At that moment I firmly resolved that this had been my last attempt to become a real person. It was something that I was simply not capable of.

"I'm out of my mind," I said out loud, sticking a cigarette in my mouth. "I'm absolutely insane, a fucking lunatic!" I repeated, trying to convince myself.

A freshman glanced at me curiously as I slapped myself in the face, knocking the cigarette out of my mouth and into the snow. Ignoring the freshman, I continued my soliloquy.

"Something is genuinely wrong with me. I am seriously emotionally disturbed. What kind of man am I?"

I passed a college tour group whose student guide appeared to be pointing out something of significance about our admissions building while simultaneously walking backwards and attempting to field questions from the small group of prospective students and their parents that followed him. The group stared at me as I slouched by mumbling to myself. Sensing their invasive eyes on me I turned to them, sneered, and menacingly said, "If any of you come to Dartmouth I'll fucking kill you!" Though I said this softly and I doubt anyone heard me.

I needed a beer (or rather, seven beers) but I doubted there was enough cold Keystone Light in the basement to fill an entire Ship game and supposed I would have to scrounge for warm stray beers left on side benches to play a single game. The real challenge was going to be finding three other people willing to forgo the rest of the day's productive hours to indulge my obsessive drinking habit. Though it was still early, it was also a Wednesday, which meant that with some convincing I could find opponents and a partner among the legions of our brotherhood who would be getting out of class over the next several hours, but it also meant the majority of our beer supply since the last purchase on Monday had evaporated. I no longer had class but ironically for once had an overwhelming desire to wake up the next morning nice and early and with the rest of campus stagger like a robot from hall to hall, filling my cover-less spiral notebook with illegible, soon to be forgotten scribble. I had even found several promising classes that had a real possibility of interesting me… this was no longer relevant. I had ceased to be a student. There was only one reason for me to remain on campus. My very existence, everything I needed or loved was contained in one red brick building.

The Chi Gamma Epsilon fraternity house was waiting for me just as I had left it the night before. A broken lawn chair, more closely resembling a grotesque arrangement of bones, sat atop an enormous pile of snow in a half deflated baby pool in the front yard. It seemed to reign over the two dozen or so empty beer cans that were littered about the snow-patched grass like lawn ornaments. I gave a cursory glance down the street before turning onto the walkway, hoping someone might see me entering this den of debauchery and shake his or her head disapprovingly.

Inside the house, a rank odor comprised mainly of warm stale beer, stagnated urine, and fresh vomit immediately set about strangling and suffocating me. While familiar and comforting, this smell nonetheless caused me to wince in disgust as I glanced about the deserted front rooms for signs of life. With some imagination, a wet-vac, and yes, maybe even a bucket of soapy water, the carpeted meetings room in the west wing of the building could look respectful, almost elegant. But in this state it looked condemned. Noxious garbage decorated every surface; the floor shining crystalline blue with Keystone Light cans. Shin high piles of empty, cracked and dismembered plastic cups were arranged haphazardly like anthills around the room. Rows of half-filled cups covered every surface but only some of these were beers. Many were filled with mysterious colorful liquids—the dead insects floating inside assured their identity would remain secret. On either end of the room, two beautifully painted wooden Beer Pong tables lay on the ground, propped up several inches from the floor by a combination of empty thirty-packs and half crushed aluminum cans.

Music was emanating from the basement but after listening for a few seconds and not detecting the bounce of a Ping-Pong ball I determined that this was from the night before and not a sign that games had already begun. It was early (even for me), but this was a special occasion and I was in no mood to wait around all afternoon. I smiled for the first time all day and at the top of my lungs, so that the whole house could hear, bellowed:

"THREE FOR SHIP!"

Chapter 1: A Dartmouth Man

"We must promote an environment that allows our students to reach their full potential, that appreciates them as individuals, and that fosters a sense of responsibility to this special place as well as to the wider community. We must encourage our students to become leaders in whatever fields they choose, as have generations of Dartmouth alumni before them."

– *Excerpt from the Summary of the Recommendations Submitted to the Board of Trustees by the Committee on the Student Life Initiative*

I am perpetually waking from a nightmare of my own design. The few seconds where I realize I am awake before falling back asleep are the only moments of consciousness that I can fully control. The rest of the time I sleep walk. My memories fade and then vanish until I'm left with only a vague inkling of the terrible things I have done.

This is the frozen home of singing giants. The infamous fraternity houses loom menacingly over the campus while the warmly dressed students slip silently from building to building. The moment you set foot in Hanover, the frosted air begins to turn the blood in your veins to granite. The surreal backdrop of the brilliantly changing New England foliage surrounds and encloses you. Then the snow arrives to bury the campus in a gleaming white coat and transform the walking paths into canals of ice, mud, and snow. This turns any commonplace excursion into a physical trial of cold resistance and outright perseverance. The massive icicles and large snowdrifts that drool off every surface expose the campus to the constant excitement of being impaled or buried by them at gravity's whim. The Dartmouth I knew was a place of unstoppable forces.

It is somewhat interesting to note that the first beer I ever consumed, well I should say, actually *remember* consuming—was handed to me at Dartmouth College. I forget who I was before this all-important event. The child who I *was* seems to be an entirely different person than the man I *am*. That first beer ushered me into the adult world, and the subsequent four or five of the evening made my decision for me. It hadn't been the extensive tour of the facilities we had been taken on, or the introduction to student life we had received at the hands of the sophomore "buddy" that Dartmouth's recruitment team had paired each high-schooler with. The allure and mystique of the Greek houses was the most magnetic force of all.

During this pre-matriculation trip I remember an encounter with a fraternity member acting as doorman outside one of the numerous frats we visited after hours. When this "brother" discovered that our group was composed mainly of visiting high school students he urged us to drink up while we still could because by the time we got to campus the fraternities might be entirely gone. I was the happy type of drunk that night, glowing from the inside out, without a fear or care in the world. It didn't matter that I overslept the next morning and nearly missed the bus back to my parent's house in New York or that on the ride back I had been sick a total of two times in the rear seats; there was no longer any doubt as to which school I should pursue my college education. The summer before enrollment I described frat row to my friends and family as Disneyland.

Only when I am home do I truly come to my senses. I tell myself that the next time around will be different... but in fact it never is. My grasp on the situation deteriorates and the periods of time without control grow gradually longer and nastier until near the end I am almost completely possessed. There are no precautions to be taken. No medicine that can be administered. No rigorous schedule that can limit this loss of control. It exists, I am its slave, and nothing can be done to stop it. My biggest fear is that this metamorphosis may become permanent, my demons finally exposed and not at all anxious to be again repressed in my unconsciousness. *Is this the real me?* This person who I have described as "possessing me," a person everyone else affectionately refers to as

Balls. Have I given in completely to the demands of this sociopath?

I find that I am a ghost on campus. I walk anonymously through darkened corridors, my eyes averting the glances of fellow students. There is nothing to be done about the anxiety raising fact that I *must* at some point leave my cocoon and brave hostile exterior environments. I do so unwillingly and without true purpose. My all too common name appears sloppily written across blue book essay tests and the professors look up at the class and squint while scanning attendance lists through tortoise framed glasses. Is *Chris Knight here?* The class echoes back smooth, blank, expressionless faces. They haven't even heard of him.

Balls is a completely social being, never alone for more than a handful of minutes each day. You would truly be amazed at the quantity of alcohol that Balls can consume in one sitting. He operates solely in the environment that has created him—anything outside of this world is misinterpreted or ignored. He is content to spend all of his days drinking with the same small group of alcoholics and feels himself better off because of it. Balls is the Jester of the Basement.

This will not be a chronicle of my descent into substance abuse. I refuse to tell you the obvious—that my detrimental habits became an ordinary and integral part of my life. I will not say that I drank such and such quantity of beer on this or that day and that it felt completely normal but in actuality I was really repressing problems A and B by doing so. Suffice it to say... things got away from me rather quickly. Eventually binge drinking was going on practically seven nights a week. For no reason other than to play Beer Pong. Once I played that first game, I was trapped. When I win I *have* to play again. When I lose I *want* to play again. These stories aren't exaggerated and are written exactly as I remember them. Together they constitute the formative years of my young life, my college years, spent almost entirely at a small university called Dartmouth College located in the town of Hanover, New Hampshire.

It wasn't always like this. There existed a time in my youth when the rigid ways of the world appeared malleable to me and I was able to slide in and out of the numerous crevices with relative ease. My imagination carried me to distant worlds so that at every avenue I attempted to bring the realm of fantasy to life. I was a constant dreamer, a voracious reader, an aspiring writer, a widely circulated cartoonist, a one-time musician, a civil war historian, a competitive basketball player, a leader among my selective group of friends and all this by the end of high school. Yet I never defined who I was by what I did. School, like everything else, came naturally to me but as with my other pursuits, I viewed my formal education as just one more realm of life presenting itself to be conquered. I made myself its master effortlessly and by senior year it became clear that I could attend any university I wanted.

Dartmouth College is the fifth oldest member of the "elite eight"—that ancient group of ivy-covered institutions whose existence has come to represent academic prestige and excellence in this country. The beloved college was founded by Eleazar Wheelock, a man dedicated to the education of the Native American tribes of New England. Wheelock's fascination with the "savage" can be traced back through several of his colonial predecessors, one of whom, John Sergeant, once fittingly said, "We must take the Indian child, 'the savage,' and change his whole manner of thinking and acting and raise him as far as possible into the condition of a civil, industrious and polished person." Though he never got to witness the creation of Wheelock's Indian Charity School, later to become Dartmouth College, its guiding philosophy and purpose would have been right on line with Sergeant's thinking.

As members of the academic elite, we are Wheelock's "savages," little more than soft balls of dough, and so singularly naive that in Dartmouth's experienced and time tested hands, we could easily be molded into just the right sort of "industrious and polished" person for this day and age.

My accomplices in these early months were a hodgepodge collection of freshmen that I met early and clung to religiously. Like any fledgling group of friends, we grabbed lunch after or between classes, met each other at the dining halls for dinner, played intramural sports, watched movies in residential lounges, drank beer in freshmen dorm rooms, investigated the various fraternity houses—we had our hands in Dartmouth's cookie jar.

Troy Winston was the first freshman I think I laid eyes on. The majority of incoming students participated in a pre-matriculation Dartmouth Outing Club, or DOC, trip allowing them to meet one another while hiking, biking, canoeing, kayaking, rock climbing, or organic farming in the pristine wilderness surrounding Hanover. These trips are staggered over numerous weeks and labeled Trip A, Trip B, Trip C and so on, as logistically there was no way to coordinate all incoming freshmen on a single three day trip. It is often quipped that the students you meet on your DOC trip turn out to be lifelong friends and given my continued attachment to Winston it seems there is solid truth to this platitude.

I had signed up for the most generic offering available, moderate hiking. This put me in one of several twelve member hiking groups led by two members of the DOC. Winston, a fellow New York native, was on the same Dartmouth sponsored bus from Port Authority to Hanover. He randomly took a seat across the aisle from me, which probably would not have made any great impression if he hadn't almost immediately reached into my seat brandishing a list of rules and regulations that the school had mailed us in anticipation of the event.

"I'm not sure if you got this," he said, while wagging a finger at the Walkman headphones I was about to put on, "but I don't think we're supposed to have those."

I ignored this good-natured oaf with no way of knowing that I would enthusiastically share a room with him for a combined four terms.

Winston was an interesting character. In mathematics and computer science he was brilliant and his aptitude for learning translated into every other field as well. He was one of those rare kids who are able to maintain a 4.0 grade point average for their entire college careers no easy feat at a school like Dartmouth. This logically tuned mind of his regimented his daily schedule in the most precise and mechanical way so that by knowing what day it was, one could unfailingly predict his exact location at any given time. Classes were dutifully attended but one got the feeling that this was more from being an entrenched habit of his than because of any true desire for additional knowledge. He knew exactly what the end goal of his post-secondary education should be—namely a well-placed and highly lucrative employment opportunity with a career trajectory vertically aligned to a lifestyle of wealth, leisure, and prestige. He never missed a lecture. The odd truth about Winston was that at the heart of it all, in a Dartmouth basement, the guy was an absolute lush and raged harder and drank more excessively than ninety percent of the student body.

On campus, I registered for my trip and met my fellow moderate hikers. Winston was among this twelve-member group. The larger section of kids, numbering approximately one hundred and twenty out of a twelve-hundred total incoming freshmen, spent the remainder of the afternoon getting acquainted with all things Hanover at the hands of the DOC. It was these crazed people who taught me the "salty dog" in front of Parkhurst and had me so caught up in the moment that I failed to notice the flash of the camera capturing the scene for posterity's sake. This was the squeaky-clean version of Dartmouth—crunchy, liberal coeds welcoming us into the fold of Dartmouth's outdoorsy, eccentric culture.

The first night was spent uncomfortably on the floor of a dorm lounge and the next morning, after a short van ride, we arrived at the entrance to a well-traveled Appalachian trail. The group set out single file into the woods—a pack of eager, wide-eyed strangers being led into the unknown by equally enthusiastic upperclassmen. These were my tripees—the first Dartmouth family any of us would have.

On the evening of our second night, we made camp at the base of an old fire tower that loomed above even the highest coniferous trees. As the others set up tarps for the night, preparing for a forecasted shower, a group of five of us, Winston included, scaled the fifty foot ladder up to the firehouse itself and laid ourselves in our sleeping bags like sardines on the wooden floor of the interior. We must have stayed up talking for half the night with a storm swirling around outside, beating at the windows with loud macabre thuds and swaying the cabin back and forth so that at any moment we all imagined it might collapse and deliver us into the abyss below. It didn't and when morning broke we awoke to a beautiful expanse of forest glistening through the window in front of us. This was our future obscured out there beyond the tree line, and what I remember most of all from this moment was how anxious I was to throw myself head first into whatever it was that awaited me.

At the conclusion of the hike, our exhausted group arrived at the Moosilauke Ravine Lodge, the final destination for all individual trips in our section.

This is actually how I met my other best friend at Dartmouth, Maxwell Beetle—first encountered stuffing peanut butter and jelly sandwiches into his bulging pockets at a banquet table stacked high with the things in the main hall of the lodge.

Beetle was at times the most and least serious out of the three of us. Socially he put himself out there more than Winston and I ever did and had a large web of friends and acquaintances that he cultivated and attended to separately from us. Often he was the one dragging us across campus to fraternity dance parties or unknown freshmen dorm rooms on weekend nights. Beetle was the builder type; he always working on a new construction project or blueprinting the design for some fanciful object he had no intention of actually using, simply for the personal joy that accompanied physically making it. If Winston was our Chief Information Officer then Beetle was our Head Engineer.

The three of us decided to start the year as friends and once school started, our core solidified with plenty of peripheral members and overlap into other circles. Whenever we reminisce about the early days we always find it funny that we met so early and were instantly drawn to each other.

❄

"Is this a black student I haven't met before?"

I was in Thayer, my head buried in a copy of our college newspaper, my mouth stuffed with gobs of chicken and cheese, when I heard this ridiculous sentence. The speaker took a seat across from me and smiled obscenely. I recognized him instantly; Stanton Williams. Like a politician, he shook my hand vigorously and asked what my name was.

Stanton was perhaps the most well-known black kid in our freshmen class. Extremely ambitious and involved with dozens of campus activities, clubs and student groups, it came as no surprise that I knew who he was but not the other way around. He was what I like to call a Dartmouth Enthusiast. Here was someone who devoted so much time to maintaining his campus-wide persona that I doubt he had any time to let someone genuinely get to know him. He was the poster boy for the Dartmouth image that I thought I was expected to adopt. Friendly, non-threatening, and involved. I'd never seen him in a fraternity basement.

"You're an '03 too. How is it that we've never met?" he asked incredulously, once I had told him my name.

I continued to devour the Cordon Bleu splayed out in front of me and wondered if he had considered the possibility that he just hadn't been trying hard enough.

"It's good that we've met," Stanton said after a moment of silence that made it clear I had no intention of responding to him. "I make a point to introduce myself to every student of color that I see."

He then invited me to a meeting of the African American Society held that very night at the Cutter-Shabaz dorm—a residential living space populated almost entirely by black students.

I actually took Stanton up on his offer, but it was the only AAS event I ever attended. There was a discussion of the passive campus-wide racism we were all still trying to wrap our heads around where being black just meant you didn't exist for most of the rest of campus. Dartmouth's campus, while fairly homogeneous for a major university, tends to operate quite democratically with regards to inclusiveness; however, it does so with a certain upper middle class swagger when it comes to social hierarchy and the rules of engagement. If you are a black student, it is guaranteed that you will routinely be in classrooms where you are the only black student. Your familial, financial and cultural background will likely differ greatly from much of the rest of the campus. You will be greeted happily and enthusiastically everywhere you go and all the while it will be plain and obvious that nothing worthy is expected of you at any time. You will feel utterly alone and come to believe, as I do, that the school largely ignores the plight of its black students. This was true then, it's true now, and it will be true a long time into the future. The AAS was a place where Dartmouth's black kids could feel comfortable and be themselves primarily because the environment they created was nothing like Dartmouth itself.

Various students came forward with their own harrowing tales of campus wide racism, but what the group saw as forming a united front against a hostile, alien environment, I saw as ultimately self-defeating in its strange brand of segregation. How can sitting there and talking about how we don't fit into white Dartmouth, in the basement of the only African American dorm on campus, before an audience of only minorities, help the perception of black students on campus? What we should do is disband the AAS right now and never hold one of these meetings again. Cutter-Shabaz, the (practically) all-black dorm, should be fully integrated. These would be the most significant steps we've ever taken to achieve campus wide acceptance.

These thoughts made me wonder if my experiences were even relevant. Maybe this racially motivated frustration was merely a symptom of what being a *mulatto* has meant to me. I looked black (or Hispanic maybe, depending on who you ask) but I had not grown up *black*, if that makes any sense. My African American, Georgia-born father had intentionally discouraged me from forming a specifically black identity. I had a diverse background, being born in Brooklyn and raised to the age of ten in Queens with an Italian mother and black father. But when I moved to a quiet, upper-middle class beach community on Long Island, where I spent my later adolescence, the friends I formed by necessity of proximity were all white as pear meat. Our small village was isolated; I didn't hang out with the other kids across the bridge, or loiter around school grounds when class let out. Didn't have a car. Never went to a football game. I proudly missed every school dance; including my own prom. Me and my friends went straight home after school and took up our own pursuits; video games, basketball, Dungeons and Dragons, elaborate team "manhunts" across the vast, deserted lots of our seasonally depopulated, incorporated hamlet. That was my day to day; I never knew group socializing of any kind growing up, except in a very controlled capacity at school, where my eccentricities during class could truly shine. So at school I excelled, and at home I lost myself. It was as content a childhood as you could ever ask for.

But in the Five Towns of Nassau County, where I went to high school, one of those towns is black and the rest are white and the kids from the most economically disadvantaged of the five towns are all varying shades of brown, sitting and socializing almost exclusively with each other, and don't even know

I exist. When I got to Dartmouth I wanted to leave all of this behind. I didn't want the kids at Dartmouth (though as I write this I realize how stupid it sounds) to define me as a *white* or *black* Dartmouth student. I wanted them to see me as just another outgoing beer loving upper-middle class Ivy Leaguer soon to be Greek. From this point forward I was no longer a part of black culture at Dartmouth. I interacted with many of these kids outside of the group dynamic but didn't socialize specifically with the AAS, except when attending their parties, and as a result would never truly know what it felt like to be "black" at Dartmouth.

My freshman dorm, Wheeler Hall, was a hike from the majority of the other dorms but was just a short distance from frat row, my home away from home for the foreseeable future. My roommate was a fellow African-American and we met two black girls living down the hall in an identically laid out L shaped room. Opposite our room was a triple of a black girl, a white girl and an Indian girl who shared a half bath and homely features. Dartmouth was about six percent black at this time, the odds of five of us all being randomly assigned to live on the same floor of a dorm seems pretty slim. I found out this was actually fairly common on campus, though we hadn't requested in our room preference note-card (filled out and returned several months before we matriculated) we be separated and quarantined from the rest of campus (though this was actually a check-box option believe it or not). Maybe it was all the white kids who had requested to live with their own race.

My roommate was very involved in the AAS for the two years he attended the University before being unceremoniously thrown out and was diametrically opposed to the Greek system. I would arrive at our room drunk on a Friday or Saturday night only to be greeted with a barrage of condescending insults.

"You're not drunk again, are you?"

Yes, I'm drunk. Congratulations on that extremely astute observation.

"So, when are you pledging Chi-Gam, anyway?"

We both know freshmen can't pledge. Don't patronize me.

"Don't you think that you should do some studying for a change?"

Thanks for the lecture. I'm a big boy. I can make my own decisions.

"Let me guess. You played Pong tonight, didn't you?"

Once again, I must commend you on your powers of deduction.

In the presence of his guests I was introduced as his frat guy roommate. Weekend binge drinking didn't seem to be on the agenda for everyone on campus. He had nothing but disdain for the Greek system and thought it odd that I didn't. Throughout the year he frequently entertained women, who by their skin color I should have known, and they gave looks at me as if to say, "Yes, you should know me, but you don't and that's your fault not mine." My roommate obviously enjoyed my discomfort during these encounters and while it was obvious that he played for the other team and didn't have a romantic interest in any of these girls, I nonetheless despised him for it.

The true source of my contempt for this man, I only recently realized, was that I was an unwilling witness to his slow unraveling at the school and secretly feared the same fate for myself. Over the course of freshman year, his failure to fully adapt to Dartmouth life continued to drive him further into isolation so that by the spring he had become a self-imposed prisoner in our one room double—in which he sat and festered all year long. The sight of him silently brooding in the dark at eleven at night on a weekend was a far cry from the images of Dartmouth I had long been bombarded with. By the end of the year, we were barely on speaking terms. I ran into him a few times randomly during the next fall but after that I never saw him again. Later on I found out that he had been parkhursted for academics and had transferred to a new school.

The word *Parkhurst* is synonymous with hard times at Dartmouth. Parkhurst was the building that housed the dean's offices. When a student was suspended from the school for academic or disciplinary reasons, he or she is said to have been "parkhursted" and has their fate whispered about in fraternity basements and dining halls throughout their three to five term exile. For me he was a cautionary tale: reject the norms of the campus and the campus will reject you.

Which fraternity are you rushing? Everyone asks this as if the concept of not being Greek was patently insane. Even then it was clear to me that non-affiliation was a near irreversible social death sentence. So I spent little time in my dorm that year in an effort to escape my roommate and the other hermits of Wheeler Hall and instead made a new home for myself in the basements of frat row and the dorm rooms of my more socially minded peers.

Chapter 2: A Sea of Optimism

"...life in the residence halls is marked by a stunning lack of continuity, resulting in an ongoing sense of upheaval and rootlessness for students. Testimony from students, faculty and administrators alike suggested that a lack of residential continuity and identity is a major reason many students are motivated to seek a sense of community by joining CFS organizations."
– *Excerpt from the Summary of the Recommendations Submitted to the Board of Trustees by the Committee on the Student Life Initiative*

During my debut month in Hanover I had my first semi-serious bout of alcohol poisoning. This was not completely new territory as I had experienced accidental incapacitating drunkenness before, but this was different in that now I was consciously putting myself in a stupor, blindly in pursuit of some cloudy and intangible goal.

A few too many games of Beer Pong (which I will describe at length in due time) had inspired me against my better judgment, to try and convince a platonic female friend to sleep with me. This spontaneous decision was extremely uncharacteristic of me and I largely attribute the sudden attraction I felt for her at two o'clock that morning to the fact that her dorm cluster, the Choates, was located almost directly behind frat row. The four prison barracks-style buildings that comprised the Choates had glass corridors one story above the ground causing the complex to resemble a hamster cage. I arrived at what I guessed was her hall at the very last gasp of night, very drunk and only getting drunker.

This friend of mine saw the dreadful state I was in and urged me to go home and sleep it off. And here I was, hoping that her bed would be home for the night! She practically slammed the door in my face.

The next hazy memory I have is that I'm in the public lounge of this girl's dorm. I can't stand up and I can't stop vomiting. Campus security shows up because someone has seen me in this compromising position and this isn't so unreasonable a reaction because the carpet in a five-foot radius around me has been turned into a lake of puke and I'm floundering like a beached whale on the floor. In all likelihood, the aforementioned female friend has actually blitzed another non-drinking friend of mine to come to my aid who, upon realizing when he arrived that extracting me safely from the Choates was not an option, called campus security.

The officer asks me my name and tells me I'm going to be all right then he asks if I can stand and I mumble yes but when I attempt this feat I wind up right back on the floor.

Then I'm in a stretcher being wheeled down a flight of stairs to an ambulance parked outside. I know this for certain because my head keeps hitting uncomfortably against the back of the stretcher on each step. I hear the screech of the ambulance as they load me aboard and race across campus to the Dartmouth-Hitchcock emergency room. I remember thinking that I was drunk, but not *that drunk*. Then it all goes black and suddenly I'm awake in a hospital bed with the sun shining brightly through the window, naked except for a hospital gown and an IV inserted in my arm. I vaguely remember the end of the previous night and shudder. I am alone in the hospital room. I promise myself that I won't drink that much *ever* again, but I don't even believe this as I think it.

❄

The feeding frenzy of freshman year released us into the wilds of New Hampshire to prey and feast on one another amid a mad scramble to meet as many people as possible, putting forth the best possible impression while doing so. For many this meant a complete identity makeover and I imagined some kids as being entirely different people the summer before. This evolution of personalities, all vainly trying to adapt to Dartmouth culture but not fully comprehending that it was their own synthesis of personalities that determined what this culture entailed, was in essence the guiding force that determined the very people who we would eventually become. Many students (myself included) made it a point of emphasis to expose themselves early and often to Dartmouth's underground culture of fraternity-centric binge drinking.

On any given night you can be sure that in Dartmouth's CFS houses, basement Beer Pong games are being played. In Beer Pong, two teams compete on a flat playing surface (at Dartmouth about the size and shape of a standard Ping Pong table) on which a predetermined number of beers are distributed into plastic cups and arranged into one of many formations. The object of the game is to successfully hit a Ping Pong ball into the opposing team's cups using a paddle; the team whose cup is hit or sunk drinks the beer inside. A game typically ends when all the cups on one side of the table have been hit or sunk away.

There is a special connection between this drinking game and Dartmouth students and a certain pride in the fact that our school was likely the origin for all existing forms of Beer Pong. One variation in particular, called Beirut, has become a familiar staple across the country and can be found under every nook and cranny where young adults are prone to binge drink. When high school and college kids refer to Pong, as in: "Come over to my place, we're going to play some beer-pong in my dad's garage!" the game they are actually referring to is what we call Beirut, where teams take turns *throwing* the ball across the table at their opponent's cups. Having played both versions extensively, I can tell you quite honestly that our version is light-years more fun.

Not to knock Beirut, but it is a much simpler game that requires less setup, space, and equipment—this adaptability is also probably why it is *much* more popular. It's easy enough to get the basics down so that anyone can play a game and the skill gap so minor for the majority of players that most games result in toss ups. Hand someone a Ping-Pong ball and ask them to throw it at a grouping of cups ten feet away and anyone who has the use of their arms and can see further than a few feet will be able to play with some reasonable amount of success. Anyone should be able to come within a foot or two of the cups after a throw or two. Hand someone a Pong paddle on the other hand and ask them to make difficult lob shots from a variety of angles and locations, having never done anything similar before, and most of them won't be able to even keep the ball on the table. I have introduced many first timers to the game over the years and it usually takes a full game before the person has even grasped the concept of how to serve and return the ball fluidly. Hitting cups with regularity doesn't come until much later. A superior Pong player will almost never lose to an inferior one if their partners are more or less equal in skill, while in Beirut, drastic upsets can and will occur on long enough time-lines.

Since the game was first conceived at Dartmouth—teams using *paddles* to return the ball back and forth across the table rather than each team taking turns throwing it—we claim our version as the original and most pure manifestation. The history of American Beer Pong has almost mythological qualities. If you believe certain sources, the invention of Beer Pong can be attributed to table-tennis playing Dartmouth fraternity members who would rest their beer mugs on the table while they played. It was eventually discovered that it was actually more fun to aim for the mugs of beer rather than follow traditional Ping-Pong rules. At first the game was played at full speed with high velocity, close to the net shots. I imagine that the constant breakages in play this style presents eventually led to the switch to lob shots, which slows the game down and makes it more about finesse and less about brute strength. Now, almost universally so, the game of Pong at Dartmouth is played with a continuous back and forth of high arching paddle shots where a hit on a cup costs a half a beer and a sink the whole thing.

This paddle version is much more fluid, requires players to possess a sufficient level of hand eye coordination, and heightens the level of athletic competitiveness in a game. We find this to be vastly superior and don't play Pong solely as a means to get drunk; to us it is a recreational activity first, a drinking game second. Many Dartmouth students, believe it or not, are actually as competitive about their Pong ability as they are about their grades. The obsession is so complete that in every basement, off campus house, or student controlled social space on campus, you could be assured of one thing each evening: Pong is being played. The first group of students you see materialize in these places set up the first contest. The last standing are those participants of the final game. In between, the ball never stops bouncing.

A second major difference between Beirut and true Dartmouth Beer Pong, in addition to the use of paddles, is the quantity of beer that the participants are required to drink. With a Beirut game it is common practice to use a single can of beer to fill between three and five cups. Each "beer" on the Beirut table actually contains only a few ounces of liquid. With Dartmouth style Pong, a plastic cup is filled as close to the brim as possible—to the very top line of the molded ridges of the clear plastic cups that are so common on campus. This amounts to a full eight ounces per cup and there is no exception to this rule. Because these cups were *clear*, it was easy to tell how high your opponents' beers were filled and you would often hear one team tell another to add additional beer to not quite full cups because they were too weak. So even with your standard Dartmouth game of Pong, you are drinking three, four, sometimes five times as much as you would drink in a normal Beirut game. And the only way to do so comfortably and with expertise is through dedicated repetition.

Dartmouth students have devised many variations of the game, the most basic of which is called Shrub and uses a triangle formation of six beers with one beer serving as the stem of the "shrub." From above, one side of the table looks like so:

O
OO
OOO
O

A Tree formation is similar but employs either eleven or twelve beers per side, depending on if house rules call for a one or two beer stem. The main difference between Tree and Shrub is the speed in which you drink. The opening of either game is normally a barrage of hits and sinks, and with Tree you are basically just drinking four more beers in roughly the same amount of time. A single two-stem Tree (fairly unusual) looks like this:

O
OO
OOO
OOOO
OO

Variations of Shrub and Tree are the most common formations found on campus—however the possibilities are practically endless for creative minds bent on dreaming up ever new ways of tactically arranging the campus' inexhaustible supply of plastic cups. Games of Death, Two-Cup, Corners, Line, World Cup, Enchanted Forest, Social, Harbor and so on are played on a nightly basis in the CFS basements and occasionally games were even made up on the spot by enterprising players and subsequently never played again.

Then there was Ship, which had an allure all its own. This is what half of a Ship game looks like:

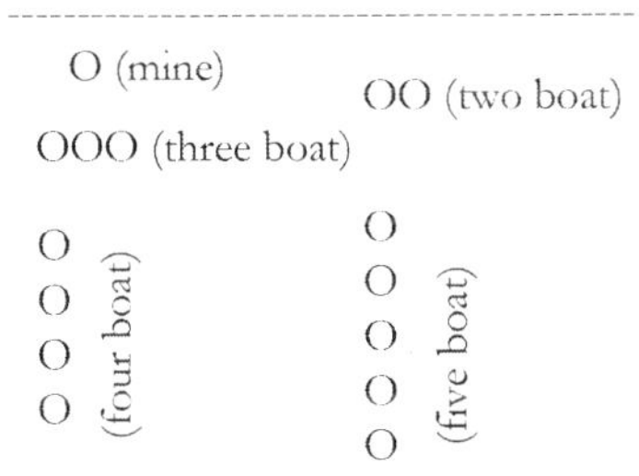

O (mine)
OO (two boat)
OOO (three boat)

O O O O (four boat)
O O O O O (five boat)

Ship certainly deserves some added attention but what is important here is that freshman year I fell in love with Pong and to play Pong I had to brave fraternity basements.

Almost completely devoid of bars, clubs, or local hang-outs and with a limited selection of off-campus residential spaces, Hanover doesn't at first seem like it would be entirely conducive to supporting a binge drinking culture, until you consider Dartmouth's location, size, and history of male-dominated drinking clubs. At Ivy's like Harvard, Columbia, U-Penn, Brown, or even Cornell to an extent due to its huge undergraduate population, students never had to rely on Greek organizations as a social outlet the same way Dartmouth kids do, as they had access to a varied citywide social and cultural infrastructure. At the smaller elite schools the necessary infrastructure wasn't in place because of a lack of historic precedence and alumni voice. As opposed to Dartmouth's sixty percent affiliation rate, only a relatively small number of the eligible student body at these other elite schools fully invests itself in Greek culture. When out in the real world, these students had to handle themselves somewhat responsibly—the boundaries of the "college bubble" extend only to edges of their own urban-enclosed campuses. Blacking out and strolling through downtown Boston or Philadelphia at two in the morning is not a recommended practice but in Hanover one could do so with near impunity—the biggest danger coming from the laughably ineffective Safety and Security vans that patrolled the campus at night in an attempt to capture zig-zagging, homeward-bound drinkers. Hanover was Dartmouth—we never had any reason to go elsewhere.

As a result, Greek organizations have played an important role in student life for a hundred and fifty years; the integration of women in the nineteen-seventies did little to alter that landscape. Sororities and coed houses quickly sprung up alongside the fraternities and adopted many of their drinking practices—Pong, Meetings, and parties for starters and since Dartmouth CFS houses are the only places for students to socialize in large groups while using alcohol, they could safely foster as extreme a drinking culture as they themselves could tolerate. Over time this has evolved into a drinking *tradition* and a certain pride has arisen that this was both a place of academic excellence *and* extreme partying. And since this isn't a few rotten apples we're talking about—it's the whole beer-soaked system really—the college administration has historically been at a loss at how to address a problem that much of the student body and alumni dismiss as being a problem altogether. Support for the system until the last decade and a half has been near universal. The existence of the SLI now threatened what has always been taken for granted on campus and many feared that this strange, wonderful world we had newly discovered was in the process of being altered irrevocably.

My own drinking habits were fairly normal during that first year and I found myself doing what most other kids did at Dartmouth and many other schools across the country—I studied and went to class during the week, while partying in freshman dorm rooms and fraternity houses during the weekends. I had struck a sustainable balance between academics and social experimentation and was enjoying my newly discovered weekend rager lifestyle. It was surprising and refreshing to see such a vibrant and engaging social scene at an Ivy-League school.

❄

Occasionally on late school nights, I would find myself across campus in the dorm room of two of my other freshmen year pals, Yogi and Trane, engaging in mini-marathons of beer drinking, pot smoking and video games.

The enormous Trane had a muscular, athletic frame and an intimidating persona that tended to react loudly and angrily to just about anything that drew his attention—as if he was the byproduct of some terrible testosterone experiment gone awry and we were all at the mercy of his imbalanced chemical composition. Yogi was a big guy too, but was more the slobbering, goofy type, who more or less stumbled through life with neither the inclination nor the patience to understand the larger world of human interaction the way he understood text-books. They were both bright guys at their core and even shared some similar interests, but clearly Yogi fit the nerd stereotype of "book smarts" while Trane was your prototypical "street smart" jock. Hanging out with the two of them was a bit like being in your own personal episode of *The Odd Couple.* Yogi was not on our DOC trip, but Winston, Beetle and I did meet Trane, which I suppose is how Yogi ended up attaching himself to us. The two lived on the first floor of Topliff Hall, a dorm next to the Hopkins Center that became a stage for the enactment of two strange and unpleasant incidents during our freshman year.

None of us had ever seen anyone enter or exit the room directly across the hall from Yogi though the construction paper name-tag taped to the door indicated that a junior girl was at least supposed to live there. We just assumed that the resident was out frequently and presumably very quiet. More than a few times I had stumbled intoxicated into this door, confusing her room for Yogi's, but always found it locked. We began to notice a peculiar smell emanating from within and as the term went on it only intensified in nastiness and reach. The running joke among us was that the poor girl had died during the first week of classes and Dartmouth had yet to discover the body. In fact, for two months the smell accumulated and spread through the dorm until the college had received enough complaints to investigate for themselves. When the Safety and Security officers opened the room they allegedly discovered a scene of extreme squalor and neglect. The source of the smell was easy to identify once her line of defenses had been breached—dozens of excrement filled jars scattered about the room. The girl was apparently some kind of recluse. She practically never left her room, not even to attend classes, didn't appear to have a single friend on campus, and furthermore, was disturbingly opting for a storage rather than disposal oriented solution to the agoraphobiac's problem of waste accumulation.

What could possess someone to adopt this terrible habit? I refuse to speculate about the probable cause of this excrement themed psychosis—the gamut of psychological disorders that can produce this result is staggering. What I do know is that this person had been completely ignored, and in a way we were all complicit. The next day they moved out the unfortunate creature and cleaned, closed, and locked up the room. Nobody would occupy it for the rest of the year.

For the next six months we told this story whenever the opportunity arose, primarily to evoke a "what the fuck?" sort of incredulous facial expression you are sometimes hoping to elicit with such a tale. As for the girl, we never learned her fate

There turned out to be more than one depraved soul living in that dormitory during our freshmen year. Those nights I spent with Yogi and Trane were the only times I smoked pot at that point in my career. I wasn't asked to bring anything or pay any money and didn't concern myself with the details of how these drugs had been purchased. Yogi had mentioned an upperclassmen floormate who had barged unannounced into their room one evening, introduced himself as their savior, and proceeded to get him and Trane ungodly high over the course of several hours. From that point on he paid them frequent visits. He would smoke them up for free and also sell them small quantities of marijuana for later use that they sometimes shared with me.

One evening, as we prepared to engage in our regular series of activities, it came to our attention that Trane's supply had run out. He suggested that we actually go to this dealer's room on the opposite end of the floor to smoke, which was something he assured us we could do for free.

The dealer's name was Dante, Trane explained as he banged on the door, but instead of a human voice answering we heard a loud bark. Trane pushed his way in and motioned for Yogi and I to follow. This room was laid out like any normal single I had seen thus far at Dartmouth. A desk sat in one corner with a near obsolete Apple computer resting on top. Dante's bed was in another corner, and above the bed a shelf housing a television, positioned so that it could be watched from the desk but not the bed. The television sat atop a VCR which had a tape playing when we walked in. I glanced at the monitor and was only a little surprised to notice it was pornography. There was no lighting except for a string of white Christmas lights that ran around the perimeter of the ceiling.

Dante sat at his desk, clutching a small glass pipe that was leaking a trail of smoke from the bowl. At his feet, a full-grown German Shepherd lifted his head and barked half-heartedly to protest our arrival but soon collapsed again on the floor.

"Have a seat," Dante uttered, noticeably not addressing the obvious fact that he had only one chair, and he was already occupying it. He seemed to be completely absorbed in whatever was happening at his computer. We sat on the edge of his bed and waited for some further acknowledgment. Without diverting his eyes from the screen he handed the bowl to Trane.

"Hit that," he commanded. He then allowed us ample time to finish the bowl before spinning around in his computer chair to address us properly for the first time.

"O.K., here's the deal. I can have hydro bused down from Burlington for four hundred an ounce. That stuff is fantastic. I also have some pretty good Mexican outdoor shit that I get from around here. A little seedy and stemmy but the price is right. It's up to you—the more I pick up, the cheaper it will be for you guys. You've got little freshmen friends to sell to, don't you? Outside of reefer, we got kizzy, crystal, boomers, acid, X or if you're feeling adventurous—a little opium perhaps? I can get it all—I just need time and a cash deposit," he paused to laugh but nobody did likewise so he continued. "These little sessions have been fun and all but I'm afraid I can't be smoking you guys up for free anymore. It's costing me a fucking fortune. I know at least *you* have money! A few questions remain, fellas. What do you want, how much do you want and how much money can you get me by Friday?"

He twirled back around to his computer and resumed typing to some presumed drug dealer who was conceivably thousands of miles away. Yogi stammered something about not being able to withdraw that amount so quickly but was beginning to promise that he would in a few weeks. Dante began explaining how much trouble he had already gone through for us (*us*? I had just met him five minutes earlier!). He then addressed me directly as if he had been reading my thoughts.

"Dude," he said as he pulled out a zip lock bag and tossed it to me. "With the ganja you already smoked this is about a twenty bag. Got a twenty on you?"

The seed and stem-ridden contents of that bag couldn't have been worth much more than ten dollars. Looking at him incredulously, I thought to myself, *This man must be out of his mind. He doesn't even know my name!* I pretended to sift through my pockets and told him I didn't but even if I did I would have declined on principle at that point. Trane snatched the zip-lock bag off my lap while snorting in Dante's direction.

"I'll take this bag but I've told you that we're not interested in any real drugs." Trane glared at Yogi who removed a twenty-dollar bill from his wallet and handed it to Dante.

"Let's go," Trane told us.

As we exited his room the drug dealer yelled after us, "Jesus loves you, suffered and died for you, and wants to live eternally with you in Heaven... please get in touch with me if you have not accepted Jesus Christ as your personal savior."

I didn't want to read anything into this encounter past the eccentric drug dealer, the porn, and the illegally housed dog. Trane on the other hand had thoughts on the matter.

"That son of a bitch thinks he can rope clueless rich kids like you as soon as they get to school, have them addicted in a matter of weeks and recruit them into selling for him."

"He's just a crackhead. I doubt he's put that much thought into this," Yogi replied.

"Why do you think he smokes us up every day?" asked Trane. "It's so obvious, dude. Listen, I don't ever want you going over there without me. Is that understood?"

That's pretty much how their relationship went—Trane dictated the terms, Yogi fell into line and we went along for the ride. The dominating alpha male personality of Trane was "cool" and thus carried weight with our peers while the reserved Yogi, lacking in confidence, was just happy to be included. The rest of our friends fell somewhere in between the two extremes. It was clear to us all that Trane had befriended Yogi as a matter of necessity. He had to mold Yogi into the roommate he wanted. Someone he could drink and smoke with, but more importantly, boss around. The constant peer pressure was having a noticeable effect on Yogi's personality, habits and general work ethic.

This was the only occasion I actually had the pleasure of meeting Dante; however, his exploits soon became infamous across campus.

Dante was widely known, at least in Topliff Hall, as being devoutly religious to the point where his passion for Christianity repeatedly led him into tirades where he not only debased the beliefs of others publicly but also actively attempted to convert them. At some point during his senior year, Dante must have snapped.

Throughout that year anti-Semitic slogans had been left on the dry-erase boards in Yogi's dorm. A Cohen was labeled "Jew bastard"—a Silverman got "Christ killer." Swastikas appeared next and decorated the doors of Jews and gentiles alike. One day the words, "Kill Kosher Kikes"—the K's emphasized and enlarged—were found scrawled onto the door of the undergraduate advisor's bedroom. The mounting trail of evidence led straight to Dante. His handwriting was found to exactly match the writing on the eraser boards and the next day he was led out of Topliff in handcuffs, accused of leading a campaign of harassment against the dorm's residents. In the subsequent days of investigation he gave an interview from the Hanover Inn that actually made it to print in the college paper. Shortly thereafter he was expelled. Like the feces hermit, he disappeared from our lives as quickly as he had entered it.

I now feel strangely disassociated from this previous life I used to live. I analyze and replay in my mind these little details that have contributed to the end result of who I have become and yet it feels as if these things are happening to someone else.

"We need new friends," I recall Beetle telling me once over a meal in Thayer.

"We'll have new friends when we pledge."

"You mean, when we pledge *Chi-Gam.*"

"Obviously..."

For the most part we ignored the aforementioned strange events of Topliff Hall, principally devoting ourselves to an earnest search to each find our proper niche on campus. A million different lives awaited us and every aspect of the campus encouraged you to dip your feet in the waters and explore the "vast and diverse" campus in any manner you saw fit. There were almost too many options, not enough time, and I couldn't decide where I wanted to focus my energies, so for the time being I felt comfortable devoting myself to my studies from Sunday to Thursday and letting my mind and body wander at the start of the weekend. At the time I, like many others, saw this as an opportunity to jump a few rungs in the social ladder. If you attach yourself to the right people, you'll find it hard recognizing yourself in two years. So for the first few months, we found ourselves parading around campus in "schmobs" from fraternity house to fraternity house, filling their bellies with beer and trying to better understand the cold world they had been banished to.

A typical Friday night for most Dartmouth freshmen began with the same sort of bizarre dorm based "pre-gaming" rituals one might find at any other college. That is to say, they were as much about rapid, self induced inebriation as they were about any sort of genuine social interaction. Small groups of students multiply in dorm rooms across campus until a breaking point is reached where their numbers can no longer be supported by the room's set dimensions and so the party must seek shelter elsewhere or disband into smaller groups. The sounds and sights of such evenings are distinct and haunting. The clinking of shot glasses. The metallic glint of airborne beer cans as they ricochet about the room. The subtle slurp that accompanies the gravity and pressure assisted chugging of entire beers—inhaled either through colorful funnels or directly from the beer can itself after a key induced puncture. The silent and deliberate loading of a bong at one end followed by the bubbling sound of water filtration and the discharge of smoke at the other. This was all deliberate preparation for a night destined to be spent in one or more of the thirty or so Coed, Fraternity and Sorority houses that dominated the Dartmouth campus nightlife. For me these nights out were spent in pursuit of Pong games.

Chapter 3: Pong and the Frats We Played In

"CFS houses at Dartmouth, although selective in terms of membership, are relatively open and democratic in the sense that the events they sponsor are usually free of charge and widely accessible. With some exceptions, social events at houses are open to all affiliated and non-affiliated students."
– *Excerpt from the Summary of the Recommendations Submitted to the Board of Trustees by the Committee on the Student Life Initiative*

In the Chi Gamma Epsilon basement one evening, a fraternity brother approached Beetle, Winston, Yogi, and I as we stood in a semicircle with beers in hand. Our eyes focused on a game of Beer Pong being played on the so-called "Varsity" side of the Chi-Gam basement.

"Kouge," this grinning brother said, extending his hand.

We introduced ourselves. Kouge responded with a series of introductory questions I imagined his type had been using to interrogate freshmen for as long as there had been freshmen to interrogate. Where we were from, what dorms we lived in, the classes we had enrolled in, which fraternities we had been to so far and what we thought of them, what we thought of Dartmouth in general—friendly fucking banter. He said that he had seen us in the basement a few times now.

"Ever play Ship?"

Nope. Just watched. Played a whole lot of Shrub though, we said.

"We'll fix that—you'll play your first game tonight. If you're going to hang out in Chi-Gam, you might as well be playing Ship."

Kouge started off towards the other wing of the basement, slipping through a throng of students holding beers and mixing in front of the stairwell, past the brother-manned keg behind the bar (from which beers were being extracted furiously and placed one by one onto a milk crate rack that sat beside the keg's operator), and finally to the far side of the basement, nicknamed "Junior Varsity," where two Pong tables sat spaciously mid-game. The four of us followed close behind. Kouge approached the table closest to the bar, where a lower ceiling and general lack of space cramped the playing conditions, and snatched the ball out of mid-air—right in the middle of a point.

"Guys mind moving your table over two feet?"

Not at all, they said.

Two of them gripped either end of the table, keeping it suspended in air, while the other two inched their garbage can supports over about two feet in the direction Kouge had indicated. They lowered the table into its new position and Kouge returned their ball. He next halted the game on the table furthest from the bar, but did so with words rather than actions, and only at the end of a very long rally. These players were obviously brothers and showed no signs of being thrilled with the impending interruption.

"Gonna' be bringing a table over," Kouge explained, as apologetically as I imagined he was capable of.

No problem, the brothers said.

We were instructed to grab a badly damaged table that leaned precariously against the back wall directly behind the table occupied by brothers and carry it over to the newly formed space.

A Pong table is essentially a flat sheet of plywood, about half an inch thick and in this particular basement measuring nine feet by five feet. Often they are painted with a design or insignia meaningful to the organization or person who created it, however the table we had been told to move was without a design at all and resembled a flotation device one might use to survive a shipwreck with its numerous knobs, cracks, chips and dents that would surely provide a serious challenge to any players who attempted to utilize it for its intended purpose, yet by the time we had carried this "table" over, Kouge had already set up two garbage cans to support it. It was clear he intended us to play on it, gross imperfections and all.

"I'm going to show you how to set up a game of Ship," he next said.

We all filled beers. Fifteen full cups per side, we were told. A sixteen ounce can of Milwaukee's Best, a.k.a the Beast, the standard non-keg beer on campus when I arrived in the fall of '99, could fill two twelve ounce plastic cups with eight ounces. Each empty can of Beast was thrown towards a stack of cans and cups splayed out near a non-functioning fireplace along the eastern wall, a practice we had observed the brothers doing with the cups they routinely emptied into their mouths just one table over.

Kouge then used a Ping Pong paddle (with the handle snapped off) to measure the precise placement of cups along the table's edge. In a few seconds, he had lined up four full cups in a row, equidistant from the table's edge and positioned so that the lip of each cup just barely touched its neighbor.

"All boats are measured the short side of the paddle in from the table edge," he said. "Start with the back cup and work your way up. The four boat runs up the left side. On the right side—the five boat. Then a two boat in that corner and the three boat at the median. Here, watch this."

He formed a little square of four beers at the long-wise dividing center of the table half-paddle in from the edge and below the median which split the table in two. He then took the beer closest to both the median and the edge and placed it at the other end of the cups so that there was a row of three beers with a single beer in front of the middle cup.

"The mine," he revealed triumphantly, "protects the three boat."

We set up the remaining boats on our own but Kouge checked each one for accurate table-measurements. When the boat setup was judged adequate, we stepped back to admire the table.

A full Ship game is a formidable sight. With its eight boats and two mines it gives the appearance of an army of beer cups marching towards you in strict military unison. Your initial thought is to wonder how exactly it is going to be possible to drink this much beer and you resolve yourself to the fact that indeed you *must* win in order to survive, either that or be utterly destroyed by the onslaught of drinking that will accompany consistent poor play. I stood on one side of the table with Yogi, who had a paddle in one hand already. He kicked at a second paddle half-hidden under some beer cans underneath the table and nodded at me, implying that I should grab it.

"Leave it down there. One paddle per side in this house," Kouge said dismissively. "Boats are sinkable at two and a half cups."

He summoned a Ping Pong ball from the depths of his cargo pants and tossed it in our general direction. Yogi caught it and paddle-bashed it down against our side of the table, aiming towards Beetle and Winston, who were able to loosen their aggressive stances when it became clear that the ball would outdistance their side by two or three feet.

"A little overzealous, no?" chirped Kouge. "Two serves in this house."

Yogi served once again, this time less violently and keeping the ball in play. The two teams rallied back and forth until eventually a cup on a back five boat was struck and not returned as a save.

"That's a hit," said Kouge. "Drink just half the beer for now."

We nodded, the half beer was downed with no argument, and play resumed, the two teams continuing to trade shots, hitting a cup here or there (but with no real regularity) and sending quite a few balls out of bounds where they would bounce and roll quickly out of view on the filthy basement floor. The retrieved balls were caked in a blackish wet grime but no water was in sight to wash them off.

"Just pour a little beer on it, and try to keep the ball on the table, fellas," Kouge advised with a grimace.

Play resumed unabated.

More shots, a few hits and even more misses followed. One of the back boats was hit dangerously low, a fact that peaked Kouge's interest in the game. A few more shots and the ball landed right inside this boat's half filled back cup.

"A boat sink," said a delighted Kouge. "That one's for the history books, boys. Now you each get to enjoy a beer. Drink up."

We did. By now we fully had the hang of things and Kouge's commentary subsided as the game transformed from one in which our primary focus had been to impress Kouge to a battle of wills from which only one team could claim victory. We were by no means competent players, but Kouge remained focused on our game as the back and forth continued with occasional hits and plenty of botched plays. The beer was beginning to add up. Each player had consumed four or five full beers within twenty minutes and each hit or sunk cup was taking longer and longer for the players to finish, a fact that did not elude our patron.

"Quit nursing your beer," Kouge said after the next boat sink, while Beetle and Winston attempted to nonchalantly extend their drinking period by disguising their duress with a banal side conversation.

Play resumed with the gravity of each hit or sink increasing as we became drunker and more liquid full. A timely shot not only crippled your opponent but also provided some much needed recovery time. And always, Kouge's inspirational commentary echoing in the background.

"Jesus Christ, I don't know which one of you is worse," he said, during an uninspired rally.

"You're supposed to aim *for* the cups," he said, after a particularly bad miss.

"Fuck, can't believe you didn't sink that shit," he said, after a closer miss.

"That shot was so low, dude. Get it up," he said, after a botched hit.

"Are you playing Pong or are you singing each other love songs?" he asked, after a prolonged delay in the game.

And then... we all froze in anticipation as the ball caught the air somewhere above that last boat and to me seemed engulfed in flames, a sign that the game had ended and there was no longer anything that could be done to stop the inevitable; a jet stream of purposeful wind carrying the ball up and out of the trajectory of normal misses and into an invisible line just above the table that abruptly snagged Beer Pong balls and delivered them into their natural habitats.

"That's a wrap... you fellas feel free to run that back."

Kouge had watched our entire game.

Each of the CFS houses has its own distinct personality but the lifeblood that powers them is universally beer. On any given weekend at least four or five of the bigger fraternities and sororities can be expected to have dance parties while the others are hosting unofficial nights of Beer Pong playing. For impressionable freshmen males it was hard not to see the fraternity brothers as nobles among peasants. They effectively dictated the entire social scene. The upperclassmen who failed to affiliate themselves with a organization roamed the campus without direction, the social equivalent of de-clawed zombies. I decided in the first week that I would pledge.

I should point out that the social landscape of Dartmouth's CFS system is always changing, and the perception of each house in the eyes of the student body evolves over time as well. While I was a student, there were three fraternities considered to be "power houses" on campus, though nobody actually called them that. These were the popular houses; home to the major sports teams, the socialites and the campus leaders. It was mostly from these houses that Dartmouth's most prominent senior societies hand picked its members each year.

The Alpha Male fraternity was, and as far as I know still is, Theta Delta Chi—home to hulking, brutish, jock types. Nicknamed the *Boom Boom Lodge* due to a notorious whiskey-related murder committed within its walls during the 1920s, Theta-Delt drew from a mix of athletic clubs, which included a large percentage of the basketball, lacrosse, and soccer teams. Parties and social events at Theta Delt also tended to attract the very small pool of ultra-desirable Dartmouth females. The brothers exclusively played Tree in their basement and were pretty darn good at it, often able to win entire contests just on cup saves. Many of my brothers were friends with Theta Delts and some would come over to our house to play Ship or vice versa; these were sort of like Pong play-dates. Theta Delt has an immense house away from Frat Row, behind Thayer dining hall.

Being the inspiration for *Animal House*, the Alpha Delta brothers tended to hold themselves to a higher bar of zaniness and wanton depravity than the other frats. A sobering fact you will learn immediately after stepping foot in their house is that it is rancid in a way you didn't previously think possible. The source of this foulness is the dungeon-like AD basement, which they called the "vomitorium"—easily the filthiest on campus due in part to a drainage system forming a perimeter around the walls that is openly used as a urinal by the brotherhood. AD played a Pong game called Two-Cup, where, as the name implies, two cups are continuously refilled as they were sunk and hit into nothingness and the game only reached its conclusion once a score of twenty-one, fifty or one-hundred is reached. I think that this strange Pong game, in conjunction with the hell-like conditions in the basement and the bizarrely aloof brotherhood, was too intense of a mess for me to contemplate dealing with on a consistent basis, so I was rarely at AD outside of party conditions and as a result don't really know too much about the house outside of its reputation, house game and physical appearance.

The last of the three power houses was Chi Heorot; a bastion of warm blooded athletic Nordic types, hockey players mainly, who had thick beards and loud booming voices. These thick armed giants could drink vast quantities of alcohol with seemingly no effect. They threw excellent dance parties and had bleachers set up around the Pong tables in their basement for spectators to watch and cheer while they awaited the inevitable start of their own games. Heorots loved anything that involved drinking and so played an exorbitant amount of Shrub, Tree and sometimes even Ship. They were unpretentious yet still, for someone like me, unapproachable.

Most other frats were considered middle-tier and appealed to their own specific subsets of the campus. We had hippie houses, nerd houses, jock houses, even a D&D obsessed milk and cookies house—it seemed as if there was an organization with the right fit for just about everyone on campus. Some of these organizations were more into bigger themed dance parties, while others focused on smaller scale room-to-room cocktail events or hosted acapella concerts and round table discussions with resident and visiting professors. They all engaged in local community service and periodically sponsored non-drinking events in their chapter rooms that were open to the campus. To stereotype all CFS members with the standard "frat guy douchebag" or "sorority girl slut" label is not only simplistic, it's also factually incorrect. These were really a diverse set of democratic drinking clubs and not the homogeneous, authoritative, elitist cults that many would have you believe. The makeup of these houses was at all times fluid; one single pledge class could at a blink of the eye transform an entire fraternity's identity and in three years that house could be unrecognizable to previous generations. The point of pledge term was to implant the essence of those specific philosophies, traits and traditions that a house felt vitally important to propagate, into the very fabric of a pledging sophomore's DNA.

Gamma-Delta-Chi was a former nerd house that had been invaded by football players one year when a block of like forty of them all rushed at once following the derecognition of their own fraternity, Beta. Gamma Delt's consensus best feature was the Pong galley they had instead of a basement. This was a room with immense ceilings down a flight of stairs off their first floor that had ideal Pong conditions for any style of play and room enough for three or four tables to operate simultaneously but not much else. Because of this exceptional setup, they hosted the annual cross-house Pong tournament held each summer with little complaint from other houses. Gamma Delt had quickly become the meatiest house on campus, at the time almost entirely football players, and solidly on the periphery of the Dartmouth fraternal hierarchy.

Bones Gate has always had a reputation on campus as the druggie house—a collective of paranoid, wastoid, basket-case, anarchists—and it seemed a certainty that this would always be the case. The brothers were for the most part friendly (if you cornered them long enough for a conversation), but kept to themselves and rarely threw open parties. An over-sized ladle hung from one of the pipes in the basement and if one accidentally knocked it down the Gatesmen would start chanting "LADLE, LADLE, LADLE". The ladle would be filled to the brim with beer and the offending party would have to immediately drink the whole thing in front of the crowd of brothers and guests—either five or ten beers, depending on which of the two ladles had been hung that night. A night could break down quickly at BG. A room full of visitors and three active Pong games could turn into four or five brothers passing a blunt around a dormant Pong table in the darkness in an unbelievably short amount of time so usually you had to see the writing on the wall and get the hell out. You didn't want to get stuck in one of these BG binge caves after hours with a group of blitzed brothers because who knows when you might emerge, and what might have happened to you once you did.

SAE, a widespread national fraternity, had an impressive mansion next to Baker Library and seemed primed for a hostile takeover. This was the country club of Dartmouth fraternities where pastel colored polo shirts with popped collars seemed to be a strictly enforced house rule. They hosted a beach party once a term where several inches of sand replaced the usual hardwood floors, the guests all wore beach attire and flip flops, and the house was adorned with palm trees and tiki torches. A fun party to be sure if you could get past the disconcerting fact that a large percentage of the party goers were SAE brothers and their friends. They had nice Pong tables, but I've never played on them.

Alpha Chi Alpha was a fraternity frozen in time, giving us a hint of what Dartmouth might have been like way back when. Times have been harsh since the days of the long-haired seventies but still there was an undeniable mystical feeling permeating the Alpha Chi house that overpowered you despite a sincere effort to stay on your feet in the AXA "Barn," stuck in the middle of a seven, eleven or doubles game while Stealers Wheel's "Stuck in the Middle with You" drowned out all sounds in the vicinity. A standard Shrub and Tree house, this brotherhood recruited us hard during the second half of freshmen year and then those same brothers ignored us entirely the second we pledged Chi-Gam.

Tri-Kap was known for both the ravenous intensity with which its brothers engaged in Pong and the fact that it was composed almost entirely of minorities, a far cry from the piles of white-faced composites surely stacked somewhere in the attic. The brothers here had mastered the art of the spin-shot and for a Ship player this was a difficult place to win an away game in. The brotherhood was about half Asian, with the other half split more or less equally among the other races. Unsurprisingly they threw popular dance parties, staged rap battles, and supplied a large chunk of the deejay pool for the campus.

Zeta-Psi, another big national fraternity, was on the rise as one of the cool "geek" houses on campus, mostly on account of a weekly Tuesday night "tails" event that had been gaining popularity. Home to computer science majors, Star Trek fans, and social misfits, they drank just as much as the bigger houses but accepted their role as a sort of hipster geek mecca. If I pledged a house like this I could assume a larger than life persona. I could effectively be king of the nerds. This was a role I had assumed before in High School but I consciously decided that when the time came I would pledge upwards—higher up on the social ladder than the rung me and my friends seemed stuck on.

There were plenty of other fraternities, sororities and co-ed organizations; each shared the same Pong based normative hang out structure and it was obvious to us all that anyone on campus who knew at all what they were doing was drinking a whole shit-load of beer and enjoying themselves mightily while doing so.

My own future fraternity, Chi Gamma Epsilon, was the black sheep on campus and served as Dartmouth's all-purpose party house. They threw dance parties every other week and the basement was constantly full of freshman and sophomores who had found little else on Frat Row to keep them interested. Chi-Gam was a welcoming place, truly open door compared to many other fraternities I visited but as with the other houses, the brothers operated with a strict set of invisible rules that they forced on themselves and any visitors. Upper-class students typically preferred AD, Hereot or Theta-Delt, while the first and second years frequented Chi-Gam. Because of this, the brotherhood was known for its romantic engagements with the younger classes and had a reputation as the "sketchy" frat on campus. Chi-Gam was a Ship house and any Shrub games played in its basement had the potential of incurring the wrath of the brotherhood, who were prone to flip these tables as a show of force.

As freshmen technically not allowed to even enter Greek houses during our first term on campus, the various brotherhoods effectively ignored me and my friends and were under no obligation to extend even the smallest courtesy. We were forced to find creative ways to gain access to parties that were strictly off-limits and were routinely frustrated while trying to find a Pong game at any of the bigger fraternities on weekends. Into our second term, when the freshman ban was lifted, it became remarkably easier to do so and we learned that each house even had its own designated Rush Chair—a brother who deliberately went out of his way to meet and greet visiting freshmen who were prospective pledges and arrange events where they could better get to know the house. Chi-Gam had welcomed us despite the prohibition on freshmen entering Greek houses during fall term and when winter began and the other houses suddenly began similar courting practices, this fact was not lost on us.

Seven Webster was a brick mansion situated in the middle of frat row between a fraternity (Phi-Delt) and a sorority (KDE). Anyone who ventured inside (and literally *anyone* could just walk in off the street) was faced with the stark reality of an interior that looked like it had been recently blasted with a fire-hose of sludge.

Inside the house, a strategically designed foyer allowed access to all rooms on the first floor, the basement by way of back staircase, and the upper floors. There was an ongoing battle to keep the largest and most inviting room on the first floor, our Meetings Room, in a presentable enough shape, however this was a war we were destined to lose in the face of Wednesday night Meetings and the occasion afternoon Pong games that could be observed taking place within. A house composite showing the fraternity's current members hung above a fire-place situated between two side doors that let out onto a patio of sorts where we sometimes barbecued. This Meetings Room also served as the dance floor for our well-attended "DJ and Kegs" party hosted every other Friday. The second and third floors were a cell-block of member occupied bedrooms—fourteen in total that were divided into ten doubles and four singles. More house composites, from bygone eras, lined the walls of the bedroom hallways. The second floor had a kitchen and three-stalled bathroom while the third floor had a more private single stall.

As you entered the basement, you were greeted with a long wooden bar running along the back wall. A narrow walking space behind the bar allowed brothers to dispense beer from two cold kegs that were on tap twenty-four hours a day. My freshman year was the last in which CFS houses had no limit on the number of kegs they were allowed. Following the implementation of certain elements of the *Student Life Initiative* a limited number of kegs were allowed during registered parties only. The school would give you say four tags for kegs and if you were caught with more kegs than you had tags the house could incur disciplinary action. Fraternities after this point were also no longer allowed a permanent bar, so this whole setup was abandoned the following year and a pointlessly removable bar was installed. This is when the campus made the switch from Beast to Keystone Light as the staple non-keg beer for nights of Pong.

The Keg Cave was what we called the back room, which was accessible from behind the bar and housed our beer cooler and music system. The cooler could keep up to ten cases cold at a given time, however from November to March refrigeration of beer in the unheated keg cave was entirely unnecessary. The music system controlled a series of speakers set up in the basement, meetings room, and perimeter of the house.

The Trough was the basement's only bathroom—a three-person urinal located just behind the basement stairs that was constantly being clogged with vomit.

Brothers usually booted publicly in one of the basement's many garbage cans or in one of the two snow piles that flanked the rear entrance to the house, but non-brother male visitors often opted for the privacy and convenience of the trough to expunge their bloated beer bellies, not having to concern themselves with the logistics of how this mess is cleaned up. Once the trough did become clogged, guys would obliviously continue to piss into it, causing the waste level to rise until an inevitable breaking point was reached and subsequent spillage occurred. This didn't deter most from continuing to urinate into it though, but it was advisable to change your method of doing so and enact a high arching stance well behind the lake of piss and vomit that was rapidly forming underneath. This dance would play itself out regularly until the next house cleaning.

Our back "Mud Room," located next to the trough, had a laundry machine and dryer and let out into the parking lot behind the house. Also in this room was a short staircase leading down to a tiny sub-basement that contained the boiler and additional storage space.

Varsity was the name we gave to our premier Pong Table and by extension that whole side of the basement. The ceilings were just the right height, allowing a player to put a nice high arc on his shot but still gave a savvy player the ability to use the ceiling as a deadly weapon. This was advertised as a brothers only table but that just meant a brother had to be one of the four participants in a given game and if it was a Pong intense day/time then really one brother per team was required. The other side of the basement was double this size and home to two additional tables. These were the "Junior-Varsity" and "Super Junior-Varsity" tables, where anyone could play. To acquire an additional beer, one only need approach the brother manning the tap who had to do nothing more than hold an empty cup under the spout for a few seconds and manage the fairly simple coordination involved in handing off a beer while grabbing another empty cup at the same time. The taps never shut off. Not while there were still people drinking.

Without fail, Kouge was in the basement every time we were at Chi-Gam. We would walk through the entrance and see him perched up there on the bar, or behind a Pong table mid-game, or entertaining visitors near the entrance. All other basement dwellers seemed to know and respect him; he ran that place as far as we could tell and to an extent we were hypnotized by him. He always wore pretty much the same outfit: a hooded Chi-Gam sweatshirt, rugged green cargo pants and barely held together Birkenstock sandals. In warmer weather he donned a Chi-Gam t-shirt instead of the hoodie. There was a permanent five-o'clock shadow drawn on his face, suggesting that he never had to shave after a certain point of stubble growth.

"Come play Dice," Kouge said to me once while I was standing alone with a beer watching Beetle and Winston play Ship in the Chi-Gam basement. Sipping my beer and thinking about how long it would be before my own game started, I shrugged and said: "Why not?"

We joined a small circle of students that crowded the bar surrounding a near full beer that rested between them. Kouge ducked under the bar joining two brothers that I vaguely recognized. I remained on the apparently non-brother side with a pair of girls I thought might be freshmen and a guy who I knew certainly was. I didn't introduce myself.

The brother standing next to Kouge had a pair of six-sided dice in his hand which he rolled on the bar scoring a four and a five. He passed the dice to the next person in the circle who also rolled, scowled, and handed the dice to Kouge.

"What is going on here?" I asked.

"You're about to find out," Kouge said, shaking a fistful of dice in preparation for his roll. The dice rolled out of his hand and skidded across the bar coming within an inch or two of the edge and displaying a pair of fours.

"Doubles, fantastic. Ready for a quick lesson?"

Using the edge of his cup of beer he pushed the dice closer to his clenched fist. He then set the cup down in front of me and cupped one hand over the dice, careful not to touch either of them.

"Drink that as fast as you can," he urged.

At once the cup was at my lips and the beer running down my throat. Meanwhile Kouge had made a lightning quick move for the dice and was now rolling and re-rolling them on the bar. He stopped when they read:

"Eleven. You drink."

"I thought I just did."

"Didn't finish your beer in time. You drink again."

He snatched my empty cup, reached over for a fresh beer from a rack of twenty that presumably had been filled for the game and filled the original cup about halfway. He again set this down in front of me.

"You'll have to be quicker than that," said Kouge.

"Seven, eleven or doubles," one of the girls explained to me as if it were the most obvious thing in the world. This time I downed the beer quickly, only giving Kouge enough time for one roll. He passed me the dice and handed me a beer. "Now fill that and roll."

I poured in a quarter of a beer and rolled a seven.

"Excellent." Kouge lit a cigarette. "Now you make someone drink. Move the dice closer with the cup but don't touch them yet. Now give the beer to someone."

One of the participants seemed to be on the verge of wandering off so the beer went in front of her.

"Can't touch the dice until she touches her cup, otherwise it gets reversed... you drink and she rolls," I was advised.

She calmly laid her hand against the bar and began inching her fingers closer to the cups. She was hoping that I would overreact and go for the dice too soon. I continued to wait for the exact moment her fingers came into contact with the cup.

My opponent took a fake swipe at the cup to try to throw me off but I was too deep in concentration to take the bait. She tried two or three more decoy grabs before actually raising the cup. Now it was my turn to frantically roll the dice. First I rolled a seven and she drank. On my next set of rolls I began intentionally rolling the dice slower, allowing my opponent to drink a little slower. Still I rolled a pair of twos as she began to drink.

When she finished her beer I poured in what was basically a single large sip. Not embarrassing but not difficult. As soon as I set the cup on the table Kouge picked it up and drank the entire thing in one gulp. The girl, while surprised, was clearly happy that this occurred.

"That's a steal," Kouge said with a laugh.

"This game has steals?"

"It sure does," he said, "Also, you still get a roll. You always get one roll no matter how fast I drink the cup."

I rolled an eleven for him.

"Fuck me." he said

Dice continued for some time and probably only ended because the two brothers were called upon to start a game of Pong they had called next on. Without the brothers, the girls didn't want to drink and neither really did we, so Kouge and I grabbed a beer each to sip and walked over to the exclusive brothers only table to watch the end of a Ship game that was in its advanced stages.

This was as intense a Pong game as I had ever seen. Players were diving around the table, tossing paddles back and forth, furiously pounding cups of beer, cursing violently when forced to drink and otherwise just having what looked to be a profoundly important experience, or at the very least one that appeared to be great fun for anyone participating.

We watched the game together for a few minutes and then Kouge slapped my knee and motioned towards a new arrival to the basement, a character who swaggered down the stairs and at the entrance surveyed the scene carefully as if he were a farmer inspecting his fall crops for insects or mold. An obvious brother this one was.

"See this asshole?" Kouge said. "There's one like him in every house."

The new arrival was being greeted by some of his friends and had begun to tell a story or joke or something along those lines that these friends of his were clearly enjoying and he didn't seem to be giving any indication of being quite the "asshole" Kouge described. In fact the whole basement scene seemed a serene and inviting place where the behavior of assholes just wasn't going to be tolerated by the group.

"Here's what we do to assholes."

Kouge sprung up from the side bench we shared, galloped across the room, and jumped on the back of the unsuspecting brother, who toppled over with Kouge still on his back and collided into a garbage can that had been propping up the Pong table that Beetle and Winston had until that point been playing on. My two friends shrugged as their table, beers and all, crashed to the floor as if to say '*What can you do?*' while Kouge and the second brother (who had apparently at some unknown point seriously offended Kouge) rolled around together in the filth of the basement, quite oblivious to the fact that they were in the middle of ostensibly throwing what would in normal circles be considered a party. The assaulted brother struggled to bring himself to his feet and then garbled something unintelligible at Kouge, while re-erecting one of the fallen garbage cans next to him. He then bent over this can and vomited into it violently and for a prolonged period of time—some students didn't even seem to notice this affair while others looked on voyeuristically—the music blasting the whole time and the never stopping Pong balls providing a hypnotic background beat. I was at once amazed at the utter ridiculousness of how we were all treating this as inevitable or pretending like it wasn't occurring at all. This whole scene taken in one long gulp forced an envious smile to my face.

❄

"Shrub is *seven* beers a side," Winston was saying as he dislodged the first of six beers from a *Milwaukee's Best* plastic six-pack neck ring. "Knight, haven't we played Beer Pong to the point where you should know that by now?"

I had already filled at least ten for my side.

"We're not playing Shrub in Chi-Gam," I replied, continuing to fill cups with a mocking expression, "And why would I waste beer, even if it is *Beast*?"

"Are you thinking Ship?"

I looked at Winston cynically, "Bro, you suck at Ship,"

"We all suck at Ship," Beetle said with a laugh. "Winston just happens to be exceptionally terrible."

"What!" exclaimed Winston. "I'm in no way worse than either of you. Fact."

"The only way we're finishing a game in time is if we get at least one halfway decent player."

"That ain't Yogi..."

"No, it is not."

I began to set up a standard game of shrub. After placing the extra beers around the stem of the shrub, I quickly rearranged a few cups to form a cross. "How's this for a shrub?"

Winston smirked and began arranging his cups into the Star of David. "A little *Holy War* perhaps?"

This was not the first game of Pong that we had spontaneously invented.

Beetle meanwhile was sifting through a pile of cups and empty beer cans on the floor. A moment or two later he popped up with both a paddle and a ball. Yogi, who I could only guess had wandered off to avoid filling any beer, entered the room with a second paddle in his hand.

The four of us were in the Ship Room on the morning of Fenway Fiasco, unofficially considered by just about everyone to be the culminating event of pre-rush and consisting of a house barbecue followed by a Red Sox's game—expenses all paid by the fraternity. This was an occasion for the brotherhood to meet and court their next prospective pledge class privately but in the context of the group. It was the spring of our freshman year and fraternity rush for our class would be the following fall. While I had already decided on Chi-Gam, anything could happen, either jeopardizing my chances of getting a bid or pulling me in another direction. In those days the frats were still near the height of their power; it could be expected that anywhere from fifty to seventy kids would rush Chi-Gam and only thirty or so would get a bid. There were no guarantees.

After Holy War (the outcome of which is lost to history) other freshmen had arrived and the first floor was filled with fellow potential pledges as well as actual brothers. A few games of Ship were being played in the basement, but primarily people were holding casual conversations and drinking cocktails in the

Meetings Room. We were left largely to ourselves in the Ship room.

The bus transporting us to Fenway prepared to leave following a second game. We split up and scrambled around the house to pack as many stray beers into our pockets as possible. We also created several mixed drinks in emptied soda bottles with the cheap alcohol the fraternity brothers had set out in the Meetings Room. Now in possession of an impressive arsenal of beer and booze for the bus ride, we had signed our own death warrants. None of us would be able to fully recall the events of the next few hours and only after piecing together testimony from a dozen or so sources have I mustered the ability to narrate the unfortunate events that transpired.

We became separated on the bus. A lack of seats coupled with a general drunken confusion proved too overpowering for any kind of group coordination. Yogi and I found ourselves in the back of the bus with the majority of the alcohol. Beetle and Winston were somewhere towards the front. We traded shots and hungrily immersed ourselves into the group dynamic of the house, excited that at least temporarily we were in some small way brothers.

Yogi polished off one of our prepared rum and cokes before the bus left Hanover. As it had been for me, Dartmouth was his first exposure to serious alcohol consumption, which made him, despite his size, a quick drinker with a dangerously low tolerance and as I recall, he almost immediately passed out with his head banging rhythmically against the windowpane as the driver careened dangerously around the interstate. With Yogi unconscious, I was on my own. The brotherhood that I thought I knew so well seemed foreign. The alcohol was beginning to do its trick.

I stumbled down the aisle toward my other two friends but was stopped after two rows by a hand that reached across the aisle and grabbed hold of my shoulder.

"Where the fuck do you think you're going?"

I recognized my assailant as a sophomore—only his second term as a full brother. His eyes betrayed a man who was anxious to "haze" another after the eight weeks of pledging he had endured earlier in the year. The reality of the current situation was that even though I wasn't officially a member of the organization, I was effectively auditioning to be a member and it was important that I didn't seem afraid in the face of potential hazing—the full nature of which largely eluded me at the time. The sophomore Chi-Gam pulled me closer and handed me a bottle of cheap rum that had been sitting on the seat next to him.

"We call this game *Island Rum*," he said. "See the little island there?" The label displayed a tiny shipwrecked man drinking under a lone palm tree, which I imagined to be his attempt to quell the certain loneliness of being stranded on so tiny an island. The bottle was still three-quarters full.

"Drink that until the rum is below the island."

As it dawned on me that this would be almost half of the remaining bottle, I looked around for a familiar face but the bus had become a moving photograph of a bus. Nothing I could reach out and grasp and no allies in sight. With no other option at hand, I surrendered myself to the task at hand.

"You mean... sort of like this?"

I raised the cheap rum to my mouth. The stuff was foul, fire all the way down, something maybe stirred in my stomach. I was already so sauced that after a few moments it began to taste like flat root beer.

"And... you're done," the brother declared, a painfully long moment later as the rum dwindled its way toward the little island. "Dude, I back this kid. He's fucking hardcore."

The brother sitting directly next to him nodded with obvious disinterest and then resumed an apparently more interesting conversation with someone on the other side of the bus. In fact everyone in the back of the bus seemed to be talking to people in the front. The drunker I got, the louder these voices seemed.

I was released and allowed to make my way towards Beetle and Winston a few rows back from the front. Either my friends were asleep or I never made it there at all—I honestly can't remember this particular detail. I do know that soon I was making a return trip to the back of the bus, and brothers were calling for me to "sit my ass down." Not anxious to pass Mr. Island Rum again, my only course of action was to somehow make it back to Yogi without being intercepted.

My mission to return to my seat without being captured failed. I wasn't sure exactly when it happened or who did the capturing, but I was once again given a drinking assignment. Instead of a bottle of rum, this time it was a plastic Snapple bottle that did not look like it contained any Snapple.

"I'm giving you a little break," this brother reassured me. "Drink this, you'll sober up." He handed me the bottle and instructed me to begin chugging.

I fully expected this to be some horrific concoction and was relieved to find out it seemed only mildly alcoholic, although granted I was probably beyond estimating alcohol content at this point. I polished off his drink and staggered on my way.

I retreated not to my seat but to the bathroom, thinking at first that I was about to vomit at any second, but my body decided that it would prefer to expel the rum and everything else through the other end. The toilet stall in the coach bus consisted of a two-foot hole that led down to the dark, oily, scary compartments of the bus with only a flimsy piece of plastic for a seat. There were rubber flaps a foot below the bowl opening, presumably designed to prevent any splashing up of excrement, but when I had finished this particular nasty business, I discovered the remains of the previous day's meals resting comfortably in the middle of the flaps just a few inches below the seat. So I kicked the contraption as hard as I could. No result. A black hole couldn't dislodge this shit.

Someone started banging on the bathroom door. "What the cunt are you doing in there?" This unfamiliar voice demanded to know.

A terrible moment of drunken panic set in, and I couldn't bear the humiliation of opening that door to this huge pile of fecal matter defying gravity in the toilet bowl. It seemed sensible then, in my staggering state, to wrap my hand in toilet paper and begin forcing the shit through the flaps. A lane change thrust me up against the wall of the bathroom, my now feces covered hand rose to protect my face automatically. You can imagine the subsequent moments of terror. After regaining my balance it occurred to me that now both the bathroom and myself were speckled with little brown dots of dung. The banging on the door continued.

Smiling devilishly I quickly washed my hands and began trying to smear the mess into the walls to disguise what had happened. I thrust open the door and marched confidently back into the bus, maybe even whistling. The awful stench that accompanied me and my casual stride fooled nobody. I took the first empty seat I saw but was instantaneously deposited on the floor by the person in the next seat.

"He shit himself!" this person laughed.

The bus exploded in hysterics.

In fact I had not shit myself, though to this day nobody believes me. But think about it. Who in their right mind goes to the bathroom to shit their pants? My underwear, I would discover, was clean. But evidence covered the outside of me head to toe.

I was dragged to the last row of the bus and seated beside Yogi, who had also been relocated. He was covered in a good deal of vomit (his own I assumed) and seemed to be continuously burping up more of it onto his shirt like a bubbling hot spring. Sitting next to him, my head resting gently on his shoulders and my eyes dimming, I began booting on his shirt as well. He was strangely cognizant enough to change his trajectory and then his puke began raining on me. The back and forth vomiting bonanza lasted the rest of the way to Boston.

I must have sobered up enough to follow basic instructions by the time the bus off-loaded us at Fenway but to a blind man it would be clear that Yogi and I had no business being admitted into the game in the shape we were in—covered in vomit and dung and barely able to stand. A couple of scholarly brothers came to the same conclusion and purchased us Red Sox fan-gear and we tossed our boot n' shit covered clothing in a nearby trash receptacle, hoping jean rigidness and body stench would be less noticeable.

Miraculously, the entire stinking, drunken Chi-Gam congregation went through security uneventfully and made its excited entrance into the ballpark. The seats purchased by the house were among the worst in the whole stadium. Yogi and I were placed behind even these seats, in the last row, on account of what I'm assuming was a horrendous smell. The scoreboard blocked a full half of the field but I could faintly discern a handful of tiny men running around the diamond what seemed like several miles away. I remember wondering if the game had begun or if the cleaning crew was still prepping the bases.

The first inning came to a close with me still sulking in my extreme upper-deck seat, enviously watching the Chi-Gams and freshman guests yucking it up below, and smelling strongly of shit. Yogi, who by my distorted perception was the very reason we had been ostracized from the group to begin with, was fishing around in the trash of the stadium around us and smirking wildly as he threw each peanut casing he came across into my lap with a flick of the wrist and a delayed, ostentatious chuckle. He then let out a shriek and sat upright in his seat, quivering like a school boy and brandishing an already opened beer can he had discovered on the floor, which he immediately held prone in a pouring position over his mouth and then crushed in an attempt to quickly extract its contents. A few drops of who-knows-how-old beer sprinkled down around the outside edges of his mouth and he groaned in disappointment.

"Empty." Yogi said, seemingly stupefied.

The crushed can was hurled into the air out in front of us where it hung for a second before descending rapidly right into the mass of Chi-Gams that chattered loudly below. The projectile perfectly intercepted Beetle's head and then ricocheted down two more rows into an innocent bystander who sheepishly glanced up at our group and then quickly looked away—wisely deciding to pretend as if the offense hadn't occurred. Beetle, on the other hand, not fearing Yogi in the slightest, and perhaps feeling slightly emboldened because of his current standing with the group in relation to ours (being allowed to sit with them for one) jumped out of his seat, spun around and pointed a finger directly at us while declaring something I could not make out to the gang of frat brothers in his midst. In slow motion, I watched him climb into the aisle, ascend the stands and punch Yogi full on in the face before poor Yogi even had a chance to fully comprehend what was transpiring. Within seconds a swarm of security guards had surrounded and apprehended all three of us and we were being forcibly ejected from the stadium.

Out on the street we hit the curb with no real choice but to wait out the remainder of the game but before long, two brothers and three freshmen were also escorted out of the ballpark in much the same fashion as we had been—draped in a security detail that watched their every move. That's when Rats, a freshman who I had seen in the basement before but wasn't personally acquainted with, defiantly knocked over a kiosk of Red Socks memorabilia and the group sprinted off, security following close behind. My curb-friends and I looked at one another, shrugged and joined the pursuit, not wanting to miss this chance of getting the hell out of Boston.

The three other prospective pledges, I learned much later, had also been kicked out for disorderly conduct and general drunken behavior. One had apparently made a game of sprinting up and down the stadium steps, tripped, and rolled down nearly the whole flight before colliding into a beer vendor, whose carrying case erupted, spilling cups and cans across several rows of seats. A second pledge, this Rats character I just mentioned, had come to the fallen pledge's aid as security approached and was tossed for his "threatening posture" during the brief encounter. A third pledge had nearly come to blows with a die-hard Sox fan and was ejected mostly on his future potential in the realm of beer-throwing, stairs-plummeting or aggressive posturing.

The two brothers, one drunk but functional, the other stone-cold sober, had been assigned by the house to make sure none of us died. I've imagined the headline in the college newspaper the next day, *Fraternity Linked to Death of Freshmen, One Covered in Feces.* Not very good publicity for the Greeks who were already on the chopping block. If the college even found out the trip had occurred in the first place, the frat could be in big trouble—probation, or worse, de-recognition.

For several weeks following the Fenway debacle I avoided the house. Rumors were flying that the bus company had reported our obscene behavior to the school and that Chi-Gam might actually get accused of hazing freshmen, which would be considered significantly worse than being accused of hazing pledging sophomores. My chances of getting into the fraternity seemed shattered. Not only had I completely humiliated myself in front of the group but I had endangered the very existence of the fraternity in the process. Why would they want someone like that as a permanent member when they had the very easy opportunity of just not letting me in to begin with? I didn't know this at the time but all it took was three votes saying no. That's it. No amount of support gets you in once you have three "dings" during deliberations.

When I finally swallowed my shame and dared set foot in the house again, I was not thrown out, ignored or made to feel uncomfortable or unwanted in anyway. Everyone sort of knew the story and many wanted to hear it firsthand. Raucous laughter typically ensued during the telling, and after the climatic finish, wiping tears of sheer joy from their eyes, to a man each listener offered me a symbolic gesture acknowledging my misfortune—affirming for me that while yes, everyone endures such hard times at some point in their life, not everyone has the pleasure of doing so quite as publicly. Somehow, being covered in shit became a badge of honor.

Chapter 4: Two Men Enter

"The committee noted that fewer than a fifth of students report that they are likely to join a CFS organization when they are surveyed before matriculation, but in fact half ultimately do join. A potential explanation for the much higher percentage that ultimately joins is that the dominance of the CFS system at Dartmouth has led to a lack of other social options—or that the absence of any consistent effort to create other options has reinforced the dominance of CFS organizations. Whatever the case, many students believe that they have little choice but to join."
– *Excerpt from the Summary of the Recommendations Submitted to the Board of Trustees by the Committee on the Student Life Initiative*

I arrived back on campus in September of 2000 after my first summer away from Dartmouth consumed with thoughts of rushing a fraternity. This was an opportunity to participate in something unique and there was no way I would pass that up.

Rush took place on the Tuesday and Wednesday of the second week of classes. Each fraternity on campus opened its doors to potential sophomore recruits and hand-picked their next pledge class from among the truly interesting or interested parties. This obviously allowed the fraternities an opportunity to evaluate the personal characteristics of the rushing sophomores. At the same time the candidates had a chance to investigate different houses and meet the brotherhoods; they would then signal their interest in the frat of their choice. In many cases, the two sides had already met in the darkness of the basement but some sophomores were meeting brothers for the first time. The brotherhoods deliberated and voted on each rushee and once the final list of new inductees was decided, teams of brothers were sent out across the campus to offer up "bids" to the accepted candidates, who were then brought back to the house to celebrate.

Students wore formal wear and mingled in the chapter rooms of each fraternity house. Food was generally served, ranging in quality from Taco Bell and KFC at Chi-Gam to a catered lobster feast at SAE, the school's obligatory preppy house. Rush was one of the few non-alcoholic events any frat held and these forced conversations with people you had never seen sober could be awkward. In a little over a year I would be on the opposite side of the spectacle, dressed in a suit, yet still wearing sandals, a strongly spiked rum and coke in hand—which was a near mirror image of many of the brothers I met that night.

For those who had not made up their mind as to which house they wanted to join or who didn't think they were guaranteed a bid at their first choice, the game was to strike as many good impressions as possible in the houses you were interested in, before indicating your first choice by "shaking out" at one of the frats. In that way you could have a backup. If you didn't get a bid at your first choice it helped to have a second lined up. If it was already a foregone conclusion that you were getting a bid, then you just showed up at that house during rush, said hello, and went home to wait for your bid. Our strategy was to drop by Zeta-Psi for thirty minutes to let the brothers know that our first choice was Chi Gam but insinuate that if we didn't get in we'd go Zete. We spent the rest of the night at Chi Gam. Assuming I was already in, I got high with Kouge upstairs towards the end of rush and spent the remainder of the evening at the food table, a bucket of fried chicken in my hand, joking that the choice of food was a brilliant minority recruitment initiative.

Following this meet and greet reception, the entire brotherhood lined up outside along the shaft of the cock to greet the rushing sophomores who exited the building one at a time and shook the hand of each brother as they departed—a tradition termed "shakeout." Now the waiting game ensued. Winston, Yogi and I walked back to our triple in New Hamp Hall to wait for the brothers to pick us up to sink our bids and welcome us into the fold. Beetle, who lived on the opposite side of campus, did the same.

Few things are more frustrating than waiting for something that you know must come, but for some reason or another doesn't. After two hours, two Chi-Gam brothers visited a couple of kids down the hall we sometimes smoked and watched *Family Guy* episodes, and the Chi-Gams spent the better part of an hour convincing them to rush the house. When they eventually accepted their bids and left with the brothers, this frustration turned to anger. Soon we couldn't avoid the fact that nobody was coming for us and that, in fact, we had been intentionally passed over.

In the third hour of waiting we heard a knock on our door which I eagerly sprung up to answer. It was two of the Zeta Psi brothers we knew from hanging out in their basement and with whom we had discussed the possibility of pledging earlier that night. They said they knew we intended to go Chi-Gam but also said they honestly thought we would be happier in Zete and could play a large role in the future of their house and that the Chi-Gams were not who we thought they were. Yogi decided to leave with them to accept a Zeta Psi bid. Winston and I remained behind, still with a glimmer of hope that Chi-Gam was on its way.

At any moment I half expected a familiar face to burst into the room spouting congratulations and welcoming me into the fold, but as the night dragged along it became clear this wasn't going to happen. Thoughts of inadequacy filled my mind as I reexamined the details of the past year, searching for an explanation among my fuzzy memories. Was the previous year a complete farce? Was the kindness shown to me by the brotherhood fake and contrived, designed to bolster the frats image, not welcome new members? Maybe they knew they weren't going to take me and strung me along because no one had the heart to tell me otherwise. Or maybe it was because I shat myself during Fenway fiasco.

Whatever the reason, by the morning we had received callback emails from Kouge inviting us back for the second night of Rush. We hadn't been dung but we hadn't gotten bids either. I sent several frenzied blitzes to Kouge that went unanswered. But Winston had an explanation that made some sense.

Earlier in the term Winston had identified a similarly minded computer science geek of a Chi-Gam brother named Pope, and the two had become close friends with Pope almost acting as a sort of fraternity benefactor on Winston's behalf. He was able to glean from Pope that the problem was we didn't know enough brothers. We had our supporters, Kouge and Pope among them, but if we wanted into the fraternity we would have to meet the guys we didn't know and by way of a contrived five minute conversation convince them we were Chi-Gam material.

Winston and I repeated the entire process the next evening. Although at this point the kids who had been accepted the previous night (Beetle included) were invited back as new brothers. We had to accept the stigma of having been passed over the first night. This time I left nothing to chance, sought out the brothers I may have avoided the previous night and put on a calculated facade that I deemed as appropriately "Greek" in nature. Winston and I stumbled home from frat row unwilling to concede that we didn't belong in Chi-Gam. We blamed Yogi, and the Fenway trip, our friendship with Kouge; we didn't consider the possibility that just maybe the brotherhood might be doing us a favor. My brain told me the obvious—I wasn't a frat boy and neither was Winston and we had no business pledging any fraternity, let alone *Chi-Gam.* I was a pretender, and the brothers realized this and were going to allow me to continue pretending, perhaps even privately enjoying my pathetic attempts to curry their favor. The real Chi-Gams effortlessly integrated themselves into Dartmouth's world while I was clearly putting on an act. My routine was not fooling anyone.

Thankfully we didn't have long to dwell on such thoughts. Waiting in our room were Kouge and Pope. I looked at Winston and saw that his eyes displayed a look of euphoric relief. Minutes before what now lay before us seemed like an impossible dream. I remember only three distinct thoughts. *This is something that is actually happening! Tonight I am going to pledge a fraternity! Everything is going to work out after all...*

Kouge handed me a purple Mad Dog, a fortified wine artificially flavored and colored, typically with an alcohol content between 13 and 18%. Pope had a yellow "banana flavored" bottle for Winston. We were told to chug these immediately because tonight we'd be *sinking our bids*—a special fucking moment apparently. We chugged our Mad Dogs, and then vomited purple and yellow into our trash can. Next we were blindfolded for no discernible reason and driven to the Chi Gamma Epsilon fraternity house. It is important to note that because this was the second night of rush and a Wednesday night, we wouldn't have the same bid night experience as the rest of our class and since I didn't experience "bid night" directly I will leave those details out—scandalous though they may be. Meetings were just beginning as we arrived and we were instructed to line up next to the rest of the new pledge class against a back wall. Needless to say, everyone was extremely excited to welcome us to the fold. Hugs, handshakes, smiles—everyone laughing and a table of beer and chugging, shouting—merriment of every variety. Anytime a chant of: "HERE'S TO ALL THE PLEDGES! THE PLEDGES, THE PLEDGES..." broke out amongst the brothers we had to chug a beer and this was done over and over again, a countless number of times over the course of the night.

Meetings themselves! Try to imagine sixty individuals excessively drinking in a room together; all inhibitions disappeared, nothing would leave the room and all pretensions were dropped. I was too drunk to remember any specifics of that particular Wednesday night, but I remember feeling like a very small part of something much bigger than myself. A living and breathing brotherhood, its independent parts all interacting with and influencing each other. Becoming a part of this cult was no longer an abstract idea. That night Winston, Beetle and the rest of the new pledge class got absolutely shit faced blacked out together for the first time as a full group and other than a couple stories recanted afterwards about pledges vomiting or urinating various places around the house, I strangely (or maybe not so strangely) don't remember any specifics at all concerning how we ended up in the miserable conditions we found ourselves in the next morning.

The following evening we were summoned to the house for our first real "pledge event." The previous night had been strictly a drinking celebration. We still knew next to nothing of what the rest of the term would look like. Kouge met us in the Brothers Room and introduced himself as our pledge trainer. I observed immediately that his demeanor towards us was changed. No longer did he carry himself like our equal. An aura of authority now surrounded him that was displayed so confidently none of us dared question it. With the group of pledges gathered before him, Kouge next outlined the obligations and expectations of the following eight weeks.

"This little green manual you've just received isn't a book of love poems I wanted you to read to each other so stop looking around with those dick licking expressions. This is your fucking pledge manual. You are expected to know everything in it. I would open them up and start reading, NOW. House history. School history. Memorize everything. This is important. Turn to page three. The contents of your pledge pack. You must carry these items with you at all times. I recommend one of these—yeah it's a fucking fanny pack—get used to wearing it, *Gorgeous*. If your pledge pack is not with you at all times along with every item you are expected to carry in it—penalty beers. You will purchase one six by four inch black notebook, unlined and hardcover. One of these here in my hand. Every week you must get the signature of five brothers in this book. Some will be easy to get... some not so much. By the end of pledge term you must have at least fifty signatures. You must get every executive in the house, your older brother, and your pledge trainer. Do not attempt to get my sig unless you know your pledge manual cover to cover and every last detail about my family, history and personality. This is not a joke. If you do not get the correct number of sigs you will not be let into this fraternity. I can guarantee that. Pledge cleanings are twice a week. Duties will be blitzed out before cleanings. I am also your Houseman. I will expect you to be at cleanings. If you are not at cleanings—penalty beers. You must spend two hours per week at the house during the daytime—not in the basement. The Brothers Room, Room M, one of the bedrooms on the second floor. Somewhere there are no Pong tables. If you do not hang out in the house—penalty beers. Any questions so far?"

"What's a penalty beer?"

Though shocked that someone actually had the gall to ask this question, I was sure we were all thinking it.

"You'll find out soon enough." Kouge said.

At that first gathering, I got to meet the rest of the kids I would be pledging with; together we constituted the future of the house. Out of the thirty of us I only recognized half and had only spoken to five or six. Most names remained a mystery until we were all wearing our pledge signs the following week. As a general rule, Chi Gams won't learn your name until it is written in bold black lettering across your chest.

We were required to wear these pledge signs at all times (a laminated rectangular piece of poster board with our name, our Greek letters and the identifier: pledge written in black marker).

Pledge
Chris Knight
XRE

We carried pledge packs also, containing brother essentials (condoms, playing cards, Pong balls, cigarettes, dice, tobacco dip, chewing gum, etc.) and would need to pass an "interview" administered by each brother and be present for every house event regardless of other obligations or even sudden ailments. To this end we worked as a group. Someone purchased all the black books. Another pledge brother picked up the fanny packs. A few others split up procuring the pledge pack contents. We shared information about what needed to be known for each brother's specialized sig.

The sig process was really genius. A sig was basically an interview between a pledge and an existing brother designed to both reinforce what the pledges were supposed to be learning as well as introduce them to the brotherhood at large. Depending on who you were getting a sig from and what state of mind they were in at the time, this could be an extremely casual conversation (one memorable sig I managed to snag from a notorious stoner in the basement had as its sole requirement that I be able to name ten animals) or a *Spanish Inquisition* style interrogation. Brothers who you had only seen in the basement before or standing in a corner at Meetings, you now felt a legitimate connection to and all you need do to talk to that brother is say "Hey, can I have your sig?" and the door is open.

Here's also where I sort of started experimenting with truancy for the first time. I enthusiastically pledged, and committed a large amount of my free time to the house, which led naturally to drinking more often during school nights. Three games of Pong on a Tuesday night for example could lead to a missed alarm on Wednesday. Classes begin at nine am, and since I would often arrange my schedule so I had three in a row it was easy to tell yourself: "Well, my nine is a fifty minute lecture in a huge auditorium. I can easily get the notes from one of the four Chi-Gams in the class and it'll be as if I didn't cut at all." Thus you skip your nine, go to your ten and then either skip or attend your eleven, depending on how you felt that particular day. So as Chi-Gam violently crashed into the rest of my life, I grew accustomed to missing a class here and there but was able to keep up with the work and do well enough on essays and tests to justify my inconsistent attendance. Many around me either had already or were now developing similar habits.

I took an oath of sorts when I became a brother: *What goes on in the house STAYS in the house!* Some may argue that I've already violated this oath many times over and I suppose this is true but I must point out that I have also carefully avoided any in depth discussion of the specifics of our fraternal practices, traditions and legacies in this book. Outside of Ship and some of my own isolated and bizarre actions, you may safely assume that everything I describe was fairly commonplace on campus and that none of this would be considered all that shocking to even non-affiliated students. All the major fraternities engaged in these practices; everyone, the administration included, was aware of them. This was especially true of our "hazing" practices.

There was a time when the administration could largely accept Dartmouth's so called hazing because what we did pales in comparison to many other Greek-infested schools and is not (generally speaking) the potentially damaging sort of hazing that everyone worries about. On any objective scale, Dartmouth's initiation rites would be considered relatively low-key, for the most part effectively hidden from view, and deemed appropriate in their intensity by the vast majority of CFS members. We were never excessively or systematically humiliated, intimidated or coerced into legally questionable activities, physically or mentally assaulted, put in dangerous situations, forced to do drugs, or even insulted beyond a reasonable threshold. Sure, I had to endure the occasional "shit-break" comment but gentle ribbing certainly didn't affect me in any damaging way.

Our institutionalized "hazing" consisted of a very specific kind of forced drinking that wasn't necessarily mandatory—only heavily suggested. We drank almost exclusively beer. Think about that for a minute because you never hear about a kid drinking himself to death with beer. It just does not happen. "Pledge X dies at said state school after consuming thirty-two shots of vodka in two hours." That's the usual headline. That is not to say that there aren't very real risks that come along with excessive binge drinking on beer. The reality was that someone *could* die doing what we did and everyone was aware of this possibility but viewed it as remote and preventable. Even so, we did have kids who would dry-pledge and nobody had a problem with that as long as you kept your commitment. One could not abstain during the week to avoid pledge events and then drink on the weekends to be social. It was all or nothing.

There was one night towards the end of each pledge term where some borderline hazing abuses did occur and I'm pretty sure most other fraternities on campus had their own version of such a night during this period in time. I can't go into the details of what Chi-Gam's "Hell Night" consisted of for obvious reasons but I will say that as pledges we were warned in advance that this was coming and I wouldn't quite characterize anything that went on as being technically abusive in nature, however it was pretty close to that gray line. Hell night was eventually ended as a practice while I was a brother at the school and nobody was too upset to see it gone. As far as I know it hasn't made a resurgence. That said, it wasn't even *that* bad.

The ridiculous nude group hazing you might be thinking about was completely a no-go—for us at least. As a rule none of us wanted to see each other nude. The even worse physical, mental or sexual torture doesn't exist at Dartmouth at all (at least as far as my knowledge of the fraternity system goes) and I have spoken to many members of other CFS houses about their own experiences and feel comfortable in stating this. Were bodily fluids sometimes involved? Yes certainly. Did we voluntarily vomit on each other, absorb insults, wear outlandish costumes, eat disgusting combinations of food products, sometimes wrestle one another, get "mind-fucked" by the brotherhood, drink unquestionably gross penalty beers, drink even more real beer... was this a part of our initiation? The answer is emphatically yes. We did all of that and more but this was the reality we had volunteered for. We all knew exactly what pledging would entail long before we sank our bids and anyone who tells you otherwise is lying or deluded. Submission to the will of the brotherhood. For a variety of reasons this is what we all wanted.

I didn't then and still don't see these more harmless initiation rituals as primarily being about exercising power over the powerless or forcing conformity through intimidation and humiliation. The act of pledging merges you irrevocably to the fraternity—it creates within you the sense that only your pledge brothers have gone through what you've gone through, that this is the price you pay to get into the frat, and most importantly that it's *worth* it to do so. Many of us believe that the strength of the bond between us would not have endured as it has if not for the shared experience of pledging.

We were expected to participate in what Kouge termed "Pledge Events"—special nights during pledge term where we'd be given group drinking assignments and what a corporate strategist would probably refer to as "team building exercises"—traditions that were intended to manufacture a sense of camaraderie between us and that we knew we'd be expected to pass down to the next class of Chi-Gams the following year. There was Basement Appreciation night where all twenty-eight of us spent the night in the basement, some sleeping in bags they had brought with them, others such as myself pulling an all-nighter of Beer Pong games and group song and dance routines. Pledge Olympics, held on a different evening, pitted pairs of pledges against one another in a series of team based physical and drinking challenges. At another point in the term there was a Greek themed scavenger hunt. We were hazed of course during these events—at any point a brother could hand you a Mad Dog and demand you chug it instantly, or a different brother might ask you nicely (or not so nicely) to pick him up dinner at Thayer. You really couldn't say no to any of these requests, but I didn't see anything that crossed the line in my own fraternity. The things we subjected ourselves to voluntarily, without coercion, were the most bizarre and extreme acts I witnessed during my stay in Hanover.

At Dartmouth we unleashed our inner animals for four short years and then poof—we were released into the wilds of the real world with the full knowledge that the occupants of said real world had not subjected themselves to the same monstrous lifestyle that we had. This was an empowering feeling as a pledge. We heard stories that were half boasting ("look how hard we are") and half cautionary tales ("don't be that guy") meant to impress upon us what others had done with their opportunity of being Chi-Gams. These were the "get to know the house" stories and it became clear that we were a part of a living history creating new stories each evening. We studied the composites that lined the hallways—a glimpse into a past when hard guys ruled the campus and now, as we imagined, the world. We were told that the school was dying a little bit each year and that the golden age of the fraternity had come and gone—days before the information age when what went on on campus truly stayed on campus but this had all changed. Our actions seemed like they were examined under a microscope with the college waiting for the slightest excuse to kick us off campus—no fanfare, no frenzied twenty minute climactic sequence in which we are allowed to ruin a school parade and triumphantly best the college deans. Just empty bedrooms, silent basements. In actuality the college is balancing a delicate tightrope walk of respecting the tradition of fraternities amid powerfully vocal alumni support and the increasing pressure that comes along with ensuring the safety of its students in the face of an unprecedented visibility for fraternities. The last thing that either the Greeks or the college wanted was a dead student on their hands. And now here we are (lest the old traditions fail) faithfully carrying on and trying to replicate or outpace the antics that made our forebears legends of the Ivy-League while keeping in range of what was perceived as allowable or tolerated by the administration. Our reputation as Dartmouth men and women on the line—the college appreciative and tolerant of who we are but expecting us to behave appropriately by minimizing or at least hiding our misbehavior.

On a Tuesday night, Kouge and Pope invite Winston and I over to Chi-Gam for a game of what they call "3D Ship." This was much like regular Ship but had an extra layer of cups stacked on top of the normal boats thus nearly doubling the alcohol payoff of the game. We are both encouraged to finish a bottle of Mad Dog before the game ends and Winston gets blisteringly drunk and finally breaks his bed-booting, class-missing cherry. He is so upset by his actions that he informs Kouge and Pope that he will be "dry pledging" for the remainder of the term but by the conclusion of the weekend he is once again playing Ship in the basement.

A pledge passes out in the basement and combo urinates/vomits himself. At our next Meetings he is given a hefty cinch sack plastic garbage bag to wear around campus for a week—debatably our worst pledge gear. Anytime someone asks why he is wearing this bizarre getup the pledge must recite: "I am a filthy mess. Known to expectorate on myself and others around me. For your safety and mine, please keep your distance."

❄

A co-ed Pong tournament pairs newly pledged girls of a sister sorority with our own pledge class—the elder Social Chairs of both organizations playing Pong match-maker. As with many of my early tournaments, this a first round exit and I forget the identity of the sorority (either KDE or Tri-Delt) and my partner (a girl who did not come close to sleeping with me).

❄

Kouge leads our pledge class down to the basement after a pledge meeting where we are greeted with a Pong table completely covered in full cups of what appears to be beer—something like two or three hundred cups in total. Before we can leave we must clear the table. After their third or fourth drink, certain pledges uncharacteristically start booting (we are all used to chugging seven or eight beers easily before vomiting at this point) and it is only after we finish the beers that Kouge reveals to us that he has poured whiskey shots into about a third of them.

❄

When an old house alum in his sixties visits campus one weekend and stops by the Chi Gamma Epsilon fraternity house, he challenges three brothers to an old-school rules Pong game with a two cup setup in the Meetings Room. The two cups are placed where the stem of a Shrub would normally go and low and fast shots are hit across the direct center of the table with the alum smacking the ball with absolute precision. The two brothers he faces as opponents are drinking beer at a continuous clip while the brother who is the alum's partner laughs at their misfortune. A crowd of brothers and pledges has gathered around the Meetings Room to watch this spectacle. Someone asks when in the world the game ends, a logical question given that the old guy doesn't seem to be keeping score and continues to urge the refilling of the cups as they are hit and sank over and over again. The white-haired retiree, but still brother, tells us: "We drink until we boot!"

❄

One night we gathered at the BEMA, all of us, and a sister sorority as well, for a pledge mixing event on this great expanse of a lawn. The upperclassmen of the fraternity and sorority are once again watching on together with amusement as the girl and boy pledges awkwardly mingle like newly introduced toddlers. I am actually consciously avoiding interaction with the opposite sex. A reformed baseball player, now an established house drunk, pulls me aside at some point and says: "Knight, you have to start talking to girls, buddy."

❄

In an unnecessary show of strength, a brother drunkenly punches his arm through a piece of wood paneling in the basement, shattering it into splinters and badly lacerating his arm. The walls around Varsity are dripping with alcohol saturated blood. This unfazed brother calmly retrieves a BIC lighter from a nearby pledge pack and carefully cauterizes the wound with an emotionless face in front of the basement regulars.

❄

Two or three pledges have their signs stolen by rival fraternities over the course of the term. A stolen Chi-Gam pledge sign is a coveted item to display at meetings for other frats. We are commanded to retrieve these signs by any means necessary—a feat we normally accomplish through a combination of diplomacy and group intimidation tactics.

❄

An enormous balding Javelin thrower with a round face and a terrifying demeanor patrols the basement at night with the long pointy tool of his sport, brandishing it in a threatening manner, assaulting unsuspecting pledges and inflicting property damage in the basement. The house executives ban him from drinking alcohol for a week in the house.

❄

Three or four pledges hatch a daring burglary of the Bones Gate ladle and make it all the way back to the foyer of the house before being wrestled to the ground and stripped of their prize by six or seven gatesmen. We break into their house later that night and steal all of their beer.

❄

At the Homecoming football game, one of the pledges purchases two full trays worth of concessions—beverages, hot dogs, hamburgers—practically swimming in condiments. As the chosen pledge carries this gross collection of items up the steep steps of the football stands (heading up to the top bleacher where a gang of Chi-Gam brothers watches and waits) he clumsily stumbles over one step that is higher than the others—a step with a yellow stripe of paint offering the timelessly prophetic warning High-Step! The full tray of soda, mustard, hot dogs, ketchup, buns, mayonnaise, burger meat, relish and grilled onions splashes in the laps of the unlucky spectators who had decided to sit in the seats adjacent to the *High-Step* that afternoon.

❄

One early evening at the beginning of pledge term I remember stopping into the Brothers Room on my way to the basement and finding a Chi Gam standing alone in the middle of the room with the lights off and a whippetizer jammed in his mouth. He is furiously sucking down nitrous oxide and constructing a tiny pyramid of spent whippet canisters at his feet. I remember this distinctly because at the time I had no clue what drug he was doing or what its effect might be but was intrigued.

❄

I was no longer Chris Knight; I was a Chi-Gam. I can accept this. I know it is not something that is impressive to people. Furthermore I know that in fact the opposite is true. Most of the campus looks upon on me and my pledge sign with disdain. But I don't mind this, no, in fact I am partially inspired by it. I crave not only to bear witness to the spectacle but to absorb it completely within my being.

❄

Here lies the body of Eleazar Wheelock, STD. Founder and first president of Dartmouth College and Moore Indian School. By the gospel he tamed the ferocity of the savage and to the civilized he opened new paths of science. Traveler, go if you can and deserve the sublime reward of such merit.

These haunting words, read by flickering lighter, were inscribed across a large granite slab which I climbed atop to stretch out on my back and gaze up at the dense canopy of trees that blocked the spectacle of stars and other astrological phenomenon. I then closed my eyes, delicately wrapped my finger around the string of my pledge sign, and sighed.

"Gentlemen…" Kouge said from somewhere out in the darkness. "Prepare for the most exhilarating, visceral experience that Dartmouth has to offer."

Obediently, I got up and trotted toward the voice, finding Kouge only a few yards away standing in front of five noir silhouettes of my pledge brothers superimposed on drooping cemetery trees.

"This is a whippet run," Kouge announced, untangling one arm from his knapsack. He unzipped the bag and produced a small red and white box containing twenty silver nitrous oxide whipped cream chargers. The box of whippets jingled in his hand as he pulled them out. Kouge next removed an average culinary whipped cream maker, known as a whippetizer to college students and drug users, from his bag. The metallic base was designed to hold the cream, sugar and whatever other ingredients you might need for pastry decoration, but for our purposes, it was merely a receptacle for the dangerous gas we were about to inhale into our lungs.

Kouge unscrewed a knob sticking out from his whippetizer, loaded the first whippet in, and twisted it back on, producing a hissing sound indicating the successful transfer of nitrous. He then double and triple loaded the 'tizer, depositing each empty canister onto the ground.

"I picked you fucks because out of your pledge class you're the only ones who will actually appreciate this." He paced back and forth like a drill sergeant reviewing his cadets. "I discovered the whippet run sometime…oh I don't know, let's say…last term, and it's tremendous! I recommend keeping your eyes closed, get your hands up in front of your face and run as fast as you fucking can. Mole, time to man up!"

Mole stepped forward and received the whippetizer from Kouge. After four large breaths that cleared the device, he whispered, "dear god" and suddenly swayed backwards at such an extreme angle it seemed likely he would fall over entirely. Kouge, reacting as if he had planned for this possibility, seamlessly caught and steadied Mole upright and next spun him towards the interior of the cemetery, administering a strong shove that sent Mole flying down the embankment. We heard his yelps as he rushed headfirst into the darkness but these cries quickly faded into the night.

One at a time Kouge fed his victims three whippets each and forcefully sent them down the hill. Next Davis, then Thalen, Rats, and finally Beetle. I was the last to be called.

First, a quick lesson on the mechanics of the 'tizer. Next, some brief words of encouragement from Kouge. Then the tizer is in my hand and the end that normally dispels whipped cream is being jammed into my mouth as my fingers press down on the handle to introduce the chilled nitrous gas into my respiratory system. The nitrous is held in my lungs for as long as possible. Kouge meanwhile grasps me by my arms, and spins me as he had done to the others. He then points me towards what he deems the correct direction, and propels me forward.

This catches me by surprise even though the same sneaky tactic had been used on the five previous pledges. I stumble across the arbitrary boundary into the second inner circle of the cemetery and feel my altered consciousness being left behind as the shell of my barely functioning body accelerates down the hill. My momentum brings me to the first steep incline and I have no choice but to further quicken my pace to prevent a headfirst dive. Soon I'm essentially sprinting down this hill, eyes closed and hands in front of my face to hopefully block any sharp sticks or branches that might try to blind me.

I feel myself produce an impressive, piercing scream, but I actually hear nothing. A distinct yet subtle droning in my brain amplifies and recedes with each whack of a tree branch I receive. This wondrous nitrous melody continues as I thump through what seemed to be a dense forest and I couldn't care less what's in front of me. I keep sprinting, picking up speed, out of control but I can't stop myself and it doesn't matter because I don't want to stop. Before I know it the terrain has leveled out and I'm able to slow down just enough to begin to make out objects around me.

When I finally came to a stop I was in a simple clearing containing scattered tombstones. Directly above us the tree line gave way and allowed the moonlight to illuminate the faces of my fellow pledge brothers for the first time all night. Seconds later a screeching Kouge emerged from the forest and our party was complete.

"Well?" said Kouge with a wild uncontrollable smile on his face while wheezing and reaching for his cigarettes. "How was it?"

Thalen was the first to offer his opinion. "Awesome."

"You're a madman but yeah it was real tight," Rats concluded.

"Holy shit," was all Beetle said.

Davis, a heavy smoker, had already collapsed on a crumbling tombstone to light a cigarette and catch his breath. "Never again," he growled taking a long drag but smiling contently all the same.

Mole was the most enthusiastic. "That was easily the coolest thing I've ever done," he gladly admitted.

Kouge nodded as if he had known we would each say that exact thing and produced a pre-rolled joint, which he lit, and we smoked. After the doobie and some playful graveyard antics, we begrudgingly headed back to the house for basement cleanings.

Everywhere we go, whether it be class, the library, food court, or other frats and sororities, we do so in great big packs, our pledge signs hung either backwards or frontward around our necks. In the Thayer dining hall, we are Vikings feasting on the day's kill of cheesesteaks, mozzarella sticks, chicken wings, burgers, and other frozen goods, grilled or fried to moderate perfection behind the counter at the main hot foods line. Near the soda machines I might spy fellow sophomores, a group instantly identifiable as Theta-Delt pledges by the random patterns buzz shaved into their heads as part of their own fraternal initiation. I notice two or three Alpha Chi pledges with bright red house baseball caps negotiating a pizza transaction from someone who I assume is a townie sandwiched in between the counter and a pizza oven—this next to the milk fridge.

We are like gangs of droogs—our distinctive pledge outfits singling us out in bright highlights for the rest of campus. The next generation of frat boys lining up at the banks of the Connecticut River to drink from puerile waters. Non-affiliated students do their best to ignore us but I see the curious glances; they know we have given in completely to the Greek Life and I detect both envy and pity in those eyes.

Rats has been given a dress by the elder members of the brotherhood at our most recent Meetings that he must now use as a prop to assist him in finding a date to our approaching Fraternity Formal. This is a tradition termed "The

Thayer Challenge." Our group of pledges, providing emotional support mainly, is also accompanied by Kouge and several other upperclassmen brothers to record the occurrences of the evening for an update to the rest of the house on his and our performance. Penalty beers and pledge gear are likely in the balance. Most of us have been drinking all afternoon and a few of us are actually quite drunk—this is magnified to a level of unreal insanity because once intoxicated and out of the safety zone of the house we all act pretty fucking obnoxiously. Yelling at each other, flinging dining trays through the air like Frisbees, making a mucky mess of the food that's put out—a third of which ends up on the floor, a third in our mouths and the final third paid for and eventually discarded in the rotating conveyor belt of partially empty trays that the work study students will clean and set out to be soiled anew at the entrance to the dining hall.

Winston has procured several orders of French Fries and I can see that he is picking out ketchup packets from a large pile on the condiment counter and squeezing them into a round tub that had recently been holding the packets themselves. Beetle is creeping up behind Winston with one finger on his pursed lips and then suddenly applies a right foot to his friend's backside and runs off laughing maniacally while Winston grabs the ketchup jug and sprints off after him to exact revenge.

"Ever been to a Chi-Gam Formal?"

I overhear Rats asking this beside the salad bar as he brandishes his dress at a girl I fail to recognize while making my way past the checkout counter. There is a table of Chi-Gams organically forming near the back entrance of the dining hall. I see that Winston has somehow cornered Beetle near this location and the brothers all turn to watch the outcome of their entirely localized conflict. I imagine a spotlight turning on as Beetle jerks to a stop against a back wall of linoleum tiles. Winston then lifts his arm to aim the artillery shell of ketchup. There is a moment of concentrated focus and suddenly Winston hurls the ketchup bomb at Beetle, who emits one of his trademark cackles and dodges back in the direction he came from, the projectile colliding harmlessly against the wall and exploding in a four foot radius so that now there is a Rorschach ketchup blood stain marring the dining hall back wall.

This to the frenzied delight of the Chi-Gams.

Chapter 5: The Association of Ship Professionals

"Two additional matters related to alcohol are discussed in this section: Wednesday night house meetings and drinking games. In the end, the committee decided, for strictly pragmatic reasons, not to propose specific rules to change the time of house meetings or to ban "pong" or other drinking games. However, the committee believes that both large-scale, organized drinking late on Wednesday nights and widespread games designed to promote rapid drunkenness are inimical to the community that Dartmouth wants to be."
– *Excerpt from the Summary of the Recommendations Submitted to the Board of Trustees by the Committee on the Student Life Initiative*

One morning I regained consciousness abruptly, as if waking from an extended vegetative period. I sprung to my knees on the bottom mattress of a familiar bunk bed, inadvertently tearing aside the window shade to reveal an ominous orange hue of dwindling sunlight that confirmed I had once again slept through the majority of the waking hours and missed my brief window for much needed productivity. In a flash it dawned on me that I was in my own bedroom, a double on the second floor of the Chi Gamma Epsilon fraternity house.

Moving into the fraternity house was rare during one's first term as a full brother. Winston and I were allowed that distinction because we had both decided to take classes during the winter term immediately following our pledge term, something few sophomores elected to do. Dartmouth is on a trimester system with fall, winter, spring and summer terms lasting ten weeks. Students take classes on campus or study abroad for three terms a year. The winter term has the lowest enrollment of the year outside of the summer term, and Kouge had blitzed out to the new pledges about vacancies on the second floor. We responded with zero hesitation, though it required Winston and I to relinquish the triple we shared across campus with Yogi. That part of our life, the dorm life, had come to an end.

This was a period of time in which I did practically no studying at all. I had gone to class only a handful of times, at some point lost track of most of my textbooks and days went by without even thinking about school, so that I felt so far behind that it seemed unreasonable to think I could possibly catch up. The classes I had enrolled in required heavy reading but not much else as far as daily or even weekly assignments. Reading could be done while high on a couch with the television on in the background in short frenetic bursts, which allowed me to learn the material without having to go through all the trouble of actually learning the material—the relevant phrases underlined in yellow or blue highlighter, the knowledge retained overnight to pass a test or finish a paper and then forgotten post subsequent binge period. I knew that I would eventually have to locate my textbooks, crack them open, and spend frenzied hours cramming for finals and cranking out term papers but not now. This was the soft, creamy, center of the term and class was far from my mind.

I groaned an obscenity and feebly began searching my body for signs of injury. My ribcage was vaguely sore to touch and I observed a minor abrasion on one knee-cap but neither injury seemed too severe so I hopped off the bunk bed and began scanning the room for the navy XRE hooded sweatshirt I knew was about somewhere—in the pocket of which I hoped to find a not quite depleted bag of weed. Noticeably limping, I located the sweatshirt, but the pocket yielded only seeds, stems and not more than a half bowl's worth of shake.

My intention that Friday night had been to get utterly destroyed and the slow restoration of memory brought a crooked smile to my face. First just flashes—then gradually I began to piece together whole events. Licking my lips, I noticed something stuck in one of my teeth. When I rubbed my tongue over this anomaly I realized the tooth had been chipped. Shrugging this off, I allowed inertia to propel me into my desk chair but my skin caught on the jagged plastic edge of the chair's arm as I sat down. This was perhaps the fourth time I had lacerated myself in this fashion, but since only surface blood was drawn I ignored the wound and opened my blitzmail. Most of my blitzes were spam and I began talking aloud to myself as I deleted each penis enlargement, teen girls website, or debt consolidation announcement.

"—wow, started playing games *real* early last night. Beetle showed up at around six. We smoked, obviously, then played some Dreamcast. After that… called next on JV and played that first game against Turner and Pope. Shut those kids out too. Beetle got three boats…but I got three in the next game. Costanza and Words. Terrible at Pong. There were actually a lot of women in the basement and not too bad looking either for Dartmouth girls. Now if only I had actually talked to any of them. I think I can safely assume that we came upstairs after that second game and took a shit load of bong rips. What was Beetle going on about again? Something about ninjas... Fuck we were high. Winston and Facts even filled up our next game while we smoked. Chumps. Hmm…though we did lose that one. Didn't even get on Varsity. It was seniors and juniors all night pretty much. Can't seem to remember anything else, wait... AD! I went over to fucking AD at some point... it's impossible to forget the stench of that basement but certainly don't remember making it to my room. Late night games most likely. My shoes are still fucking on. Now how about this chipped tooth? A fall down the stairs at AD maybe?"

Before I could solve this mystery, the door to Room G opened.

"You're up," Kouge said, stepping into my room. Jim, a delivery guy from C&A's accompanied by a huge mutt of a dog I knew to be named Sarge, followed behind scratching Kouge's credit card number onto a piece of carbon paper with a pen that appeared largely out of ink.

"What's your query?" I asked Kouge, giving the impression that I was already more confused by my response then he would be.

"You know you have a penis scrawled on the side of your head, right?"

Kouge paid for his meal, walked Jim out to the hallway, and reappeared in my room with a bong in one hand. I was rubbing possibly the wrong side of my skull with saliva soaked fingertips in an attempt to smear in the presumed phallic ink stain.

"Jim is the fucking man," Kouge stated definitively as he handed me the bong and ushered me out of my desk chair to check his blitzmail and devour his sandwich. "This is my last eighth—the campus is fucking dry, dude." he said in between two large bites. "But I was talking to Jim…he can probably get us a bag. Some high school kid who delivers for C&A's sells bud. That's where Jim gets his weed. I've never seen him delivering though. Here, pack a bowl." He tossed me a rolled up ziplock bag which I caught and hastily unrolled.

I sat on the couch and began packing his weed into the plastic double chambered bong we called the "Purple Monster." It had rubber tubes connecting the two chambers. Any smoke you inhaled had to go through the first water filled chamber, then the rubber tubes and finally the second water chamber. The double filtration made the smoke easier to hold in your lungs, ensuring crisper, healthier, and most importantly, larger bong rips.

Kouge spun around with a disgusted look on his face. "Hey, what the fuck is this?"

Ignoring his question, I lifted his bong to my lips and prepared the first hit, being careful to burn only half of the exposed marijuana in the glass bowl.

Winston and I were in an ongoing competition to see who could come up with the most offensive computer desktop background. Winston's current entry was a close-up from a Peter North money shot. It was frozen mid-frame, catching a continuous stream of sperm seconds away from blasting a shocked brunette in the face. Kouge was staring at my current entry, a crime scene photo from the Chris Farley overdose. A bloated corpse sprawled out on the floor of his apartment. In one hand, he clutched a partially rolled up twenty; foam and vomit had recently been expelled from his mouth and nose. High Balls looking at a speed-ball. People who came into our room to check blitz were confronted with these two disturbing images and generally agreed that I had won this particular round.

Kouge was staring at the twisted image on my screen and shaking his head. "Have I ever told you how fucking weird you are?"

While I considered this question, the Room G door swung open again to reveal Winston, who walked in and deposited his knapsack beside me on the couch. He then took a seat at his own desk as if Kouge and I weren't even there.

"And where are you coming from?" Kouge asked.

"Library."

"Good for you, Winston. You should take your buddy here with you. He can certainly stand to hit the books a little more frequently." Kouge raised the bong to his lips.

"I ask and he says no. So I stopped asking."

"I'm not even sure I know where the Library is."

"It's that big building at the end of the street."

"I thought that was a church."

"Winston—want a rip?" Kouge whispered in one long breath as he exhaled a bong's worth of smoke into the room.

"Troy doesn't get high," I said automatically, before Winston had a chance to formulate a response himself.

"And I've always respected that about him," said Kouge, the smoke from his previous hit rising from his shoulders and head in such a way that it appeared as if he was about to explode.

"Well, I've seen the effects," Winston replied, nodding in my direction.

My computer emitted a chiming sound, indicating the arrival of a new blitz in Kouge's inbox.

"ASP rankings are out." Kouge said, his eyes locked on the screen. "Magpie got the number one spot, good for him. Let's see... I'm twelve. That's fair I guess."

"Where are we?" Winston asked.

"Doesn't look like either of you fared particularly well. Knight is forty-four. Winston, you're forty-three. Congrats fellas on being in the bottom ten of the house. Means you need to play more Ship... or at least play against better opponents. I suggest Varsity."

The Association of Ship Professionals House Rankings was emailed out to the entire fraternity each term and ranked all active brothers based solely on Ship playing abilities. It was the job of the House Ship Chair to compile this list and he was expected to do so based on firsthand knowledge of each brother's skill level, requiring him to play or observe an exorbitant amount of Ship games over the course of the term. The release of the ASP rankings list was considered a serious affair by the majority of the brotherhood and despite the sheer fantasy aspect of the whole enterprise, we couldn't help but nervously check our own ranking immediately. In response to the list's release, the Ship Chair would always receive a flood of replies from brothers, either angrily disputing the validity of the rankings or praising his accuracy and keen eye for good Pong playing. The Ship Chair also served as the gatekeeper for the rules of the game—which were quite a bit more complex than you might assume from playing once or watching someone else play.

The game of Ship is played on a Dartmouth style Beer Pong table the exact length and width of a standard Ping Pong table (nine by five), which is actually a foot shorter than the majority of Pong tables found on campus. The table is elevated approximately thirty-three inches from the ground by either a set of sawhorses, or the more likely alternative, two garbage cans. The playing surface is painted with a design of some sort or another with a two by four acting as the table's 'net', or median, splitting it into two sides. New tables were purchased as needed by our House Men, generally as replacements for stolen or badly damaged tables. Designs were painted on by volunteers wishing to make their mark on the house aesthetic and ranked in artistic execution and complexity of design. First the tables were primed. The designs were then either drawn directly on the primer with pencil or stenciled on before paint was applied. Once the artwork was complete, the table received two or three coats of polyurethane seal that would protect it from the thousands of beers that would be spilled on it during its tenure. Pong tables were durable and rarely wore down to the point where they could no longer be used for Pong. It was to inter-house theft that we lost most of our tables while I was a brother.

The implements of Ship—the beer, balls, paddles and cups—were purchased from an innocuous family owned delicatessen slash convenience store called *Stinson's Village Store* located not too far off Main Street in Hanover, which because of its proximity to Dartmouth's CFS houses, had grown to become one of the largest, if not *the* largest beer distributor in all of New Hampshire. We bought beer from Stinson's with comic regularity—typically every Monday, Wednesday, Friday and Saturday and in *bulk*. This was a task orchestrated by our Social Chairs with the semi-reluctant help of whoever happened to be standing idly about in the hallways of the house or waiting in the basement or Brother's Room for Pong to begin. Stinson's was a short drive from frat row—easily navigated with a light buzz—and the three or four man crews would pull the SUV, station wagon, or van or whatever vehicle they rode there in (any vehicle whose keys could be successfully pried away from their owner) into Stinson's alarmingly narrow back driveway, a location that turned out to be very convenient due to its proximity to an immense freezer housing an impressive wall of beer cases and kegs. The Social Chair would initiate the purchase of alcohol and Pong supplies inside the store while his accomplices moved cases of beer in groups of three (one in each hand and a third under the off arm) from Stinson's freezer to the storage area of the transport—its trunk in most cases, but once that filled to capacity, really any other unoccupied space that you can envision fitting a thirty pack. A Friday, Saturday or Wednesday night required a good twenty to thirty cases of beer, and a Monday night maybe ten to fifteen. Now multiply that by the number of Greek houses on campus—there being no cheaper, more convenient place to buy beer in Hanover and I'm going to take a wild guess here, but I'd say something on the order of twenty five hundred cases of Keystone Light were sold at Stinson's every week. Sometimes you weren't a part of the pickup itself but were instead left behind in the basement to play Ship with the remnants of the previous pickup, waiting for the "re-up" so to say, which could ensure that the next game (previously promised with the prospect of future beer) could proceed without any delays. The Social Chair would enter the back door of the basement that let in through the parking lot, announce that the beer had arrived and everyone downstairs would pitch in enthusiastically to assist with the carrying of said beer inside from the SUV, station wagon or van or whatever vehicle you had used to transport it from Stinson's cooler to the Chi Gam parking lot. With the beer in tow, the night was secure—we were ready for the worst that Dartmouth had to throw at us.

The setup and rules for Ship are inspired by the old pen and paper game *Battleships* with some obvious divergences in gameplay. Each team of two starts the game with four boats that the other team aims at and tries to "sink" by hitting a ping-pong ball at them. Boats are made up of full cups of beer and arranged so that each boat has its own quadrant of the table. The Aircraft Carrier is five cups long and positioned in the lower right hand corner of the table. The four-cup Battleship sits in the bottom left corner. The submarine is three cups and also set up on the left side of the table but closer in to the median than the four-boat and protected by a solitary cup, called the mine, that the opposing team ostensible avoids since they would have to drink it if they hit or sank it. The two-boat (a scout ship maybe, this was always unclear to me) was mirrored to the three boat on the right side near the median. We rarely used the naval terms for the boats and instead just referred to them by their original length, cup-wise, i.e. the two-boat or four-boat, thus I must sadly report that the phrase "You sunk my Battleship!" was never used in anything but a sarcastic capacity.

Taken together the eight boats and two mines on the table at the start of a Ship game comprised thirty cups of beer, which translated into twenty, twelve ounce cans—five per person. A random night might feature four games of Ship and if I averaged drinking two thirds of the beer in each game (a reasonable presumption) I will have consumed twenty cups of beer in that time, and with another quick conversion I can tell you that that equals 160 ounces of beer (assuming eight ounces a cup) which must exceed the standard liquid storage capacity for normal humans in my age group.

Ship, like all variations of Dartmouth Pong, is a game of lobs, both teams aiming for the cups on their opponent's side with high arching, deliberate shots. The object of the game is to sink all four of your opponent's boats before he sinks yours. This is accomplished by *hitting* or *sinking* the individual cups that make up each boat.

A *hit* is a shot that comes in contact with a cup but doesn't land inside. When a team's cup is hit they must drink half of the beer unless it has been hit once before in which case it is already considered a "half cup" and the second hit causes it to be finished and removed from the table. If a single shot hits multiple cups on a boat (this happens more frequently than you'd first guess) then only the last cup touched by the ball is considered to have been hit; however, if the ball hits two *separate* boats without bouncing in between hits, then the two cups hit on each boat are consumed.

A *sink* is what we call a shot that actually lands inside of a cup. When this happens the entire beer is eliminated whether it is a half or a full. When a cup is eliminated, it is removed from the formation and all cups in front of it are slid back one spot so that the lips of the boats remain in constant contact with each other. With the two larger back boats, this sliding is always done towards the back edges so that the boats are always a paddle's length in from the table's back edge and side. Once a boat has been reduced to two and a half total beers (counting halves as .5 and fulls as 1.0) it becomes sinkable. A boat sink occurs when the ball sinks the cup of a boat that is sinkable and results in that entire boat being consumed and its cups removed from the table. A boat that has been reduced to a single half cup can be sunk with a hit. The two-boat (which naturally starts the game with less than two and a half beers) is always sinkable.

Lobs must be hit "high" or face the danger of being called "low" by any player on the table, at which point the player who hit the low shot will start the point over with a new serve. The determination of whether a borderline shot has met the height requirements for the game is a purely subjective one that has led to countless in-game disputes over the years. Generally though, a low call is respected and the offending party serves without refuting the call.

If a legal hit occurs a team can "save" the half cup by returning the ball back over the medium before it bounces twice or lands off table following the successful hit. Saves can be hit as low as needed to cross the median but the ensuing shot (provided it isn't a save itself) must be returned at the usual height (around nipple high).

Our Beer Pong paddles came wrapped in plastic and covered with a light sandpaper layer that was glued on and difficult to remove. Some players preferred to leave the sandpaper on as it allowed for an application of spin that was impossible to achieve without it. Otherwise you counted on the dank conditions of the basement to degrade the top layer to the point where it could be stripped off gradually over the course of several games. The handles were broken off before use (this was a universal practice on campus) and the paddle was ideally gripped so that it rested in the palm of your hand with your fingers curled around the edges to grasp it. Pong was a sport of doubles and in almost every house on campus each participant in a game had his or her own paddle but in Chi Gam teams were limited to one paddle per side, which meant they had to pass the paddle back and forth in-between shots. This is a learned skill that proves to be a strong home court advantage for our brothers.

Ship and all its variants were the only widely played Dartmouth Pong games I am aware of that could require you to drink more than a single cup as a result of any particular play. A full boat sink was three times the beer you'd drink from a successful tree or shrub sink—a fact that further limited the appeal of the game outside of our brotherhood. Faced with the daunting task of consuming one and a half cups in a matter of seconds on an already beer-filled stomach just to continue a game in which it is certain I would be expected to drink even more beer, I frequently found myself hunched over garbage cans vomiting up a stinky mess of beer, stomach acids, and whatever else I had consumed food wise that day, if anything at all. Disturbingly enough, I saw this same happy hobby pursued by every one of my friends and acquaintances. This public display of the binge-boot cycle would appear grossly offensive and totally out of place in pretty much any other socially constructed environment but conditioned as we were to see "booting and rallying" as a natural byproduct of Dartmouth culture, the practice was carried out with enthusiastic pride. There was a certain hunch to your step; your eyes would glaze over slightly. Some poor souls would even begin to inch over towards the garbage can, knowing full well they might explode at any second. Blow they did—the smile and nod always meant the same thing, "don't worry about it man, this shit happens to everyone."

A Ship game could be expected to last anywhere from twenty minutes to an hour, depending on the competency level of the game's players. As with any game of Pong at Dartmouth, if you won a Ship game you had the option to retain rights to the table and faced as opponents whoever had called next on the previous game. If you lost, you were moved to the back of all current lines and it was your responsibility to call next on a new game if you wanted to play again or be picked as a partner by someone who was in line as a single. These are universal rules of the school and could only be overturned by a brother or sister of the house where the game was being played. On a big drinking night, a Ship table could be up to five deep with potential opponents making the wait for a game excruciating at times and the importance of winning any game you did manage to land that much more pronounced. The length of the game, combined with its difficulty, quantity of beer and anti-social aspects prompted some within our house to call for a change to the more social game of Tree, at least when non-brothers were over. The die-hard players never faltered in their preference for Ship. Even the most painful game of Ship was preferable to a great game of anything else.

Everyone at Dartmouth plays Pong; the school is somewhat famous for it. Our older, ivy covered dorms, built long before the integration of women, list inter-dormitory intramural sports records; if you look closely you will notice the words BEER Pong sandwiched between table tennis and racquetball. The school not only once condoned Pong but actually encouraged it. There are plenty of alumni who have tables in their apartments or houses and play on the weekends, and I've read more than one short story written by students about the drinking game. To a large degree the student body as a whole identifies Dartmouth with Pong. However, Ship belongs to us and is played almost exclusively in our house. The most exciting weekends of the year can be assured to attract alumni who come to campus on vacation or for weddings. These old guys who went to school in the late '80s and early '90s still had their worn and tattered green colored SHIP shirts, a code decipherable only by a fellow brother, and even if they promised themselves they wouldn't, inevitably they were all drawn back to the house. They had no control over it, as if gravity itself was pulling them towards Webster Ave.

On any given night the Pong Master could randomly show up at the house to victimize the brotherhood. This guy was like a Pong-playing version of the Fonz—black sunglasses, black leather jacket, freeze dried slicked back hair that talked as much as he did, and a formidable display of a special kind of blindness to the outside world and the way it viewed him. Upon entering the basement, he'd head straight for Varsity and once there slide the sunglasses off, slip them into some inside jacket pocket and then quickly slip out of this leather jacket to tie it up among the sprinkler pipes. As soon as he turned towards Varsity he seemed instantly to be playing Ship, as if during his approach to the table and subsequent disrobement, the game he was about to interrupt had been permanently halted, one of its players ejected and the beers once again filled to the tops of the cups in anticipation of his arrival.

I remember this brother vividly and fondly from my freshman year visits to Chi Gam, but didn't register his name or a single fact about him beyond his obvious love for Ship until I pledged. Only Beetle, Winston, and I called him the Pong Master (he actually had a completely different nickname) but to us the Pong Master was what he once was and that's what he'll always be. Even back as freshmen we knew this guy was just a little old to still be a Chi Gam. We figured he was a former brother who lived locally or a brother who had taken an "extended vacation" at some point and was no longer on super close terms with any of the active brothers but still finishing a degree and getting in some work on the tables. Turns out he was actually a graduate student, having walked on time as an undergrad Chi Gam four or five years earlier. You never saw him walking about around campus or eating a meal at a dining hall and really the only times he was ever even at the house was when he was playing Ship. I can't overstate how incredible he was at the game. If his skill level at all typified the Pong-playing of his era, we had let things regress to a post-apocalyptic level.

The first and last time I ever played Ship as the Pong Master's partner was a complete accident precipitated by Winston and I wandering into the basement early one night and encountering the Pong Master setting up a one versus one game of Ship against another seasoned player named Vonner, a pacific northwesterner who seemed to split his time about equally between Varsity and Dartmouth's nearby ski mountain. When they saw us at the basement entrance, our eagerness practically dripping off our face and on the floor, they decided to turn their game into a doubles match. This was probably the first game during which I was astutely aware of my luck at having been exposed to Ship at all and thereafter I was fully entranced by the game and wanted to become as skilled as the giants who loomed over me.

This is how I found myself standing just to the left of the Pong Master, watching as he examined our paddle to see if he could detect any kind of warp in the wood or a split along the seams, any imperfections at all really that he thought might affect our aim during the approaching game. When he deemed it adequate he handed it to me to begin the game.

Meanwhile Vonner was assuming a deliberately serious Pong stance on the other side of the table as he readied himself with a ball and paddle. He served and we all watched as the ball curved at the last second before hitting the very edge of the table and when I swung I missed completely.

"Ace," Vonner muttered to no one in particular as he tossed his paddle to a congratulatory Winston.

After retrieving the ball from under the table, I attempted my own serve, which was decent but still allowed Winston to come within inches of our back four-boat on his return shot. The Pong Master grabbed the paddle from me, which I had neglected to pass to him, and sliced at the ball as it made an attempt to bounce on our side of the table twice. He connected on a beautiful shot, almost lost his balance, but still sent the ball soaring through the air. Almost touching the ceiling, the ball spun upwards towards their cups and then as if depleted of all its energy, began plummeting towards the table.

"Oh.... no way," Vonner said as the ball splashed into their two boat, sinking it instantly and splattering their side of the table with beer. The Pong Master said nothing but tossed the paddle onto the table; I picked it up and imitating him, began inspecting it anew. If it became cracked or chipped, between the two of us, we would know instantly.

The game progressed as Vonner and the Pong Master continued their onslaught against the table's boats. Winston and I hit a rare shot here or there but for the most part this was a battle between the upperclassmen, and hits and sinks were coming at a near continuous pace. The Master chipped away at their battleship until it was sinkable and when this happened he promptly sunk it. The next to go was our three-boat, sunk by Vonner, which had been made sinkable on an earlier botched save attempt by me. I stared at the two and half cups of beer and actually felt my esophagus vibrating, sensing the impending flood. I looked to my partner for guidance but he didn't notice as he was already reaching for the beers. He downed one and a half of them in two fluid motions, the cups flung at the wall above the nearby garbage can, into which they ricocheted precisely. Impressed, I did the same to my single beer and flipped my cup towards the same garbage can but fell short by more than a foot and the cup instead bounced and finally landed in a huge pile of cups and cans at the garbage's base. The game resumed.

Vonner, I noticed, had this amazing ability to boot at will. He would do so every few minutes, sometimes mid-conversation even. This was something I had never seen before. He'd be casually drinking his beer, then lean nonchalantly over a garbage can and gently discharge about a cup's worth of already consumed beer from his stomach. No vomiting sounds at all, no distress in his face—he just calmly spat it out. Utilizing this method he never became full so was surely increasing the amount of beer he could consume and enhancing his playing ability as well since he never experienced those lethargic belly-full moments just before a boot where you're really just going through the Pong playing motions.

The conversation during this game I only remember vaguely, but like the game itself, it was a conversation dominated by the two older Chi Gams. The breadth of conversation was wide-reaching and touched on such academic subjects as philosophy, anthropology, and physics, but was equal parts bullshitting, telling stories, and questioning the two of us youngsters. The skill of these two players and precision with which they played along with the often lofty conversation framed Pong in a new more mature light to me. Pong was a vehicle for four individuals to exchange ideas in a way that also exercised the body's sense of athletic competitiveness; well, that and it got you drunk.

Before long the end of the game was upon us and both sides had downed the majority of their beer. We had a cup and a half left on our four boat and a full two boat. On their side of the table was the three-boat, which had given us trouble all game. The mine had blocked several attempts to make it sinkable and when it was finally gone, Vonner had saved several more. Finally I sunk the middle cup on the boat off a somewhat lucky shot and now their two remaining cups stood tittering near the median on the verge of disaster.

"All boats sinkable," Vonner observed.

At this point I noticed a serious change come over the Pong Master. It was as if for him the game, winnable by one shot, was only now beginning.

Winston served to the Pong Master who placed his shot squarely in the middle of the narrow strip of table between the three-boat and the median. Every shot he took seemed to come within an inch or two of the cups. Vonner responded with an equally accurate shot, though his too just barely missed wide. I was nowhere near as comfortable hitting to the short boats so I put some extra power on my shot to make sure I gave the other team some difficulty in returning it. My long shot and Winston's inexperience caused him to shank his next shot. As it bounced right in the middle of the table the Pong Master, paddle in hand, positioned himself to deliver the final blow.

"Game over," said Vonner before the Pong Master even had a chance to connect with the ball but his words proved prophetic as seconds later the shot splashed into the three-boat, ending the game.

The house bled money. In addition to our alcohol expenses (which were considerable), we were constantly buying little things—thousands of plastic bags, gallons of cleaning fluid, new windows to replace a never ending string of broken ones, ten-by-five wood-flats to be turned into Pong tables, semi-formals, formals, and then bigger things as well—room furnishings, the occasional renovation, physical plant upgrades. This money all had to come from somewhere and that somewhere was our House Fund.

The House Fund received its capital primarily from the rent we charged the brothers who lived there. House rent was the same as dorm rent and could be charged to a brother's tuition bill that parents regularly paid without question each term. Fourteen hundred dollars per person from twenty four residents, four times a year. I'll allow you to do the Math. This meant the House Fund was always flush with cash. The main problem facing us was that it was a violation to use this money to buy alcohol, which was our primary daily expense and the administration checked our books each term to ensure no House Fund checks had been written for social expenses, which were required to come out of the Social Fund.

Each term active brothers were expected to pay social dues, which amounted to three hundred dollars per person. This money all went into our Social "slush" Fund and was used to purchase beer and alcohol nearly every night of the week, and also paid for our dance and cocktail parties, pledge events, barbeques, house dinners and formals each term. The other source of revenue was the parking lot. Chi Gam was one of maybe ten houses on campus to actually own the physical property that it sat on. This actually turns out to be a strong bargaining chip against Dartmouth, which owns just about everything else on the campus proper and quite a bit else off campus as well (including its own skiing mountain). Possessing the deed for that chunk of property, that close to the center of campus, meant our house could never truly be kicked off campus. We had an enormous parking lot behind our house that at half capacity could hold every brother owned car. The back half we rented out each term. The rarity of parking on campus sold out the parking lot every term for us.

So with the parking lot cash cow and dues from every brother you'd think we could afford to supply the house with alcohol for the ten weeks each term that we needed it. But we couldn't, at least not while I was there. Near the end of the term we would resort to sneaky tactics to get the job done. All you needed was a receipt from a large purchase, hopefully something that looked like it could have been bought for the house. A couch, a chair, a television—anything really. And it didn't matter if said item was actually in the house or not. The house would write the purchaser a check and the item would be written off as an improvement to the facilities. The check could then be cashed by the recipient and deposited into the Social Fund, but more often than not, it was made out to cash and immediately used to buy beer.

Much of this beer was consumed on Wednesday nights which is when we held House Meetings—principally devoted to upholding our fraternity's most durable traditions: its drinking contests and physical challenges. This was a weekly no holds barred exhibition of group songs, scandalous stories, grievance settling fights, vomiting, and extreme drinking challenges. We assembled at ten every Wednesday night. The house door was locked and a full table of beers was filled and maintained for use. A stage was erected in front of the Meetings room fireplace and garbage cans were dispersed throughout for the inevitable booting incidents.

Under the non-judgmental eye of Meetings any dirty laundry from the previous week could be aired safely and awards were handed out for truly stand-out performances. The group fight songs we sang had hilariously distasteful choruses that allowed brothers to easily come up with alternating rhyming lyrics. Any brother who thought he had something clever would hop up on stage and sing his verse. He was either rewarded with laughter or boos for his effort. Everyone was encouraged to participate and most did.

The most basic drinking challenge was the single beer chugging contest. A challenge could be issued to a single friend, a subset of the house, or the entire brotherhood. The Guard counted down the participants, "*FIVE... FOUR.... THREE, TWO, ONE!*" Cups of beer would be raised to already moist lips; the mixture of barley, hops, water and yeast consumed in seconds, and then finally the brothers would embrace each other as a winner was declared. These challenges were issued periodically throughout Meetings, often for no reason at all.

Boat races were popular because they inspired everyone to drink; the higher the average brother blood alcohol content, the more enjoyable Meetings are for everyone. This often resulted in class warfare. A team of seniors would match up against an equal number of juniors and sophomores and line up so that each person faced an opponent and everyone had two beers. The two opponents facing each other at the front of the line chugged their first beer, and as soon as he had finished the second in line started chugging his first beer, and then the third began and so on. When the drinking had reached the last man, "the anchor," he chugged his two beers one after the other and then the order reversed with the first person to drink also being the last. The key to chugging is to literally open the back of your throat and pour the beer in. Using this method six full beers can be finished in about five seconds. A fabled '98 Chi Gam, notorious for the speed of his six-beer chug, used to practice this technique of opening up his throat with large quantities of shower water in the third floor bathroom. Disturbing, I agree. So in a boat race you wanted to put your fastest drinker near the end of the line since he would be drinking his two beers in quicker succession than someone near the front. By junior year I was the anchor in every boat race I took part in.

Then there was the *Dome.* This was reserved for the most egregious brother grievances and borrowed its name and inspiration from the caged semi-circle gladiatorial ring of *Mad Max Beyond Thunderdome.* Anything could instigate a Dome; the only requirement was that the offended party had to convince the brotherhood of the gravity of the charges. As soon as the story concerning the disagreement or infraction was told, a declaration of hostilities announced and a Dome challenge issued and accepted, a chant of *Two men enter, one man leaves!* would break out among the drunken masses. A solitary garbage can was set up between the two men and each of their seconds (this was really much like a duel) fetch a handful of beers to use as ammunition in the coming battle of wills. Next the two trade beers while a timekeeper/judge ensures the rules are not violated. The Dome continues until one of the two participants vomits, forfeiting the match.

The Kumite was a wrestling match, usually something like three, two minute rounds. The brothers formed a circle around the combatants, who both removed their shirts, belts, and shoes before squaring off. Anything short of punching and kicking was technically legal and sometimes the odds were so much on one side's favor that it was essentially a six-minute midget toss. I've seen some interesting Kumite set-ups. One time Winston (this was much later in our careers) took on two baseball pledges with the added twist that they were duct taped together at the wrists. Another brother was infamous for intimidating his opponents by vomiting on them and himself continuously during a Kumite match.

Every term we would inevitably have one or two "dry pledges"—sometimes athletes in season, sometimes just kids who didn't drink or didn't want to during pledge term at least. We didn't leave them out. Instead of force-drinking alcohol we made them force-eat foods. Winston eventually became infamous for his dry-pledge challenges. There was a Vienna sausage dome, a Jello dome, and memorably, a hot sauce dome. Winston won every such event I saw him orchestrate.

At the end of Meetings we all formed a circle, locked arms and sang our house song. Everyone was so drunk by this point that we were basically holding each other up as we swayed about in celebration of what everyone agreed was a sacred and special practice. This was the deciding moment of Meetings for a Ship Professional. You must place yourself in the circle so that you are the closest to the foyer and be prepared to sprint in the direction of the stairs as soon as the last words are sung. Varsity was the most coveted post-Meetings assignment and there was a mad dash to the basement as soon as the house song finished, signifying the end of Meetings. The first four on Varsity had the first game. The next eight set up JV tables. It is assured that within half an hour outside students will begin to swarm the house. We only went through about ten to fifteen cases at meetings and there were still twenty left to be consumed and with that we would need help. Many students don't have class at all the next day. Those that do have a start time of ten am or two pm and nobody stresses out about whether to drink or not. We will play Ship for as long as we can. It is a massive party of true Dartmouth warriors and the one night where Pong is everyone's primary consideration. These Wednesdays were my favorite night of the week.

Chapter 6: The Summer of Balls

"The committee proposes one change involving the summer term. To enable CFS houses to undertake necessary refurbishment and regular maintenance, no residency would be allowed in these facilities during the summer."
– *Excerpt from the Summary of the Recommendations Submitted to the Board of Trustees by the Committee on the Student Life Initiative*

Sophomore summer, two thousand and one—an entire term dedicated to second year students. If I could ever have one moment frozen in time or design the architecture of my future afterlife, this would be the model.

Constant eighty degree days allowed the student body to ditch the winter wear and adopt new wardrobes of cargo-shorts, tee-shirts, tank-tops, Capri-pants, swimsuits, open-toed footwear and vibrantly tinted, aviator-style sunglasses. With only a fourth of the campus in residency, it felt like the college facilities were finally available to you personally and yet at the same time, operationally at least, the campus was more or less in a state of stasis. Dining halls kept shortened, erratic hours. Campus-wide activities were largely suspended until the fall. Even the college newspaper, *The Dartmouth*, scaled back its publication to two or three days a week. Summer camp is a commonly used analogy, except the counselors have gone home for the summer and left the spoiled brats in charge for three months. Classes are an afterthought. Afternoons, more often than not, are spent doing nothing at all. Everyone on campus was making the slow transition from fledgling student to Dartmouth men and women. On the first day of classes, professors proclaimed that the same standard of work would be expected of us and that we shouldn't expect "Camp Dartmouth" but even having to say so meant we all did.

Most freshmen and juniors had the term off and worked internships or jobs scattered across the country; others studied abroad and presumably some did nothing at all. The seniors of course had graduated. But the vast majority of sophomores were enrolled on campus, Chi Gams included. Our pledge class was now entrusted with the full responsibility of managing the house and the property that it sat on. We occupied it, paid the bills, cleaned it, maintained it, represented it on the Greek council and conducted its dealings directly with the college. During the previous term Chi-Gam had held its yearly house elections to determine officers for the '03 class. Beetle, who like me had been off for the term, ran unopposed for one of the top positions. That put him just after the President, two Social-Chairs and Treasurer on the housing priority list.

The four singles on the third floor went to these more senior officers but Beetle snagged Room M—the largest double and designated communal living space of the house—and invited me to be his roommate. The doors of Room M, we would soon learn, were to be open for visitors twenty-four hours a day. Three couches formed a U in the center of the room with a large television facing them. This was an ideal setup for the lazy summer afternoons we would spend stretched out stoned on our couches absorbing the much coveted house cable system. The success of sophomore summer, we had been told, judged by who hung out, what they did, and the frequency with which they did it, was often determined by the occupants of the very room that was to be home. When the brotherhood had a friendly place to congregate in large numbers all other aspects of the house could thrive.

When I arrived at the house towards the end of June, I fully expected to find my new room empty. Instead it was crowded with '03 brothers as well as recently graduated seniors who would be near permanent fixtures on our couches at night. Beetle was nowhere in sight. I actually had to mentally review the faces and conjure up names.

Rats—the hero of Fenway Fiasco—sat with Davis, and Soapbox on one couch. Kouge, Pigs and Thalen were on another. Mole and Pope were on a third. The way they looked at me when I walked in made me think that maybe they didn't even recognize me.

"Chris Knight." said Kouge loudly, as if he was introducing me to the group for the first time.

Everyone offered half-hearted greetings as they realized I was living in Room

M for the term and would be a potential obstacle to their ability to make use of it. I walked over to the bunk beds and tossed the bag I was carrying on the top bunk.

Outside of my freshmen year crew I still didn't know any of these guys particularly well. We had pledged together, sure, but the following term, winter, was one in which nearly all of them had taken off to compensate for being on campus during the current summer. I had taken off in the spring instead, a term in which most of them were taking classes. I had missed out on a full term of class bonding and was fully aware that I was near the bottom of any objective ranking of the house coolness barometer. These were now my brothers and we came from all walks of life. Among us was an affluent son of a hedge fund manager, a state debate champion from a liberal mid-west city, an "old boy" southern gentleman whose family had their own livestock brand, a pothead with aspirations of becoming a criminal defense attorney, an avowed conspiracy theorist from southern California, a ten time Mardi Gras veteran with a fetish for toes, a working class New England boating enthusiast... and yet somehow we had improbably all ended up living in this same fraternity house together.

It was important to win their respect that summer and to prove how serious I was in this endeavor, I pulled an eighth of an ounce of marijuana out of my cargo pockets and tossed it on the coffee table.

"This I expect to be finished by the end of the day," I said as I went about the relatively mundane process of unpacking my bag.

Since joining the fraternity I had heard countless stories about what sophomore summer was going to be like from Kouge. Cannabis was always the primary protagonist. To ensure that our summer reached its full potential, I contacted a drug dealing friend of mine whom I'd known since elementary school, The Double, before heading up to school. He procured a few cheap ounces for me, which I naively thought would last the whole summer. Never did I take into consideration that I might be smoking every day, several times a day. A clique formed in Room M comprised of stoners and Ship players.

The nights belonged to Ship. This was the term, the rest of the house on vacation, where our skills could blossom to their peak. Every night we bought at least ten cases of beer, that's three hundred beers and at least fifteen games a night. This meant every '03 brother could play at least one game per night, but in actuality it was only maybe a third that did all the heavy lifting. The Ship players, those with a true love for the game and not just the intoxication that accompanied it, quickly separated themselves from the rest of the class. We played every night, even if a game had to be slipped in during a study break.

Playing that much Ship built your tolerance up quickly; the elite players could easily drink ten beers and then head over to the library without missing a beat.

The game had transformed into sport and became a dance of strategy. Where you aimed depended on who you were serving to, their style of play, the shot you had just returned and your faith in your partner. Because of the nature of the game, your partner was almost always a fellow Chi-Gam. Ship was the most anti-social game on campus. Best friends would play together without sharing any words besides the occasional, "good shot." A large number of students, including a large percentage of the female population, just flat out couldn't handle that quantity of beer in so short a period of time and those that *could* handle the drinking *could not* master the large variety of difficult shots a successful game of Ship required. The concept of a team sharing a paddle seemed outrageous to the campus's other Pong players. Thus the summer term was perfect for Ship. We could be assured that few people would venture into the basement during the week and we accomplished our socializing on the weekends—always after a few afternoon, first-floor games.

Our social chairs routinely set up social events with sororities. A Pong tournament with KDE one weekend, cocktails with Tri-Delt the next. We even threw what we called "invite tails," which was literally just combing the printed campus "face-book" for attractive women and adding them to an already cluttered invite list. I happily participated in the Pong tournaments (those were great fun but always resulted in disappointing loses) but couldn't endure the forced intermingling of cocktails. In concept it sounds great. You set up rows of alcohol and mixers along the length of the bar with dozens of cases of beer clearly visible underneath. At around nine pm the girls stream into the basement. At first just a few at a time, usually the ones who already knew Chi-Gams and so had a legitimate excuse to be the first ones into the basement. Brothers all over the room flash a look at the entrance but the unbashful ladies stroll confidently into the room. Their friends meet them, get them drinks, and then the party is going. More and more women appear at the foot of the stairs and then the room is packed and swirling with open mouths, and your thoughts can no longer be heard over the dulling white noise of crowd chatter. I almost always played Ship during these cocktail parties. When they took place at the sorority house I'd hop on their Pong tables to be slaughtered in Shrub games against the sisters. I was always physically present but I needed to be engaged in Pong games to maintain some semblance of control. I couldn't bear to be any of these places otherwise.

Our class gelled that summer in a way I could never have anticipated, in large part due to our shared drinking experiences in Room M and on Pong tables. We saw the very worst and best of each other each night, and in many cases it was the little things that have stuck with me. Thalen and Soapbox hurling spit-balls at a stationary bat that had landed on the wall of the third floor stairwell. Pigs, one drunken night, implying that our friendship had reached a point where he would consider having someone murdered if they posed a significant threat to me. Hitting the permanent gravity bong on the Room M coffee table morning after morning. Winston taking a long brutal pull from a Gatorade bottle full of cigarette ash, bong water, and tobacco dip that he mistakenly identified as a newly opened beverage. Davis creating homemade opium tea from poppy seeds in the second floor kitchen and throwing the foul smelling water coolers they used to brew it out of the window to collect maggots on the side of the house. Cheering Rats on as he booted during meetings. These thirty near strangers were like family to me by the end of August and for the first time in my life I hadn't chosen my own friends, but that hardly mattered. We all seemed suddenly free from the weight of chains holding back the Chi-Gam buried deep in all of us. Things would never be quite the same for me.

During a brutally hot summer afternoon in Chi-Gam, I took refuge in the second floor air conditioned double of house video game aficionado Nathan Burner. After a short but efficient session of bong rips, Burner inserts a pirated copy of NBA Street into his modded Microsoft X-Box and hands me the second of two controllers. The system boots up and the game begins to load its start screen. When prompted to enter a name for my guest character, I type out C-N-U-T-Z, utilizing each of the five characters allowed. This was done for unimportant and forgotten reasons.

"See-Nuts?" Burner asks.

I hesitate for a moment and then shrug.

Burner starts chanting: "See-Nuts, See-Nuts, See-Nuts, See-Nuts...".

Just then Burner's roommate enters the room and approaches his closet cubby-hole while Burner snaps his fingers to get the roommate's attention.

"Hey... hey!"

He points at me with his left hand and says: "See." Then he makes a twirling motion with his free right hand and directs that one at me as well. "Nuts."

His roommate laughs.

"C-Nutz?" he asks.

"See-Nuts," Burner confirms with a nod.

Within two weeks everyone in the house was calling me *C-Nutz*. A week later and it was just *Nuts*. Burner then began experimenting with variations on the original.

"Nutsack," he suggested one night in the basement to a series of groans from the brotherhood.

"Testes," he offered the next night. This was flat out ignored.

"Balls," he finally said and the brotherhood patted him on the back and adopted the new nickname with great enthusiasm.

From that point on I was known as Balls on Dartmouth campus.

❄

In early July I got a call from The Double, that eccentric friend from home whose trees we had been smoking for the last month, asking how the pot had worked out. We were on my last eighth and the suggestive tone I used to relay this information was not lost on him.

"Can you move a half pound?"

Our impending shortage was no longer going to be a problem.

"Definitely, maybe even in a weekend."

By this time word had gotten around campus that I had bud, and numerous requests had come in from contacts at a few other houses for weight. This wasn't dealing—merely distributing and really a civic responsibility if you think about it.

"It's only worth it to me if it's a HP," The Double said.

He would be on a Greyhound bus from Port Authority to White River Junction that next Tuesday afternoon and planned to stay until Sunday, meaning he would get to experience Meetings on Wednesday and a dance party on Friday. Not a bad four days to spend at Dartmouth. It was easy to deduce that The Double's visit had less to do with reconnecting and more to do with the large discrepancy between supply and demand on campus, but that didn't bother me. I was proud of this new lifestyle and wanted to showcase it to the friends from my past life who knew an entirely different me.

On the night of the Double's arrival, I borrowed Rats's Mercedes and peeled out of the house parking lot, closely investigating the streets of Hanover leading to the bus stop. The Double had a certain propensity, despite a foreign environment, to become distracted and wander off, either forgetting or dismissing his prior engagements. That night, however, he had parked himself on a bench outside the Hanover Inn and when he caught sight of me pulling up to the curb, he grabbed his knapsack and trotted over. Typically, a blunt hung from the edge of his mouth and flipped up and down as he entered the car cackling, a continuous trail of smoke rising from his nostrils.

"My black-white cookie! What's up, my nigga?"

He handed me the blunt and embraced me. The Double was never shy of showing emotion and was known to hug, pat, rub and even sometimes fondle his closest friends. Also, despite having grown up in the same upper-middle class, predominantly white suburb of Long Island as I had, The Double had long cultivated faraway street associates and spoke in a bastardized, half-Ebonics slang, unafraid at tossing the word "nigga" about in any situation, which could be understandably off-putting given his strikingly Sephardic appearance and obviously Jewish last name.

I hit the blunt with his arms still wrapped around me and released the smoke through my nose as I sped off.

The Double scanned the dimly lit campus as I circled around the green. As we passed a walking student he pursed his lips and emitted a little "Ooooleyoo" sound out of the open window that caused the girl to stop in her tracks and peer at our passing vehicle suspiciously. The Double laughed and said, "I knew this was gonna' be ill."

The house was deserted when we arrived and although the music system still raged on in the basement, the absence of the sound of a bouncing Pong ball told me that the games had ended for the night.

Approaching three in the morning, my usual Room M crew appeared to be the only brothers awake. I introduced The Double, who I had already described in some detail to the guys in an attempt to warn them of his eccentric nature. The Double began speaking almost too quickly to really understand while springing around the room and making wild gesticulations with his arms. All at once he appeared to be reminiscing with me, poking fun at my friends, commenting on the room's furnishings, and describing his journey.

"Nigga, this house is off the hook! And let me guess... Bug or Roach or whatever the fuck you call your roommate. Haha, you look like a bug—what up, my man! He he he. Get this: almost got fucking busted on the way up here, *son.* Po-Po is on the bus at border checkpoint just as this *dick* tried to lift a blunt out of my pocket, almost pulled a sack along with it. Po-po was just chillin. Yo, which one of you mutha fuckers has a scale? How about you Big Boy? They feed you good at this place! Haha. Spanish guy, right? Yo tengo mucho ganja mu-cha-cho. Necesito un scalo. Hahaha. This is my *nigga* right here! Did you know your homeboy used to be a nerd? Did you know that? Ha ha ha. CHRIS! Ha ha ha. CHRIS! You don't know how hooked up you are up here, SON!"

"Let me get this straight. You have a half-pound on you…."

"Three quarters of a pound," he corrected, winking at me,

"Okay sorry, three-quarters of a pound… and you're keeping weed in your pockets and smoking blunts at rest stops? Are you out of your goddamn mind?"

"I know, I know, always taking chances. You know I had to smoke that blunt when we stopped at Mickey D's though, heh heh."

Rats was shaking his head and laughing mostly to himself. Pigs, focusing on the word scale in The Double's speech, snickered, then laughed out loud and disappeared to his room. A second later he lackadaisically strolled back in with his head down, tossed his scale on the table and put his hand to his chin, striking the kind of intense pose he was known for.

"So, where is it?" I asked. I don't think any of us actually believed this kid had crossed state lines with more than a half-pound of marijuana.

He smiled in relish of the suspenseful moment and produced a tightly wrapped green lump from the inside of his bag with a jerk of the hand.

"Da Dahh!" he said dramatically, "I told you, *nigga*! That QP is for you, at price and this is for me." Two more QP bags were then revealed and tossed on the table. "Lets weigh this shit out."

And that's exactly what we did next, routinely packing the professor and smoking two blunts that were passed back and forth between the six of us. The room was soon dense with weed smoke. We had a lot of pot on our hands—nearly three quarters of a pound. The Double next produced a string of tiny connected baggies.

Rats chuckled from the sight of the baggies.

"Not sure if you'll need those bro. Kids up here buy by the eighth. No one I know is hustling dimes on the corner."

"We'll see," said The Double as he began breaking up the brick weed and packing it into a handful of the dime bags.

Now that the shipment had arrived, my standard summer activities could continue unmolested.

The next morning I awoke to a gust of marijuana smoke hitting me in the face. I opened my eyes and mouth to inhale the shotgun blast of weed The Double was blowing in my face. The blunt was flipped around backwards in his mouth and he was blowing through the end you normally inhale through into his cupped hands which were directing the tornado of smoke into my mouth.

"Only the best for my black-white."

He ended the shotgun, hit the blunt himself, which was already half finished, handed it to me and went back to bagging up dimes.

"Double—Rats was one hundred percent right. You're not going to sell those."

"Trust me, son! You *never* seen a real drug dealer around these parts. This shit is going to be sold," he smiled confidently. "Watch me work tonight."

I dropped it.

That afternoon I took The Double down to the Connecticut River, which was only a ten minute walk from the house.

"Nigga, shouldn't you be at class?"

We were passing students on their way to academic buildings. I laughed and told him this was sophomore summer, something he obviously didn't comprehend, and then I suggested he roll a nice joint for the afternoon, which was something he understood perfectly.

It was a beautiful day and The Double, who hadn't been around nature in years, was rightfully impressed by the majestic river, the surrounding dense and full tree line and the complete serenity of being momentarily *away from it all.* We rented a canoe and took it a mile downstream the river where it branched into two and engulfed a tiny island. Right before we reached this fork we slowed to a stop and smoked the joint that The Double had tucked into his pack of Newports.

Now high, the rope swing made an even greater impression on him. The college had recently cut down the rope for safety reasons—they did this every summer—but someone had already attached another so we took turns propelling ourselves into the water.

When this became boring we headed back to the shore and as we caught sight of the dock The Double and I somehow managed to capsize our canoe, flipping ourselves out of the boat and into the warm water. After a brief but intense struggle we were able to flip the canoe back over and re-enter it but an almost-full pack of The Double's Newports floating around in three inches of water made our mishap quite obvious.

We needed help getting the canoe out of the water and then together had to fish the cigarettes out and toss them as the Dartmouth Outing Club members running the lodge looked on.

The Double thought the entire scene was hilarious and on the walk back to the house he laughed, "*Son*! I've visited mad schools and this setup is by far the tightest."

Meetings that night finally succeeded in ending The Double's world from a sobriety standpoint and he didn't emerge from this hazy stupor for four days. It wasn't rare during the summer for visiting friends of brothers to attend Meetings and these "New Guys" were fully incorporated into the spectacle as far as they were willing to go. The Double chugged cups of beer along with the rest of us, participated in our songs and chants and even took me on in a bare-chested Kumite—battering my body to the point where I had to vomit following an easy defeat. In the basement after Meetings, he stumbled about from group to group and from my vantage point on Varsity that night I observed him conducting drug transactions with brothers and visitors alike. It seemed he preferred socializing and selling drugs to Pong. This would not do. The next day we awoke late and nursed our hangovers with weed and then when afternoon turned to night I forced him to play Ship with me in the basement. It took him a few games (all losses) to catch on but once he did he was addicted and we blacked out playing games late into the night, some of which towards the end we actually won. We woke up the next morning on the Room M couches still dressed in our clothes from the night before. That evening was the dance party and to pre-game we began taking shots in Room M with whoever happened to be around, smoked several blunts with the door closed, and played more Ship in the basement. Then I essentially just cut him loose and let him operate solo in the basement and on the dancefloor. I observed his every movement and interaction that night from my drunken pillar. We once again drank all night and into the early morning.

When we finally awoke mid-afternoon on Saturday, The Double was a shell of his former self, barely able to navigate his way around Room M, and not anywhere close to the talkative friend I was used to. For anyone unaccustomed to it, binge drinking on a Dartmouth scale for several straight nights is a trying experience. That evening Rats discovered a colossal mystery boot filled almost to the top of the sink in the third floor bathroom. This almost incomprehensible amount of vomit was a serious house *faux pas* that went uncleaned for several days. Of course following his departure, The Double was blamed for the vomit clogged sink and despite my proclamations of his innocence, the incident was given as proof of The Double's inability to keep up with our binge drinking escapades and he was deemed as "soft," at least in the Dartmouth drinking sense of the word.

As expected, The Double left Dartmouth for good and in spite of the terrorist throw-up and The Double's sorry shape as Rats and I drove him to the

Hanover bus stop on Sunday afternoon, we had to admit that he did keep his promise and had sold every last dimebag he had prepared. He never returned and I only saw him sparingly after that.

❄

Newly knighted and highly intoxicated, I have climbed on stage during a sophomore summer Meetings to do something extraordinary. I request and am handed six full beers, clasp each cup by its lip, and spontaneously say: "I present to you... the long fabled, but never realized... six beer CHUG!"

I raise the six cups of beer above my head as if preparing to drink them but instead simultaneously pour them out all over my face. The beer drenches me, obscures my vision, clogs my ears, nose and mouth so that I can no longer clearly see nor hear as I willingly allow my legs to give out beneath me. I fall in the direction of a garbage can propped up in front of the stage, my body contorting as it tries to squeeze into the can's narrow opening and then almost immediately the can buckles and crashes over, spilling me out onto the Meetings room carpet. I am soaked and battered but the brotherhood is exploding in laughter and I can feel the response pulsing through the group as I cough and dry heave uncontrollably on all fours in the center of the room.

"You'll get it next time," Beetle says as I plop myself dripping onto a couch. It is the hit of the evening and the "Balls Six Beer Chug" is requested and performed at every subsequent Meetings that I attend.

❄

Halfway through the summer a Ship table goes missing. It was one of our JV tables that had been played on extensively the night before, and in the morning it was gone. Teams of brothers set out and attack the campus in a fan-like fashion, hitting up the usual suspects and politely asking to "have a look around." We are taken on guided tours of the basements and storage areas of each house but the table cannot be found, nor any sign of a suspicious new table that has recently been painted. The likely conclusion is that the table has been stashed in a dorm room, abandoned where we can never find it or destroyed entirely. Beetle had painted this particular table earlier in the term. We called it "the Godfather Table" by virtue of its design, which was a parody of the original promotional poster for the Coppola crime opus but instead of the name of the film, the all black table had Chi Gamma Epsilon painted in white lettering and the silhouette of the hand clutching a marionette control bar has been replaced with one grasping a Pong paddle. It was a simple yet beautiful design for a Pong table. About a week after the table vanishes, Pigs learns through his cross-campus network of informants that it has surfaced at an off-campus apartment belonging to four non-affiliated sophomores who have been openly playing on it even when having guests over. In fact it is one of these guests who recognizes the design and blitzes Pigs. Five of us pile into Pigs's shabby looking station wagon and head to the identified house, which is one of these types set a significant distance in from the road so that you need to access it by way of a winding driveway, in this case composed of gravel. It is a gorgeous day, and about fifteen kids (guys and gals) are hanging out outside the building, four of them in the midst of a Pong game on a table that we can plainly see is ours—they haven't even bothered to paint over it. The five of us (Pigs, Rats, Kouge, Beetle and me) hop out of the vehicle and approach the party goers without saying a word but displaying our best thousand mile stare. Any conversations that had been taking place prior to our arrival cease immediately and the Pong game is halted. All eyes are on us as we calmly steer our way towards the table. The remaining beers of the game (in a shrub formation disgustingly enough) are flipped off the table and onto the ground. Pigs and Kouge then grab the table and head back to the car. The rest of us stare down the group. The Godfather table is lain across the roof of the beat up station wagon and we all pile back into the car—the four of us with window seats extend our arms up and out of the window, gripping the end of the table to keep it in place during the short ride. We then peel backwards down the driveway, reverse back onto the street and drive off.

❄

My bong was beautiful. Double chambered, hand blown glass, nipples covering the base. A whirlpool of red and blue swirled around the shaft—the colors always changing and growing darker. When I purchased her, she had been much lighter in color, exuding innocence and purity but our shared time together had darkened and altered her appearance forever. Now she was undeniably mine. It seems silly to profess such devotion for a bong but the sentiment was sincere and just stroking her smooth base or fingering her red and blue nipples could relax my mind. In my hands she was the most valuable thing I owned and when she sat dormant on my shelf I was comforted by the fact that she was always available if needed. Her name was Nadine.

There was nothing quite like the feeling of getting back to my room after picking up a sack—a red and orange logo with the word BIOHAZARD written across the middle. Locked in my room with Nadine I didn't have to think about anyone or anything. We had a special ritual. I would get her down from her hidden closet shelf, whisper a few words to her, dim the lights and the room filled with thick white smoke as her lips met mine—a symbol of our eternal love.

No such luck tonight. The sharp knock on my door reminds me that I live in a house with twenty-three other guys. Though it is two in the morning, the music seems like an earthquake, shaking the house and disorienting me, and I know that few, if any, are asleep. I've locked my bedroom, something I almost never do, but I make no move to answer the door and hope this intruder assumes I'm jerking off and leaves me in peace.

I groan as the lock on the door turns. Rats stumbles into Room M with a stupid grin on his face. The kind of smirk that is so ludicrous it's impossible to find any fault with anything he does—as if we all had to take it for granted that he was an idiot.

"Yo Balls, you smoking without me?" he barks mid-chuckle.

How drunk or stoned is he?

Of course upon seeing him I have to pretend that I'm thrilled he'll be joining me. Not that I have any problems smoking with my friends. In fact I smoked with Rats earlier this evening. However, now he was infringing on my personal Nadine time.

A house skeleton key dangles from his jittery hands. Only the execs were supposed to have house keys, and they were supposed to use it in emergencies only. Not only is this not an emergency, but I also know for a fact that Rats left his set in my room earlier; they are currently in my pocket.

Rats stumbles onto the couch, glares at me and says, "We should pack a huge fucking bowl right now, and get toasted. I want to be so stoned that I can't see or hear."

I immediately agree with him. Only seconds before, I was furious at Rats busting in on Nadine and me, but now a happy little weed smile is smeared on my face as I begin stuffing the tiny Christmas trees into Nadine's male slide. With the slide filled, I scan the room for a lighter, any lighter. Spotting one on the floor, halfway hidden under the couch, I pick it up and light the bowl. The lighter is almost empty and I make a mental note to steal another from Pigs the next day. And before long the thick white smoke creeps up Nadine's neck and fills my mouth. With my mouth completely full of smoke and even some smoke pouring from my nose, I begin to cough uncontrollably, sending the billowing smoke throughout the entire room. Rats bursts into laughter and I, unable to control myself, begin flailing about wildly, coughing and banging my chest repeatedly. When I calm myself and come to my senses, I am stoned.

After another hit or two, I feel the life being systematically drained from my complacent body and my consciousness floats upwards towards the ceiling, revealing a contorted body on the couch. Every moment that goes by his posture sinks lower, his eyes grow drowsier. He can even feel the circulation in his limbs grow slower. And while I watch him from above I can see Balls begin to withdraw. His eyes close and he begins ignoring his friend. Slowly he drifts away. There is nothing anymore but my inner voice and at once that is all that matters.

❄

Five hundred college students are floating like tsunami wreckage on the Connecticut River. Most are socializing on a mishmash collection of splinter dispensing homemade pontoon boats, others randomly drift about the waters between these vessels in black inflatable inner tubes—the whole dense ensemble encircled by a perimeter of police boats maintaining a watchful eye. There are two main classes of raft on the water that day. The fraternity pontoons are basically barrel-floating wooden platforms of various dimensions, each outfitted with dozens of cases of mad dog, beer and champagne—one or two even have kegs that are hidden under stacks of beer cases in the center. Even larger than the fraternity rafts are the multi-storied barges that look almost like buildings, built and manned by locals that show up every year for the event. One of these monstrosities has a ladder that leads to a wooden plank and diving board. A nude and certainly drunk individual takes a hazardous dive from forty feet up. Elsewhere brave or reckless students are treacherously leaping from raft to raft. An unwilling swimmer who has just been pushed into the water by a friend finds a floating beer. A shrieking student loses her bikini top to the waters of the Connecticut River. This was Tubestock—the most anticipated day of Sophomore Summer.

Every term at Dartmouth has its mid-term celebration. Homecoming in the fall is known for the iconic image of the freshmen bonfire in the center of The Green that the newly matriculated students will circle the exact number of times as their official class year. Winter term brings Carnival, featuring snow sculpture contests, the Psi-U Keg Jump and midnight snowball fights. Green Key is our spring celebration, attracts the most alums to campus, and various frats throw lawn parties (most notably AD) with bands, outdoor Pong and barbeques scattered around campus. Tubestock, the unofficial summer version, has since been banned by the town of Hanover due to the obvious liability issues that come along with half the sophomore class drinking all afternoon on the river, most without any sort of life-vest to prevent drowning.

The week before Tubestock the house was in a state of constant preparation and intoxication. Our Housemen oversaw the construction of the Chi Gam raft on the front lawn while the rest of us drank around them and in the Meetings Room. The design that they worked from was ambitious— envisioned as four separate carpeted sections that interlocked together at the middle, each quadrant was twenty by sixteen, which would make it by far the largest student raft on the river that afternoon. The actual construction took about a week with brothers alternating duties. Because of its size, each section would have to be carried down to the river on a flatbed separately, and then assembled on shore before being launched into the river.

The Thursday night Ship Tournament was orchestrated by the House Ship Chair. This was not an elected position but was instead passed down by the previous Ship Chair just before graduation to a sophomore who he felt exhibited the greatest commitment to the game. Mole was an excellent choice, one I could hardly argue with, although in later years I did harbor some regret that the brotherhood had not fully realized my total obsession with the sanctity of Ship until much later. As it was, Mole sent out the summer '03 rankings mid-summer and requested that we all send him our intended partners for the Tourney. I cracked the top ten in the rankings for the first time and never once looked back, and although Beetle and I did finally break out of the first round, we lost in the semi-finals to Thalen and Soapbox, the eventual winners of the summer contest.

Our dance party was on Friday night, our usual drunken affair, and finally our traditional wake your ass up, *Come as You Are* party was Saturday morning. By noon we would all be on the river.

On Saturday morning I woke up on a Room M couch with Kouge snoring loudly on the couch next to me. Kouge, though now a graduate, was once again up in Hanover visiting for the week as he had yet to decide what his future plans held in store for him. I sat up, reached for the bong on the coffee table, packed a bowl and began directing the smoke from my hits into his face to see if I could rouse him. Seconds before his eyes opened, a smile formed on his face. An instant later he had the bong in his hands. He took a large rip, handed it to me and began shaking Beetle violently by the shoulders and yelling "COME AS YOU ARE!" directly into his right ear. Despite this, Beetle woke methodically and merely said in a low, calm voice, "Bro, just stop it." Soon the three of us were stumbling downstairs in the same clothes we had worn for the dance party the night before, still drunk I might add. Someone on the second floor was shrieking "COME AS YOU ARE!!!!" at the top of his lungs as we descended but we ignored this as our top priority was locating the coveted *Come as You Are* shirts.

Come as You Are was a party we threw once a term on the Saturday morning of the term's "big weekend." The first brothers to regain consciousness proceeded to wake up the rest of the house using whatever they had at their disposal—loud-speakers, pots and pans, buckets of water and plain old throat power being the most common. Once awake we would resume drinking immediately as we began our search for the *Come as You Are* shirts. The first fifteen minutes of everyone's morning was dedicated to tracking one down of these house-made t-shirts in the appropriate size and immediately donning it. Then it was Pong upstairs and hopefully outside, and music and being awake together and drinking when we should clearly be sleeping off the after effects of our third continuous night of binge drinking. Outside guests actually show up for these parties in droves and at its nadir, *Come as You Are* could challenge many nighttime parties in attendance and sheer alcoholism.

The shirts were found scattered around the remnants of large cardboard box in the foyer that had more or less been torn apart by the first eager brothers who had attacked it. The handful of brothers loitering nearby were sporting them over *Come as You Are* shirts from previous terms. Get four Chi-Gams together in warm weather and three of them are almost guaranteed to be wearing one of offensively hilarious relics from a previous term. I grabbed one, momentarily admired the design on the back and tossed it over my winter carnival shirt (which was red with white lettering that said: "Chi-Gam Parties: Helping drunk people hook up since 1987" on the back). I had seen Pigs diligently working on the summer design several days before in Room N and the finished product looked pretty great. It was black with white lettering across the top that read "Come as You Are." At the bottom, in the same coloring and font, was the phrase "Come While You Still Can." A dartboard occupied the middle of the shirt with the letters of different frats occupying various locations around the bullseye; most of these had darts in them representing the derecognized frats (Zete, Phi-Delt, Beta) and the active frats on probation (at that time numbering four or five). XRE occupied the bulls-eye spot and was still untouched.

Thalen set up three recycling bins in our meetings room; I lined the insides with plastic garbage bags, and someone else began pouring champagne and orange juice into one of them. Twenty or so bottles went in before the champagne breakfast reached the top of the bin. Thalen then topped off the meal with a bag of ice and declared, "Mimosas are served!" In the second bin we created Bloody Marys. In the third a blue colored, grain-alcohol punch. Ship was set up in the Meetings Room and played with the colorful beverages at our disposal. Someone manned the DJ station that was still setup from the previous night's party. Kids who weren't playing Pong lounged out on the front lawn with colorful drinks or bottles of Boones Farm, watching Beetle and Davis put the finishing touches on our raft. Guests were arriving in large numbers and helping themselves to generous amounts of the alcohol we had put out. Everyone was trying to get as drunk as they had been the night before as soon as possible for our excursion on the river.

Down by the banks of the river, the raft took longer to put together than anyone had anticipated. The ground where the rafts were being launched was uneven, making it difficult to match the segments of raft up correctly so they could be linked and pushed into the water. Finally, after we had been at the shore for an hour we managed to thrust the unwieldy contraption into the water and miraculously it stayed afloat. As soon as it hit the water an army of Chi-Gams jumped in and swam out to our escaping raft. All attention on the river was directed at us. We all climbed aboard wondering if it would hold our weight; it did. Following Kouge's lead we began dancing and singing our house song at the top of our lungs, utterly amazed at our achievement.

With the largest student raft we were attracting a lot of attention as we drifted towards the center of activity on the river. When we neared these over rafts (and sometimes bumped into them) students jumped across the gap from their raft to ours or dove into the waters to begin swimming over to be pulled aboard by Chi-Gams. Several of us made trips back to the shore to re-up on booze, the cases carried underarm and doggy-paddled to the raft with great effort. It was a confusing mess but everyone was having the time of their lives.

The raft was suddenly full of people. Rats observed that Thalen had disappeared, and everyone jokingly concluded that he had surely drowned. I decided in the ensuing chatter that I would investigate and rescue Thalen from his tragic fate if that were so required so I took several steps back, ran at the end of the raft and dove confidently into the river. I heard several cries for my safety as I surfaced, surrounded by wet cigarettes, but ignored the shouts and paddled off towards the numerous other rafts congesting the river.

I was conscious of the fact that I was very drunk, and so I deliberately swam between several floating black inner tubes with relaxing students in them, using them to stay afloat and guide me towards the closest raft I could make out between the exhausting butterfly strokes. Once alongside this raft I pulled myself up and out of the water and surveyed the new location.

I had reached basically the center of Tubestock. All I could see around me were swarming human bodies on the river, the rafts I knew they stood on were invisible in the dense crowd.

"Hey man," a voice behind me said.

I spun around to face an enormous pyramid of Keystone Light cases, perhaps fifteen feet tall, and made up of what had to be at least a hundred cases. The raft the pyramid stood in the center of was actually chained to another raft some half a dozen yards away and was just barely large enough to contain the beer cases it hoarded. The raft's only occupant, the kid who had just addressed me, sat drinking a Keystone can on a throne of beer cases at the foot of this great pyramid with an open case beside him that his foot rested on. This was obviously just a beer storage raft for the larger "party" raft it was connected to.

"Want a beer?"

"Whose beers are these?"

"Does it matter?"

I shook my head as he reached into the open case and yanked out a beer to toss at me. I caught the thrown beer in a fluid motion, opened it and threw back my head to take a long gulp.

"You're a Chi-Gam, aren't you?"

"Does it matter?"

"Touché… well, it's treacherous out there. You should take a couple for the road."

This pyramid guardian was routinely launching beers from his craft to the much larger raft full of students and these beers would be caught, opened, and chugged by the party goers who intercepted them. Taking his advice and getting the hint, I filled my bathing suit pockets with beers and jumped to the nearby party raft, which had momentarily drifted close enough to the beer pyramid raft to leap across to.

This was a dense crowd and an obvious popular raft of the afternoon due not only to the nearby pyramid supply and delivery system but also because of a successfully smuggled Keg that stood in the very center of the raft, crowded by students who drank the keg beer from red plastic solo cups that were normally a rare sight in Hanover. Nobody seemed too concerned that the conditions were obviously unsafe as the raft bobbed and flowed at the will of river, routinely depositing students who mingled too close to its sides over and into the water. I slowly navigated my way through the unfamiliar crowd while pounding the beers I had acquired earlier. I was not able to make out a single word anyone was saying or recognize a soul. The kids around me might as well have been speaking in Serbian.

"You don't belong here, bro."

I heard this distinctly yelled at me but I didn't recognize the voice so I tried to focus in on who had yelled it from somewhere out in the crowd of the raft.

"It's time for you to leave, asshole."

As this was spoken by that same voice, an enormous force pushed against my chest and threw me headlong into the river. I went under, totally submerged for a few seconds, and when I surfaced I splashed around frantically, my ability to swim not fully taking hold, before an arm grasped me by the hand and pulled me free of the water.

It was Thalen. He was in the black tube that I was now thrust against and said "I got cha' dude" and began lackadaisically directing us away from the Gamma Delt raft with gentle water kicks while sipping from a Keystone can he held in his other hand.

Soon I could see that Thalen was directing us back towards the Chi-Gam raft. He pulled alongside it and transferred my hand over to the edge which helped me climb aboard. Everyone looked relieved to see me and discover that I hadn't drowned.

Almost immediately at this point the Chi-Gam raft began to break apart, starting from the middle. The four pieces were still connected on the sides but the middle of the raft had become a swirling whirlpool death trap that snapped open and shut like the Sarlacc Pit Monster. To keep the raft afloat and everyone out of the treacherous center, we routinely had to redistribute our weight on the raft by perilously jumping from platform to platform.

But the structural integrity of our raft had been too badly compromised and the mashing of the four individually linked sections against each other reaches a critical mass. The piece I stand on suddenly breaks completely free from the other three, causing four or five students standing beside me on the detaching segment to quickly leap across the widening chasm to the three pieces still barely connected. Now alone on the breakaway piece, I don't move a muscle as it begins drifting away from the group. The Chi-Gam brothers are calling for me to jump or swim across to them but instead I turn my back completely. The current is light but still pushes me and my private raft further out from the other partying sophomores. I make no attempt to rejoin them. The raft continues to drift away until it finally comes to a rest along the riverbed some one hundred yards downstream from the main rafts of Tubestock. I remove my last joint from the zip-lock bag I had been carrying in my pockets and light it with the bag's single remaining match. I sit down on the edge of the raft with my feet dangling over the side and submerged in the river.

That day takes its place among the countless that only exist as faded versions of themselves in the part of the brain that poorly maintains my memories. The summer continued, then ended and no more needs to be said about that.

Chapter 7: The Red Flag

"The deleterious effects of excessive alcohol use in CFS organizations are evident in other aspects of College life. Largely because of alcohol consumption, Wednesday night house meetings for many CFS organizations amount to little more than boisterous parties that preclude some students from attending Thursday morning classes. Moreover, institutional research demonstrates that "binge drinking," together with the adverse consequences suffered from drinking (e.g., blackouts and public vomiting), occur at a higher rate among CFS members than among the student body as a whole."
– *Excerpt from the Summary of the Recommendations Submitted to the Board of Trustees by the Committee on the Student Life Initiative*

Have you ever heard the expression: *Don't be that guy?* This was about the point in time when everyone started calling me Balls and Balls, as it turns out, was in fact, *that* guy.

At the conclusion of our Sophomore Summer, the previous year's junior class of Chi-Gams returned to campus as seniors and we reluctantly returned the keys to the house, now mere juniors ourselves. But I had a new identity to go with this new term. The person from the previous year was gone and in his place was some newly formed, terrorizing creation—a basement-dwelling, Pong-playing, hang-out artist extraordinaire. The nickname I had been given the previous summer had a sticky factor. I was BALLS—easy to remember, sufficiently distasteful, and perfectly encapsulating of the *who gives a shit* attitude my drunken antics had seemed to have taken on of late. I couldn't have shaken it if I tried.

This was the fall of 2001, a term during which I shared a double with Winston on the second floor of the house. Most nights were spent in the basement on Ship tables, though now to the freshmen who aimlessly wandered in, I was the seasoned basement dweller, pounding beers and intimidating underclassmen with a flashy bravado. But my goal each evening wasn't always to get wickedly blacked out drunk. On a Monday or Tuesday I might be drinking for the sake of Pong itself—an evening envisioned as just a couple of games squeezed in between dinner, studying, and bedtime and definitely not something to be too worried about from an academic standpoint. I couldn't accept the fact that after "just a couple of games" it no longer mattered what my intentions had been beforehand because studying or completing assignments or going to sleep at a reasonable hour was now totally off the table and even showing up to class in the morning was an escaping possibility. If others were drinking it was becoming more and more difficult for me to say: "You know what? I can take the night off. I really don't *need* to drink tonight. Just because others are playing Ship, doesn't mean I have to play Ship too."

There was something disconcerting about my complicity in all this. A switch had been turned on and Beer Pong had gone from being a weekend leisure activity to my primary daily concern. Everyone around me seemed to accept this change in my behavior and demeanor and there was never any reason not to. The benchmark for Chris Knight was the blank slate that I was as a pledge, not the fully realized young adult who had arrived at the school two years before. The warning signs fell on deaf ears.

I want to go back in time and violently shake this person by the shoulders. I want to scream into his ears at the top of my lungs. Why can't he see what he is doing to himself? How did he let it get to the point where the prospect of a night without Ship was incomprehensible?

A serious impediment to my burgeoning lifestyle presented itself only a few weeks into this new term when our fraternity was put on social probation for the first time since I had joined. I fail to properly recall the specific violation of college policy we were guilty of, though I'm certain it was warranted. We were in violation of the college's alcohol rules and regulations on a nightly basis, so it really just came down to being caught in the act. As a natural extension, CFS organizations had been conditioned to be as fastidious as possible with their rampant abuses of what many considered a broken system, holding us to what I deemed unrealistic expectations.

For example, at some point, fraternities were technically not allowed to host more than one guest per resident in the public areas of their house without first registering with the college as an official party—a tedious, red-tape laden process. Since it was impossible to predict the number of uninvited guests on a given night, we were regularly in violation of this rule. Realizing that this was wholly unenforceable, Safety and Security only required a party to be registered with the college if it already had been registered with the college, which is some bizarre sort of reverse catch-22. The truth of the matter is that fifty people hanging out and playing Pong in a basement was not a party by Dartmouth standards and even if it was, this sort of occurrence was so frequent that attempting to enforce this rule would have led to massive student unrest.

While on social probation, alcohol is banned in the public spaces of the house. This means no parties and no Beer Pong, basically the essence of the house stripped bare. The ramifications went well beyond our immediate social life. Without beer for the rest of the fall it would be substantially more difficult to attract potential pledges to propagate the future of our fraternity. We sought creative alternatives to indulge our abusive potomania.

To celebrate this shit-storm we threw a party at our neighboring sorority the night probation began. Armed with about five hundred dollars converted into beer and booze and our dormant Beer Pong tables, we commandeered the KDE basement and transformed it into a pseudo Chi-Gamma Epsilon. We set up our Ship tables and proceeded to black out.

After an amount of beers and drinks that is impossible to quantify, I found myself waiting for next on the sidelines of a Pong game that Brothers Pigs and Rats were starting. They were of course playing our version of Pong—Ship. It was early in the game and all eight boats on table were full. Chi-Gams and KDEs were chatting with each other in small two and three-person groups on the perimeter while I stood alone staring intensely at the action of the game.

Surprising everyone in the room, I am told that I grabbed a full cup from the back of Pigs and Rats' s five boat and chugged it in one massive gulp. I continued to drink the rest of the boat, one cup at a time. The KDE kitchen full of students then halted their conversations and turned to watch.

Rats looked more impressed than upset and applauded my efforts while commanding no one in particular to fetch replacement beers. I then heard a familiar cackle and clumsily spun around to face the red plush diner-style KDE booths set up on the sides of the tiny kitchen, which was barely able to support a Pong table at all. My Fenway Fiasco pal, Mr. Island Rum, now a senior, sat on the sidelines with a bottle of gin in one hand.

"Hey, Balls! You still look thirsty. Want to wash that beer down?" he asked.

"You had better believe it," I said, lowering my head and tilting it, giving him an adequate angle to begin pouring.

He missed badly, the alcohol instead spilling into my nose and eyes, momentarily blinding and choking me. I screamed out, "*My eyes are burning!*" and they were. I had to seek out something to douse on them to relieve the burning sensation so I again began grabbing cup after cup of beer from the nearby table but now was splashing myself in the face with the beer, imagining that the stinging from the beer would be slightly less intense than the burning of the gin. This sent everyone in the room into peals of laughter.

But these laughing students have not registered the fact that this is not your normal show of drunken showmanship aimed to amuse. What stands before them is a seriously afflicted individual, soaked in alcohol and blacked out, who has grabbed the broom which divides the Pong table to begin sweeping it back and forth across its surface. This person, who can only be identified as Balls, is sending full plastic cups of beer into the initially laughing onlookers with malice.

Balls is seized from behind. A brother, and if Balls had been sober he would have actually realized it was his best friend Winston, forcefully ushers him outside into the sorority parking lot and tells him that his night is over and it's best to just go home. Balls is furious to be kicked out in this fashion and doesn't quite realize he has done something completely unprovoked and unnecessary. He thinks his behavior is perfectly in line with what he perceives as the established Dartmouth norm but for some reason *he* is being singled out for unacceptable drunken behavior. To placate his friend, Balls begins walking towards the house which is right next door.

As soon as he thinks he is out of sight (though he is actually only forty feet away) he sprints off towards a row of parked cars that line Webster Avenue and rips at the door handle on the first one.

"GRAND THEFT AUTO," Balls screams.

The door is locked. He races to the next car.

"GRAND THEFT AUTO," he bellows once again, certainly attracting the attention of the small group that has followed him out into the parking lot to observe this strange progression of events unravel.

The next car Balls approaches was locked too and you can imagine how many he has to attack before he finally finds one that is not only open but started as well—parked outside of the Chi-Gam house by a delivery guy dropping off a pizza. Balls doesn't care though; he hops in, puts the car in drive, and peels off down the street.

And then Balls is no longer behind the wheel. The abandoned car with the driver's side door flung open is parked crookedly a few yards out from the curb, practically in the middle of Webster Avenue and positioned a few buildings down from Chi-Gam. Balls is stumbling back up Webster towards the house, having momentarily gained clarity enough to break off the illegal activity, when a black SUV pulls up next to him—the window rolls down and a voice says, "Wanna' go for a ride?"

I fully wake up out from my blackout to find myself sitting in the black SUV. I have three companions though I don't recognize any of them. One appears to be in his late thirties— *townies*!—is my first thought. As that settles, my mind conjures up images of *Deliverance*.

Squeal little piggy! The thirty-something seems to say with his eyes.

I have no idea how I got here.

We are driving down an unfamiliar street and I glance at the first license plate I see to reassure myself that we are still in New Hampshire.

A cigarette is resting between my fingers but it isn't one of mine. The man in the passenger seat appears to be smoking the same brand so I thank him, not sure if this was the first time I had done so.

Nobody speaks or makes eye contact. Our destination seems as unclear to the driver as it is to me. A few sudden stops and deliberate u-turns makes me think that perhaps he is trying to get lost... or lose somebody. Eventually the driver finds the parking lot he is looking for and pulls in. Then he turns to me, they are all looking at me for the first time, and says:

"Go steal one of those cars; we'll meet you back in Hanover."

This trick reminds me of *The Killing Joke*—a Batman graphic novel written by *Vendetta* writer and creator Alan Moore. The Joker is telling Batman a story which goes something like this: Two lunatics are escaping from an insane asylum. They make it onto the roof of the sanitarium but find out they will have to jump across a large gap to the building on the other side. The first guy backs up a few feet, runs at the ledge and jumps across easily. But seeing this insane stunt the second guy is too frightened and says "Go on without me." The first guy is having none of that and, getting an idea, he pulls out a flashlight and shines it across to the other side. "Use the light as a bridge," he tells his friend, "and walk across the gap" "Oh no," says the second lunatic. "Do you think I'm an idiot? You would turn it off when I was halfway across!"

Thinking of the joke I say, "Oh no! Not me. I've done my fair share of larceny tonight." Then I add "Take me back to Dartmouth," knowing full well that they intended to leave me right there in the middle of nowhere.

We all sit paralyzed in our seats on the ride back to campus. Our driver drops off the first two passengers and then returns me to the parking lot in the rear of the house, something he is able to do without first asking where I needed to be taken, which makes me realize they likely observed Balls running from car to car screaming "Grand Theft Auto" in front of the house earlier, must have known he was a Chi-Gam and decided to use this opportunity to teach a drunken frat boy a lesson he will not soon forget on the value of respecting private property. I sarcastically thank the driver as I get out of the car and try to commit his face to memory but to the best of my knowledge, never see him again. I learned a valuable lesson in all this: never trust a townie. I've been fearful of them ever since.

❄

The following afternoon was spent in group therapy. A small cross-section of Chi-Gams joined me in this enterprise in one of the few places where we could do so in a large group and still drink while on probation—Room M. A brother is recanting his story from the previous night. Balls' exploits have warmed up the crowd nicely and this brother was trying to match the response.

"So, you all know Clown-Face, right?"

A round of synchronized nods breaks out around the room. This girl, widely known across campus for the excessive amounts of makeup she was prone to wearing out in public, was no stranger to Chi Gam bedrooms and there were few innocent men among the assembled professionals.

"Bro, don't give me that cynical look," he said. "You banged her out, right?"

This question was asked as if the conversation could not progress without an immediate answer.

"Nope," said a second brother. "I made out with her, didn't fuck her."

"Is this the girl who leaves crumbs in your bed?" a third brother asks, momentarily glancing up from a Maxim Magazine he was engrossed in, while the second brother and others in the room, Balls included, laughed.

"You're thinking of Coke-Tooth."

"You banged Coke-Tooth on the president's lawn," Balls interjects.

"The only reason you remember that, Balls, is because I picked her up in your room."

"Yeah, and she put her cigarettes out in my fucking candles."

"Dude, we're talking about a girl whose nickname is *Coke-Tooth*."

"I love that Balls right now is upset about a couple of cig pieces in a candle, meanwhile the fool has boot stains covering his walls."

"Some of those stains were there when I moved in."

"The way to tell if it's Coke-Tooth is to get her to open her mouth. You gotta step on her foot or something. This chick has one tiny brown mollar." the third brother said, sticking his index finger into his mouth and bearing his gums. "Right... here."

"Correct, and it's disgusting," the first brother reported.

"Alright... and when you say she leaves crumbs—honestly, I've never heard that expression before and I'm not even sure what it means."

"Let me put it this way—the girl has never heard of a douche," the first brother replied.

"But she's fucked more than a few douchebags."

I don't know who said this but everyone thought it was really funny and paused the conversation to laugh for a moment.

"Well, anyway get back to the original story. What happened with you and Clown Face?"

"This is sort-of gross, but okay." the first brother said, rolling his eyes at the room as if telling the story hadn't been his idea to begin with. "So I was playing Pong with her at KDE like all night, dude. Pretty cool chick actually. Real nasty at Pong. We won fucking like five games in a row."

"Shrub, I assume," interrupts Balls.

"Yes, Balls, we were playing *Shrub*. Anyway, she takes me back to her place, right, and we bang like—all night. It was fantastic. Of course I've got whiskey-dick but still I'm able to bust a nut after like two hours of totally focused fucking." He pauses the story to burp-laugh into one sleeve. "Wake up this morning and I shit you not but this chick has pissed herself... the bed is fucking drenched. Sheets are soaked, I'm covered in piss, she's covered in piss, the room smells terrible. So I said 'whatever' and let her give me head anyway and when she's in the bathroom washing up, I fucking pissed on her clothes and just straight-up bounced."

Most everyone laughed—no doubt imagining a similar scenario playing out in their own sex lives and determining how they themselves would react—except for Balls, who was having a hard enough time as it was even imagining a girl asking him back to her dorm room to begin with.

"That's pretty goddamn dark, dude."

"It's a war-zone out there, gentlemen. Keep your gas mask on and your finger on the trigger. This place fucking changes you."

Gradually the other guys in the room came forward with their own harrowing tales from the previous night, some relatively mundane, others just as eventful. The entire time we were throwing back gin and tonics, chain smoking cigarettes, and trying to find something halfway decent to watch on TV, and it continued well into the evening.

This is what boys growing into men looks like. It's ugly, objectionable, and crude. This isn't who we were or how we were raised or what we wanted to become, but this is how the transformation happened. Time stands still in these moments and you lap up the affection of your friends, thinking that each second is a cherished moment all in some way contributing to your eventual realization as a person. Of course, most of these moments quickly disappear from memory.

That year, in accordance with the recommendations of the Student Life Initiative, fraternity and sorority rush was pushed back one full term to winter—which happened to be the term with the lowest enrollment on campus. Dartmouth's logic seemed to be that with CFS rush postponed, the incentive for sophomores to be on campus during the fall term would be diminished enough to relieve the challenges inherent in housing the majority of the student body each September. Though it may be true that they honestly believed a reduction in the "fall housing crunch" would be one of the end results, it appeared obvious to the Greek community that the school's real objective here was to meaningfully impact the number of rushing sophomores in an attempt to subtly loosen the death grip the CFS system had on campus life. Whatever their true intentions, implementation of winter/spring rush went forward my junior year with unintended consequences for all current and aspiring Greeks for that year and beyond.

Contrary to the expectations of the SLI Committee, most sophomores continued to elect to be on campus for the fall, so the split enrollment between winter and spring effectively meant two consecutive pledge terms as each group of sophomores had to be given an opportunity to rush. Fraternities quickly realized that desirable candidates could be enticed to "dirty rush" at rival frats during the fall and sought to mitigate this possibility by dirty rushing those same kids themselves. Basically what the school had done was ensure that pledging sophomores would be hazed all year round.

Chi-Gam was guilty of this "dirty pledging" violation during our first year with the new rush process, which in essence meant we had accepted members into our organization before they met eligibility requirements. A group of five sophomores had been identified as making up what we wanted to be the core of our new pledge class. They were popular within their class and already had a network of ten to twenty additional guys who would be interested in joining if their buddies endorsed the house—each one would then need to officially be approved by the current members of the fraternity and rushed legitimately during the following two terms. Our dirty pledges were invited to and expected to attend all house events (including Meetings) but we were careful not to implicate them or ourselves through any kind of public display that would reveal their new status as members. They took to the non-traditional nature of this pledge term with sincere effort, but one in particular did so early and intensely.

James Halifax was no more your typical "frat-guy" than I was, though for far different reasons. He had been exposed to alcohol and drugs early in life, abused substances consistently throughout high school, but was still able to breeze through classes and standardized tests as if they had been designed for infants. He was from the southwest, had peacefully endured but obviously ignored his Christian upbringing, was socially and fiscally conservative and totally unsympathetic to just about everyone around him. He was a multiple-gun owner, and in favor of an aggressive expansionist foreign policy about which he would speak at length when high. He could take apart and reassemble a car engine at the drop of a hat, clean and accurately fire a hunting rifle at a distance of several hundred yards, re-tile a roof and so on. The one thing our past lives did have in common was that they had nothing in common with the world we now lived in.

Despite the stranglehold that probation had on our ability to play Pong, a small contingent of Ship Professionals insisted on continuing to play our version of the game in the basement of our neighboring sorority, KDE. We acquired beer by any means necessary, since the social fund had been effectively cut off until probation ended. I took Halifax on near-nightly raiding missions—we broke into other houses through windows and back doors and tippy-toed our way into the basements where the beer supply could be located and pilfered. The stolen beer was brought back to KDE's back door where we would let ourselves in using the four-digit numeric pass code the sisters had provided. Then we'd set up Ship, always on Chi-Gam's slightly shorter tables that had been left behind in the KDE basement and play for as long as the stolen beer held out. Halifax was a daily participant in these games, as was another sophomore, Gunter, who wasn't technically one of the dirty pledges himself but was a close associate of theirs and a clear must bid candidate the next term. After two weeks of using and abusing their basement, the KDE sisters unceremoniously changed the code to their door, sending a clear message that we would need to seek asylum elsewhere.

This allowed for new types of recreational behaviors to surface. During this period I remember once running into Halifax and Gunter in the foyer one early evening before our quest for Ship games was to begin.

"Want to burn?"

Halifax plunged his hands into his pockets and quickly pulled them out again to reveal two clenched fists with what appeared to be outdoor, mid-quality weed sticking out from every seam of his fingers.

"Desperately, where?"

We went upstairs to the bedroom I lived in during my first term as a resident of the house, now a converted single housing Pigs, who was sitting on a couch with Rats drinking cocktails and listening to music when we entered. There was an obvious strange object in the room that stood out like a sore thumb—what appeared to be a water cooler jug fastened with octopus-like makeshift plastic tubes that protruded from the midsection. The top of the jug, which you'd normally connect to the water dispenser underneath, was outfitted with a miniature flower pot further modified with a little hole born out of its center and clamped securely to the top of the water bottle.

"Our new hookah." Halifax said.

As he filled the flower pot with one fistful of weed, Halifax explained how the week before, on a trip out of Hanover, he had convinced another sophomore to buy an entire pound of marijuana that they could bring back to campus to smoke and distribute together (hence the pockets of the stuff) and how he had constructed the hookah that sat in front of us after an old design of his from high school in celebration of the purchase and how we wouldn't believe the amount of pot he had at his disposal. This was the third eight-man hookah he had constructed, he told us. The first had been the original, built in high school, and the second he built the previous spring which he then sold to AD at a pretty high price. He further elaborated that the gullible sophomore he had been describing earlier, the one who had been dumb enough to actually front the cash for all that ganja... yeah, once they arrived back on campus and parked behind their dorm, this asshole managed to lock both the keys to the car and the pound of weed in the trunk. Halifax told us that he and Gunter, amidst what he described as a powerful smell of marijuana manifesting itself around them, decided that their only recourse was to break into the car through a rear side window using a rock. They then unlatched the locked door, entering cautiously to avoid the lacerating glass shards which were now scattered across the interior, and once inside Halifax cut a six inch hole in the rear leather seats using a fucking hunting knife in order to reach the car keys and pound of weed that were trapped in the trunk, due to the lack of any kind of a front trunk release lever in this painfully old shitty ass American-made car, rented, Halifax added, by the only rental company in town sleazy and fucking irresponsible enough to rent a functioning automobile to a nineteen year old asshole. Once the weed and keys had been extracted, a break-in was reported to the rental company and the trio successfully avoided any added re-windowing or upholstery charges. This eventual solution was one that Halifax and Gunter considered a foregone conclusion.

When the flower pot was completely full, Halifax instructed all present to grab one of the tentacles sprouting from the mammalian nipple area of the water jug's underbelly. He then told us all to begin sucking as he set fire to the greens stuffed into the flower pot. We were pulling as hard as we could, seriously concentrating on filling the two cubic feet of the water cooler with smoke and trying to expose our alveoli to as much THC as was possible. The marijuana in the bowl lit all at once and began the slow methodical burn to ash.

Then we had one of those conversations, a conversation you are absolutely sure everyone else involved has forgotten, but because of some personal revelation, almost every word is stained in your memory.

Gunter was talking about his dreams.

"I can never tell when I'm asleep," he was saying. "My problem is that my dreams are too fucking realistic. Even after I wake up I can't tell if it was a dream or a just a really shitty memory."

"I'm not sure I follow you," I said, but then my stoned brain finally caught up with his words and his further explanation was unnecessary.

"It's like my dreams are so mundane…this could be a dream for instance, this right here. Talking to you, Balls. Nothing ever happens in them, I'll be playing Pong in a frat basement or in a science lab working on some boring experiment or something. Everything that happens is so perfectly realistic that even after I wake up and think about it I still can't figure it out. It's like I never really get to sleep."

"I'm no expert but that doesn't sound entirely normal."

"What's even worse is—have you ever heard that you can't read in a dream?"

"I've never tried"

"Sorry to spoil the surprise but you can't. *Nobody* can. Not the case for me though. The last time I remember trying to read in a dream I was in a bar I went to all the time but it wasn't like a warped dream replica of a bar; you know how familiar shit gets distorted in a dream. No, this was an exact version of this bar I went to. I'm walking around, doing whatever it is people do in bars while dreaming and come across this bookshelf with a copy of *Catcher in the Rye* somehow staring at me and glowing on the shelf. I pull it down and flip to a random page. Okay, then I start reading out loud and not only could I read it, it was word for word the exact text of the book."

"Are you sure it was a dream?"

"Positive. It really scared the shit out of me."

"I have had some fucked up dreams." I found myself saying, "The worst are the tooth dreams. My teeth will be cracking apart, and rotting away until eventually my mouth is full of the crumbling pieces and I'm spitting out tooth shards all over the place. Every so often I reach in my mouth and yank out a whole fucking tooth that's black with rot. And now I have a huge hole in my mouth that I can't stop tonguing. The whole thing is fucking disgusting. I feel this incredible pressure on my mouth that hurts and feels good at the same time. Other teeth are coming loose and getting pulled out too."

Halifax and Rats laughed at this description but a serious expression came over Gunter's face. "Have you done much research on dream analysis?"

I shook my head.

"Supposedly, dreaming about rotting or crumbling teeth can mean that something seriously bad is going on in your life and you're either involved in some way or experiencing anxiety about it which is causing things around you to fall apart—represented by the rotting teeth obviously."

"Sounds about right."

The next time I slept I tested Gunter's theory. I was in the basement, during the very early stages of the sensation. I walked calmly over to the bar where oddly enough there was a stack of books and grabbed the book on top. Upon opening it I was greeted with thousands of meaningless symbols—shapes and colors that seemed to dance around the page preventing recognition. Even if I had been able to understand this alien language each line of text would have looked like a stock ticker randomly flashing numbers and letters. I turned around with the book in my hand coming face to face with Varsity. Gunter was standing with his arms folded watching my progress thoughtfully behind the Pong table so I approached him and showed him the book saying, *Gunter! You were right, meaningless symbols, this must be a dream!* It was only in this last instant that I realized I was dreaming. *Yes, now you see,* Gunter said then nodded toward a book that seemed to have instantaneously appeared in his hand. *But unfortunately that is not the case for me.* He resumed reading mid-volume and turned away from me in deep concentration.

Something was rotten all right but it wasn't just my teeth even though the binge drinking and frequent vomiting was wrecking havoc on my mouth. Here I was at Dartmouth, paying dearly to be there, and yet the longer I was there the less desire I had to *actually be* there.

Sometimes I would be walking around campus and pass someone and get so close to him or her that I could smell them. I could see them for who they really were. Then I'd get sick to my stomach and I'd have an overwhelming desire to just grab that person and puke directly in their face. The desire was so bad sometimes that I had to turn my head away from them as I passed to ensure no chunks surfaced in my throat.

There is no easy way to explain what was happening to me…

By the end of that bizarre term I had just about entirely stopped going to classes and put forth, at most, marginal effort on take-home assignments. For two of my classes I only showed up for the final and midterm and for one of them not at all. The professor of this class (which at the time I think I planned to drop) didn't bother to contact me even after I failed to appear for the midterm; this wouldn't have even mattered so much if I had managed to successfully drop the course on the last day you could do so, but unable to locate the professor (whose signature I would need on a blue index card, registrar drop slip), I instead tracked down the Department Chair (allowed in special circumstances to sign for a professor) but was told that this wasn't a special circumstance at all and that *it would be necessary* to locate my professor, who was certainly in her office, out and about on break, or in the department's kitchen/pantry/lounge common room combo or elsewhere—somewhere in the building certainly, except for the fact that it became clear after thirty-five minutes of searching that she in fact was NOT in the building. Yet upon hearing the details of my exhaustive search, the Department Chair still refused to acquiesce and sign the drop slip and I was left desperate, bewildered and running out of time.

I looked for some disaster to befall me—a freak accident leaving me with broken limbs or some disease banishing me to a bed for many months. I wanted an excuse for my lethargy because a tragedy could be used to explain what I had become. If I was temporarily paralyzed I wouldn't be expected to do anything. I could sit alone and brood, or read or sleep all day and nobody would say anything in protest. In fact it would be expected of me. But as long as I remained healthy, both physically and mentally, I had to accept full responsibility for my failures.

Forgery. Deception. Desperation. Fraud. These words all describe what I had been reduced to that afternoon. On a squat brick wall along the walking path just outside Rockefeller Hall, I scratched my professor's name onto the drop slip using the best cursive I could muster. I staggered toward the registrar, arriving with no more than five minutes to spare before the office closed for the day, and turned in the falsified document. I'm still not sure how I didn't expect to get caught... I guess my brain rationalized that these forms were simple formalities and I had never heard of a professor refusing a student who wished to drop a class so why would they bother cross-checking a drop slip? Of course each professor would be notified of all drops submitted for their classes. How did I not see that?

One thing I now find puzzling is that nobody seemed to notice or care that I stopped going to classes and taking tests. I'm not sure that the school was even capable of keeping track of such a thing, and as long as the school didn't know, my parents couldn't either; I certainly wasn't going to tell them. The most humiliating thing for me was not being able to escape from the obvious fact that not everyone succumbs to these obvious temptations that undid me. Even those that did largely came out unscathed. Unlike those around me, I didn't try to balance the two contradictory lifestyles I was living, opting for one in favor of the other. There was no compromise for me; the two personas I found myself being divided into could not occupy the same brain and body at the same time.

Somewhere on my journey my entire attitude toward college had changed. For the first time I began to question why I had decided to go to Dartmouth in the first place. How important would an Ivy-League degree be anyway? Certainly I wasn't maximizing my time here academically and simply having a degree without acquiring the attendant knowledge wouldn't make me any s marter or more qualified for a job once I left. Literally thousands of dollars a term were being wasted by dropping and not passing courses. Each term I reported to the student financial aid office and signed the loan documents enabling me to register, not fully registering myself that essentially I was signing myself up for a prolonged, post-college, monthly payment plan. By not maintaining an academic standard of just "okay", I was also jeopardizing my access to these federal loans. At that point I would have done anything to continue playing Ship in the basement and if the student loan office had required me to sign over my first born child to enroll in classes, I would have done so without blinking.

A week before the end of the term I got a envelope from the college containing a xerox copy of my forgery and a letter informing me that I was being brought up on disciplinary charges. I failed the class and was suspended for three terms due to a combination of poor academic performance and that disciplinary action. I left at the end of that fall term not to return to Hanover for nine months.

❄

During this homeward sojourn I had an opportunity to analyze my two plus years at Dartmouth from a distance and realign my priorities accordingly. From an outside perspective it probably looked like I was well on my way to accomplishing this task. I worked twenty hours a week as a field interviewer for the University of Michigan and volunteered for a Brooklyn-based nonprofit healthcare organization for another ten. I also started writing what was to become this memoir, though at the time it was merely going to be a series of short stories about my nameless frat-guy protagonist. I drank sparingly, a few times a week maybe and usually in moderation and alone. I rarely went out or socialized. Most of my Dartmouth friends were on campus and my high school friends were at colleges of their own.

I found it easy to categorize my suspension as accidental. The pendulum had swung too far in favor of Balls, that much I was willing to admit, but it needed adjustment, not replacement. Missing classes was an easily manageable task but missing exams entirely was an inexcusable lack of judgment. The person responsible—*that frat guy*—didn't seem anything like me. How could I, a reasonably intelligent young man, allow such a thing to happen twice? All I had to do was not fall asleep at the steering wheel and keep my foot on the gas pedal, not stopping or slowing down once until graduation.

I saw a psychiatrist to determine if there was anything clinically wrong with me and was almost immediately diagnosed with "mild" depression. I added the mild part—it was just depression, but everything not Ship-related seemed mild to me at the time, this so called depression most of all. It was recommended that I attend weekly therapy sessions and begin a regimen of antidepressants to balance my mood. I remember thinking in a way that the diagnosis was reassuring because it seemed to explain my behavior and complete reversal of priorities. But then the order of things tormented me. Did I drink because I was at Dartmouth, which is why I became depressed, or was I depressed because I was at Dartmouth and so I drank? Maybe I've been genetically predisposed to this behavior all my life and I don't have a choice but to recognize it, treat it, and learn to control it. Perhaps the medical community was unknowingly providing me with a convenient cop-out and in fact I was not depressed, in the way say, David Foster Wallace was depressed, and what I was really looking for was a *Get out of Jail* card—a carte-blanche to act however I pleased with no accountability whatsoever under the misguided notion that I was somehow accidentally living a meaningful existence.

If I concentrate hard enough and close my eyes so tight that my mouth involuntarily tightens up into a little Grinch like-grin—then I think I can actually feel the synapses in my brain misfire. The serotonin is misdirected or ignored. It collects in little pools, festers, and is wasted…as a result, my mood depresses. Air escapes and my brain deflates. The Zoloft, my therapist tells me, is like a bicycle pump. Giving my mind the correct balance of hormones to make it run smoothly again. This change takes time. The "happy pills" don't take effect immediately and only begin to work their magic after building up and coating the system for four or five weeks. This was an eternity. I start taking them, continue for a few days or weeks but noticing no perceptible change or really even thinking there was something that needed to be changed to begin with, I abandon them before they start to work—and I do this every couple of weeks. My supply is dried up within a year and I can't even tell if the pills worked or not but I tell my mother they work so her mind is at ease and I keep refilling my prescription.

❄

While parkhursted I saw Kouge for the first time since sophomore summer during a weekend he spent in town visiting some of the kids who had helped him pledge me the year before and who now worked and lived in Manhattan. We met one afternoon for lunch at a pizzeria on Houston Street, close to the apartment of the other graduated Chi-Gams he was staying with.

I will never forget that slice of pizza. Sitting across from Kouge and discussing the relatively mundane details of our recent lives, I felt self-conscience in a way that had never struck me before. It was as if I had floated out of my body and was soaring at high speeds towards the stratosphere, watching first Kouge and I shrink into the pizzeria, then the pizzeria into Houston Street, and Houston into the city, and then finally zooming back to reveal the full splendor of planet Earth. I felt as if all over the world there must be people just like us, perhaps identical in appearance and even sitting down to pizza just as we were. They might even discuss the same insignificant bullshit. My perception and concept of individuality evaporated in an instant. We looked so clueless and silly going about our everyday lives and trapped in our own little worlds that continuing to exist seemed almost nonsensical in a way. Could I handle that there was nothing special or unique in Kouge or I at all?

Even now I cannot put my foot on exactly how I felt as Kouge told me about the new condo he had purchased in downtown St. Louis, close to the medical school he had just been accepted into, and how he was outfitting this condo with a brand new top of the line surround sound home theater system. I only know that this was perhaps the queerest sensation I have ever had. At any moment I fully expected Balls to walk into the pizza joint. The sight of this, my double, would hardly faze me at all. We would look at each other, nod, and each realize that we knew exactly what the other one was thinking. I would have no ability to influence his actions, and yet he could easily influence my behavior through his own. His transgressions would be attributed to me and my successes to him. I am forced to wonder, why are his goals and mine at odds?

These thoughts raged through my mind as I sat across from Kouge, trying to look as calm and composed and as close to a normal human being as possible.

On the walk back to the apartment our conversation changed its course. Kouge asked me to tell him the story of my suspension and as I did so he was somber and pensive. I felt relieved to be finally coming completely clean to someone. Kouge was the only person besides my therapist who heard the full story. When I finished he pulled out a pack of Camel Lights, removed two cigarettes, lit one and handed it to me, then lit the other and said, "I can't help but feel this is partially my fault."

We looked away from each other and were silent as we smoked and measured the implications of his words.

"When you go back up there, you need focus solely on graduating," he continued. "It's all that matters."

"Kouge, what happened to me had nothing to do with you."

"I was the one who introduced you to this life. I encouraged you but I didn't do anything to help you."

"It was a fluke," I told him. "It's not going to happen again."

"I know you, Knight, and you have to realize that the life you lead up there is a fake—completely meaningless. As much as you want to believe otherwise, everyone up there is living for himself, and what happens to you doesn't concern them at all. You are just another Ship opponent, or kid to hang out with, or stoner to waste the afternoon with. Don't let your environment and those people destroy your life. This is about you, Chris." This was the first time I could remember him using my first name in a long, long time. "I'm not telling you to cut Chi-Gam out of your life. You have to see it for what it is, a distraction. A distraction with the serious potential of fucking up your shit. Learn to control *it*, not the other way around. Until you do that, not only will you be miserable and hate yourself, but you will struggle in school. I myself barely graduated. I got two Ds and a C minus senior spring but I managed to finish…and you want to know why? Because I sucked it up, swallowed my pride and got the work in. If you do that and listen to what I've said, you'll be fine."

At that point I decided to ask a question that had been on my mind for more than a year.

"Kouge?"

"Balls, that's really all I have to say about that."

"No, Kouge...I wanted to ask you about my pledge term. What really happened sink night? Why did Winston and I get callbacks?"

"Honestly Knight, I don't even really remember and it's not at all important," he looked flustered at what he must have perceived as an accusation. I, at least, thought it was important. "I think what happened was we put the names of the kids who had shook out into a hat, pulled them out one by one and deliberated. Both you and Winston were among the last names to be pulled out and we already had a class of twenty-six. Too many kids didn't know you, or knew you as the Fenway shitter and the kids who wanted you in knew that if you came back for a second night you'd get a bid. The brotherhood just had to meet you."

This political answer was hardly one I could challenge. Maybe Kouge was right and it didn't matter one way or the other. What answer was I searching for—a confirmation that the fraternity's initial reluctance to offer me a bid was correct in its instinctive appraisal of my character? It was foolish to expect Kouge to be so soul-crushingly honest with me at this vulnerable period of my life. He was doing me the ultimate favor—protecting me from my own dark thoughts.

"So…you called us back?"

"So we called you back," he agreed with a shrug.

"And that's the story?"

"That's it. Nothing more."
And then back to Dartmouth.

Chapter 8: Man Alive

"Some CFS members behave, at least on occasion, in ways that clearly violate norms of civilized behavior and the College's Principle of Community. Indeed, students observed to the committee that membership in CFS houses seems to confer on many students the idea that they can operate outside these norms on a regular basis."
– *Excerpt from the Summary of the Recommendations Submitted to the Board of Trustees by the Committee on the Student Life Initiative*

I have subjected my body and mind to assorted acts of vile wickedness.

"There's really only one thing you can do," Beetle tells me in his Room J bedroom as we smoke a J just a few minutes before the scheduled start of Meetings.

"Not..."

"I'm afraid so," he says, gently exhaling a dense cloud of smoke. "I don't see any way around it. What you did last night was pretty fucking obnoxious, even by your absurd standards."

"It's a fraternity house, not a nunnery."

"See, that right there is your main problem, Balls. This isn't a 24/7 deal. Kids have to be able to opt out. You don't let them."

"So you call me Balls now too?"

"The name is suiting, even you have to agree." says Beetle with a smile.

A brother we called Gonzo and I had sparked a bit of outrage the previous night, which had all started after spontaneously deciding to have an epic beer fight in the basement with four random freshmen (three gals and a guy) with whom we had been playing Pong late into the early morning. Gonzo had apparently met this foursome of freshmen through one of his many extra fraternal organizations and had been regularly inviting them to hang out at the house. I happened to be in the right place at the right time. We obliterated the basement. Each of the JV Pong tables had been flipped over during the battle and as beer had been our primary ammunition of the night, by the time we were done there wasn't a single plastic cup with liquid in it sitting on a flat surface anywhere throughout. In the aftermath of this carnage, our clothes and bodies still dripping with Keystone, we came up with the even better idea to take these same freshmen upstairs to shower off with us in the second floor's large two-nozzled shower stall. We did so loudly and with zero regard for the second floor residents. The best idea of all was to after this cleansing, venture up one more flight of stairs to the third floor bedrooms (with sleeping house executives primarily), and to stand outside these bedroom doors to serenade the occupants inside. It was three in the morning on a Tuesday night and the execs were threatening imminent bodily harm through closed doors. Over the course of the following day it became clear that the house planned to exact their vengeance on Gonzo and me later that night.

Gonzo's punishment was levied about halfway through Meetings at around the point in time where inhibitions had been sufficiently lowered to allow the brotherhood to flex its beer-covered muscles. Our crimes were first read aloud amid of series of shocked interjections from the audience with them practically demanding our blood by the end of the charges. Gonzo was then called on stage by Rats and Thalen and compelled to complete a quick six. The beers were downed easily enough but next a Kumite was announced against Winston, one of those brothers who had been unceremoniously awoken and who had about forty pounds on poor Gonzo. Winston proceeded to toss him around the room like a rag-doll until the brotherhood felt satisfied that he had endured enough physical retribution for the time being and declared the Kumite over. As a drunk and exhausted Gonzo collapsed onto a Meetings Room couch, the Chi Gam brothers turned their ravenous attention towards me.

But Balls doesn't wait for the brotherhood to issue its decree of punishment. Balls and Beetle have already worked out exactly what needed to be done, and as Beetle drags a can towards the center of the Meetings Room, Balls climbs up on stage amid the boos and jeers of the preempted brotherhood. By the intensity of their disingenuous outrage he can tell that they are ready for something special, something they didn't see on any old Wednesday night. This was one of those traditions that was completely unfathomable to attempt sober.

From the stage Balls addresses the room of brothers, who demand he chug a beer. He does so quickly and then says: "It seems not everyone was appreciative of our house tribute last night. To rectify this wrong, I encourage you all to boot on me as much as you like. This is Poncho Night."

Balls then strips down to his boxers and dives into the empty can Beetle has set up to catch him. This can buckles under his weight and flips over, dumping Balls on the carpet and as he crawls back inside a laughing group of brothers lifts and props it right side up. Now squatting in the can, Balls begins provoking the Chi Gams to assault to him.

"Boot on me!" he screams. "Boot on me, assholes!"

Beetle is primed and ready at the can with two full beers that he downs in a matter of seconds. He then leans over Balls and sticks his index finger in his throat to induce evacuation. After a few moments of dry heaving, a pint of puke erupts out of his mouth like a geyser and splatters across the front of Balls' face. Other brothers are coming forward now to replicate this feat by chugging their own beers and also leaning over the can to empty their stomachs. It takes a minute or two for the ordeal to really get going but once it does the booting is continuous, contagious and assaulting Balls from every angle. He has no choice but to close his eyes as the sea of vomit washes over him.

By the end of this strange affair nearly the entire brotherhood had at least attempted to throw up on Balls. Many who hadn't intended to had been compelled by the sight and stench of the others. It was a crazed five minutes of wanton debasement and impropriety. When the ordeal was over, I hopped into a large plastic cleaning bag that Beetle prepared beforehand and bowed to the cheers of the brotherhood before wobbling upstairs to a shower.

The feeling of being vomited on is entirely unique and will probably stay with me forever. While it was happening I could actually feel the individual chunks streaming down from my face, chest and back towards the bottom of the can as the vomit of each brother passed over me. In the comfort of the can I was enclosed in a vast tunnel of cringing, ugly faces. Vomit flowed like molasses out of some mouths, from others more like a waterfall, then of course there was the rare summer opened fire hydrant, blasting me full on in the chest, the force of the discharge even knocking back the head of the assailant. And through it all there was no end in sight, only boot. There was almost something maternal in this experience, as if by being covered in the boot of my peers I was being born anew as a more fearsome person, impervious to all forms of public disgrace, digging and scratching my way out of the womb on this strange path towards repugnant and self-abusive objectives.

❄

When I returned to Dartmouth following my "parkhursting" I enacted what I thought would be a foolproof plan. First and foremost I decided I could no longer continue to live in the fraternity house; it no longer made any sense from a practical standpoint. Instead I took a tiny single in a quiet little dorm that was more like a cottage just behind Chi-Gam and frat row. Though I was still close to the house, not sleeping there every night meant that with any luck I would play potentially dozens of fewer Pong games each term. My incidence of class attendance surged, especially in the months immediately following my return, and I took classes I considered safe—social sciences where my grades would be judged primarily on anonymously written papers.

But despite my best intentions I had picked up more or less exactly where I left off drinking-wise before my forced exile from Dartmouth. Balls, I soon realized, wasn't gone; he had merely been in hibernation. He resurfaced every Wednesday, Friday and Saturday night and had even begun breaking through to Mondays, Tuesdays and Thursdays again as well. He had an insatiable appetite for Pong but when on table was a totally focused individual. It was in the hours following Pong games that Balls was at his worst.

It was post Pong on one of these evenings that Gonzo strode into Room M flanked on either side by his new freshmen cohort—a bottle of tequila in one hand and tightly wrapped up in a full length American flag.

This tattered flag was an old house relic, maybe from 1920, and sported the 48 star design that was the norm before Alaska and Hawaii achieved statehood. Gonzo was pointing this out to the girls and describing the flag as a "historical curiosity," which prompted me to suggest we burn it, since it no longer accurately reflected the makeup of the United States.

"You wouldn't burn the flag," Gonzo proclaimed, waving his arms emphatically, his speech so slurred that the sentence seemed like one long confused word. "You can't; it's unpatriotic!"

"Bullshit," I said.

"Nobody rages anymore!" Gonzo exclaimed frantically.

Gonzo at core was a wildly excitable, yet harmless drunk who at all times appeared genuinely invested in increasing the enjoyment level of everyone who surrounded him. This was all well and fine but the danger with Gonzo was his whole *laissez faire* attitude toward drinking and mischief-making and his apparent belief in his own invulnerability. This obsession with "raging" inspired his campus wide network of friends and supporters (that he had been accumulating since before pledging) to often try to best him in the hardcore drinking performances he was famous for across campus. The truth was that a seriously inebriated Gonzo was much more prone to hurting himself than others and the intensity of his "hanging out" routine tended to result in those around him hurting themselves just as often.

"Gonzo, you're right, I wouldn't. I'm ardently opposed to forest fires and accidental arson, plus I really like our house the way it is. A pile of rubble doesn't quite make the same impression. I would, however, boot on the flag… that wouldn't faze me in the slightest." I phrased this last statement as a proposition.

"Do it, Balls." Gonzo said, winking at the interested group of freshmen that flanked him on either side of the couch,

"Fine."

My eyes are lowered and intense. I feel like something strange is coming over me and I am no longer myself. In fact there is a third Chi-Gam in the room with us and he has just assumed control of my body.

"I'll do it," Balls says. "Not because a blacked out asshole wants me to, but because I can."

By this time Balls has taken the flag from Gonzo and stretches it out across the table. He then makes an indent in the shape of a bowl and turns to Gonzo's freshmen guests. He smiles and in a mocking tone says: "You are about to witness one of the most disturbing anomalies Dartmouth College has to offer. My activities could possibly scar you for life so I urge you, for the love of god, please leave this room."

Nobody moves as Balls reaches for stray beers on the floor and coffee table. He cracks one open and pounds it, the warm, skunked Keystone going down with surprising ease. Two more beers follow before the familiar and unmistakable feeling of his throat and stomach convulsing tells Balls it's time to pull the trigger. He jams his index finger into his mouth, leans over the flag and unleashes a tremendous boot of mostly beer onto the flag and coffee table, splattering several of the freshmen who are too shocked to move.

"He did it! Balls did it!" Gonzo screams happily.

Balls says nothing and strolls out of the room laughing to himself. He is positively bellowing, laughing as loud as he can, as he sprints two stairs at a time down to the darkness and comfort of the basement.

What does Balls do during the hours I have no memory of?

❄

Zoey was one of the freshmen who had participated in the beer fight and been present for my patriotic booting display. At Gonzo's invitation, her small group of friends had been recently spending significant amounts of time in our basement during this, their first term in Hanover, and I had made it a point to befriend them—which at first meant little more than acknowledging them when they entered the basement, setting them up on Pong tables if they looked bored or thirsty and acting like the obligatory fraternity bad-ass I thought was expected of me when outsiders were around. But I soon found that I was drawn to Zoey in a way I wasn't normally drawn to girls at Dartmouth—and I truly enjoyed this new kind of intoxication, being with someone so carefree, unspoiled, and free of the basement Pong table leg-irons and tortured servitude to the endless boot and rally cycle that haunted the inhabitants of my daily routine. Being around Zoey reminded me of how I had felt as a freshman and seeing her group of friends interacting made it crystal clear that I had completely missed out on the sort of coed fun-times group dynamic these newcomers seemed to exude with every step. Attaching myself to them now and pretending to be another happily optimistic Dartmouth freshman made me realize just how jaded, bitter and utterly revolting I had become.

We corralled Gonzo's freshmen over to the house whenever we could. Invitations to play Pong in the basement during off nights (when nobody could see us playing shrub with freshmen). A scheduled viewing of the *Wizard of Oz* played alongside *Dark Side of the Moon* in Gonzo's upstairs bedroom. Always on these nights it was Gonzo and I vying for Zoey's attention in a misguided attempt to impress her with our hard drinking prowess and disregard for established etiquette. But Gonzo could never beat Balls at this game... he was merely a tourist in a world in which Balls reigned supreme.

"I don't know if any of you have noticed but Balls and Gonzo have made some new friends recently."

Rats says this from the Meetings Room stage to the assembled brotherhood the following Wednesday night. "And it seems they've both developed a crush on the same homely freshman sliz."

Beetle was already staring at me with a fiendish smile when I looked over at him in horror. It was obvious to the whole house that Gonzo and I were spending quite a bit of time with this new group of ours, but I didn't think it possible that the brotherhood could have found out about *her* without help from a close source. Beetle's shrug said it quite plainly: *well, what did you expect?*

Rats smiles broadly, "So the question I pose to the rest of you is: what do we do about this Zoey situation?"

"Who fucking cares?" says one brother loudly amid some snickers.

"Let them *Dome* for her," suggests another.

"Are we sure this girl is real and not a blow up doll?" a third skeptically asks.

"A *Dome* is perfect" says Rats, "Two men enter. One man gets the girl."

Gonzo is showing no sign of hesitation as we step forward and lock eyes around a garbage can. The traditional *Dome* acceptance ritual chant is echoing around us. Beetle fetches two beers apiece for the combatants. Winston meanwhile rolls up a sleeve and begins studying his wristwatch, which will serve as tonight's stop-watch.

"Sixty seconds for your first two beers. Thirty seconds per beer after that," Winston states matter-of-factly. "You guys ready? Five... four... three — two — ONE!"

With a *Dome* it's all about proper balance and pacing. I always preferred to drink the first two beers in quick succession to allow my body time to settle before moving onto the third. The third beer I want completed at the top of the thirty second mark so I have a full sixty seconds if needed for the fourth. With this method you can be assured that if the need to vomit did arise, you would have enough time before your next required beer for the feeling to subside.

Gonzo on the other hand attacks his beers in a less than deliberate manner and displays a pained expression while doing so.

"You're going to lose this one, Balls" he says, looking perfectly ready to vomit on the spot.

"Not likely," I reply.

Beetle fetches more beer and Winston gives a time check.

"One minute," he says. "Thirty seconds for beer number three."

The cup that is handed to me is easily downed in one long slurp so I just watch silently as Gonzo struggles to finish his sip by sip. By the time he has (and he really looks just awful at this point) it is already time for our fourth.

"Twenty-Five seconds," Winston reports.

My ability to win this Dome is without question, I think as I start in on beer number four but my stomach disagrees. Someone down there has pulled the fire alarm and suddenly it's every chunk for himself. Pre-boot surfaces in my mouth but I swallow it quickly along with the remainder of beer four. Gonzo has also finished his cup and is leaning heavily on the garbage can as Beetle hands us each our next beer.

"You both have forty seconds for the next one." Winston, who hasn't looked up from his watch once, declaratively says.

I already know that there is nothing I can do. The beer in my hand has to be finished to win Zoey but doing so will ensure involuntary vomiting. My only choice is to wait and hope that Gonzo blows his load before I do... but he doesn't. He finishes his beer with twenty seconds to spare and even starts in on beer number six. Acknowledging defeat with a lowered head, I down my fifth beer and lean over the can just in time as foul smelling regurgitant is soon gurgling out of my mouth at a vinegar and baking soda pace. The crowd cheers at the definitive outcome and Gonzo bows to the room, finishes his last beer and joins me at the can.

Rats is back on stage: "Gonzo gets the fat girl. Balls—you stick to Ship, bro."

"Zoey's not fat." Gonzo protests, still bent over the can, and now wiping vomit from his mouth.

"She will be if she stays in Hanover much longer!" Rats retorts.

Fresh beers for the gladiators and meetings continue!

❄

Later that night Balls allows me a sneak peek at his late night activities. He's on a Room M couch, chatting with a new cast of characters and looks blacked out or at least rapidly approaching that point.

Brother Soapbox, up on his namesake, is lecturing the group about various strategies to deal with corporate interview riddles. He sits next to his girlfriend, Sheila, opposite to the couch where Balls sits. Sheila, by Balls' estimation, is one of the coolest girls in Hanover and well placed on most fraternity top ten lists of attractive females on campus. Plus she smokes a ton of pot which Balls considers an added bonus. From my vantage point I can see that Balls is not processing the events around him correctly and can no longer make informed decisions as to how to properly interact with his surroundings.

Balls knows in the back of his mind that Gonzo is with Zoey in the basement. From his perch on Varsity earlier, he noticed her group enter the basement after Meetings but resisted the temptation to engage them. Gonzo of course had immediately gone over to them with open arms to claim his Meetings-won prize.

Balls is upset with himself but he doesn't understand why. He is oblivious to the fact that the basic human emotion of jealousy is causing him to look upon the two friends in front of him with disdain. Balls thinks he should be the one with the potential to date Zoey and the fact that he's not and that others around him, Soapbox and Sheila most of all, have some special ability to break through each other's cold exterior masks to something underneath that was more honest and warm and worth sharing was an earth shattering revelation to Balls in a *I'm mad but I still don't give a shit* kind of way.

Then apparently Balls is saying something along the lines of: "Sheila, why are you even here? The only thing you're good for is fucking Soapbox!"

I'm horrified that Balls has said this, mostly because I know he doesn't mean it, and I'm not even sure he has said it. He thinks Sheila is a terrific girl and probably, along with the rest of Soapbox's friends, he is secretly in love with her. But the impression of the room is that he has said something completely offensive and grossly uncalled for and what that was exactly will never be known.

Soapbox is livid as he grabs Sheila by the arm and storms out of the room, slamming the door shut behind him so hard the nonfunctional Room M wall clock falls to the floor with a clang. Balls curiously follows them out into the hall, not entirely sure what he has done to provoke such a response, but Soapbox has already locked himself in his single on the other side of the floor.

"Soapbox!" Balls yells through his locked door.

"I'm not talking to you right now," the muffled voice replies.

The door remained shut and Balls' frustration doubles.

"What did I do?" Balls slurs with his arms and forehead pressed against the locked door.

No recollection of his previous comment remains.

A small crowd of brothers and guests has now gathered in the hallway and is watching this amusing spectacle, most having no idea of its origins. Balls continues to bang on the door until finally he resorts to throwing his shoulder into it to try to break through. This he eventually does, shattering the door frame into thousands of tiny splinters. Soapbox is speechless as Balls makes his entry.

Some part of Balls knows he has taken things too far. He slowly backs out into the hallway, pausing in front of the fire door exit leading downstairs. Then he clenches his fist and throws his entire arm through the wire mesh reinforced safety glass, shattering it in the middle where his arm now rests in a tangle of broken glass and wire mesh.

When Balls removes his arm from the wreckage he is not at all surprised to see a three-inch shard of glass protruding from his forearm. Calmly turning to the horrified onlookers Balls says: "Can someone *please* pull this piece of glass out of my arm?"

I wake up from another blackout. This time I am in an ambulance applying pressure to my arm with a bloody gauze. A police officer is asking me: 'How much have you had to drink tonight, son? It's very important... we need to know how thin your blood is."

"A beer or two," I lie, "…hours ago."

At the hospital, what looked like two doctors operated on me, first shooting my arm up with some kind of anesthetic, though I doubt I would have felt anything even without it. They then split open what is left of my forearm with a blunt instrument to probe it for glass.

Beetle was the one to pick me up from the hospital, certainly a few games deep himself. My arm throbbed with pain the whole ride home through the blood stained gauze wrap which covered the Frankenstein stitching job I had received. Even so, when we returned to the house, I tried to call next on Varsity.

❄

The next week I got a blitz from the house executives requesting a sit-down for what I assumed was a discussion revolving around repayment of the cost of a broken window, so not worrying about it in the slightest I strolled in ten minutes after the designated meeting time.

All of the executives had been assembled in Beetle's Room J single. Beetle's desk chair faced me in the now open doorway so I took that as my seat and asked my friends why it was they had asked to see me.

"You've been on quite a streak lately," Beetle said but the way in which he said it felt like they had planned for some time how to approach me and just now in the last second had scrapped the plan.

"You could say that," I responded with a shrug.

"Do you remember last night?" Winston asked. "Do you remember trying to borrow my car and lying to me, telling me you were sober?"

"Hang on, Troy," Rats said.

"Is this a Judicial Committee?" I asked.

"Yes"

"You're going to JC me for trying to borrow Winston's car when I was drunk? He didn't even give it to me. Anyone could tell I was hammered."

"It's not just that, Knight," Soapbox interjected.

"We're JC'ing you for breaking your promise," Beetle said. "Last week after you put your fucking arm through a window you told us you were going to tone it down during the week. Today is Thursday; you were a mess last night. If you can't do it yourself then maybe we can help you."

"Meetings were last night."

"That's precisely our point"

"We want to put you on social probation. We think you have a problem and want you to function for a week sober."

I was shocked. This group of alcoholics was bringing *me* up on charges? I felt like the child killer in Lang's *M*, condemned by my peers simply because my crimes brought unwelcome attention to theirs. My drunken exploits of the past few weeks, while a bit extreme even for me, served mainly as a mirror that reflected the ugly truth back at the officers. We all had a problem. This punishment was not a response to my actions but a preemptive strike against theirs.

"We all know I'm not going to stop playing Ship."

"Then why did you agree to stay sober?"

"I felt cornered. What did you expect me to do? Tell you to fuck off?"

"So you're arguing due process?" Thalen asked, as if that would completely validate my defense.

"I guess I am."

"That actually makes sense, which is why we felt we had to call this meeting. It's not because you specifically drank yesterday. It's because we're beginning to see a very destructive pattern and this is a problem for everybody." Beetle was always rational and usually right.

"I'll go on social probation, but I want this to be my decision, not yours. That's the only way this is going to help me. I acknowledge that lately I've perhaps been a bit out of control." I stole a glance at the football scar on my forearm. "Look, I'm not going to make excuses; I just wish you guys had come to me as friends, not execs."

"We already tried that, Chris. If we let you do this of your own will, who's to say you'll stick by it? You've already proven that you can't."

"I want to do this but I'm not thinking of it as a punishment…more like an intervention"

"Are you prepared to guarantee a week of sobriety?"

"I am."

"Then we're satisfied."

The meeting adjourned.

Sometimes the ingrained obvious facts of my insignificant existence seem otherwise, and I am left wondering if perhaps I am a special person after all. There doesn't seem to be anyone quite like me, at least anyone I've come across. Nobody with the same cognizant ability to fully understand the implications of his pernicious activities yet still rationalize them 100% in the face of overwhelming evidence that he should stop. I stayed true to my word and didn't drink a drop in the house all week but at my first opportunity attacked Varsity with a renewed hunger and determination.

Chapter 9: DJ and Kegs

"In recent years, alcohol rules on campus have been complicated, poorly enforced by the College and widely ignored by students. There are multiple requirements for registering parties with alcohol and strict keg-use formulas that appear to be circumvented with great regularity. In addition, parties with alcohol have been banned from residence halls, a fact that appears to have driven more students to drink heavily within the CFS system"
– *Excerpt from the Summary of the Recommendations Submitted to the Board of Trustees by the Committee on the Student Life Initiative*

Long before I joined Chi-Gamma-Epsilon, the house had earned the reputation of being the "sketchy" fraternity on campus. Students called us misogynists or rapists behind our backs, some jokingly, others with earnest, and occasionally even issued warnings to freshmen girls to watch their drinks for fucking date rape drugs in our house, as if that were even necessary in the gladiatorial ring of slain pussy that was your typical frat basement.

The most damning accusations (namely, that awful roofie business) were utter nonsense, though I have a theory on how this rumor may have started. Some years before I matriculated, a group of (non-pledge) Chi Gam brothers "roofied" themselves (though what they took is still a mystery to me) and then departed from the house with a car of sober brothers following behind them. This was a challenge to see who could make it the furthest from the house without passing out or being picked up by campus security. A dumb game I admit, but really one harmful only to themselves and I am merely speculating that this story, once leaked, created the roofie image, and while I have never witnessed or heard about a Chi Gam brother using Rohypnol (or any other "date-rape" drug) on a woman, there is no way I can know for certain that this has never happened, nor would I exert such a claim.

Our continued association to this abstract and somewhat meaningless concept of "sketchiness" is really due to two simple things. One: the repetition around campus of an easy play on our fraternity letters. *Chi Gam? Isn't that the sketchy house, don't they call it Chi-Scam?* Very clever. And two: we admittedly did attract a shit ton of freshmen guys and girls. We ignored the freshmen guys and let them do their own thing (as long as they played Ship), while trying to hookup with the prettier girls. These younger visitors flocked to the house, in my opinion, due to our general lack of giving fucks when hanging out, along with our generous nature in dolling out our beer supply and that famous Chi-Gam open policy.

Now with this open invitation were we encouraging underage women to drink excessive amounts of alcohol in our fraternity basement in the hopes of hooking up? You betcha. It's also true that these sorts of sexual escapades were held in a ridiculously lofty light by the group hive-mind, fostering an environment where it was acceptable and even encouraged to pursue women who came into our house in this fashion. But is there really anything wrong in that? After all, these women were voluntarily putting themselves in this completely transparent situation. The opportunity to opt out is always on the table. Doesn't the fact that they want to be here make it acceptable?

I don't want to dismiss the very serious problem of sexual assault on college campuses, Dartmouth included. Sexual assaults did occur on campus, although to my knowledge, not in my house while I was there, and nobody I knew was condoning, encouraging, or covering up sexual misconduct of any kind while I was a brother in the house. I just want to be clear. I can only speak about what I saw personally and that was basically just a bunch of mutually drunk college kids, girls and guys, running buck wild in CFS basements.

Degrees of truth and consent aside, everyone was bound to find themselves in our basement at some time or another during their stay at Dartmouth, even if for curiosity's sake. It didn't matter if you disliked or were just flat-out disinterested in the individual brothers or the house in general. If you weren't a girl, we were too engrossed in our own games of Ship to talk to you anyway, but the beer was plentiful and easily accessible. Our doors were open each and every night to outsiders; if we were drinking, we let everyone else do so as well. Chi Gam was at the same time the most social and anti-social organization on campus. We wanted people to hang out in our basement; we just didn't want to have to talk to them. These were two different worlds. I could be on intimate terms with someone in the comfort of the basement's darkness, but ignore, in fact not even recognize, that same person in a dining hall.

Just about anything goes at a sketched-out Friday night bacchanalian dance party. We did this every other week. While the setup followed a logical sequence of events, the outcome (a series of wild and unpredictable dramas bound to unfold) was what kept me interested. Still, the pathway to this unknown was rather foreseeable. Binge drinking. Early, and for as long as physically possible. Pre-DJ cocktails with cheap liquor, even cheaper mixers and plenty of neglected women. The unsettling prospect of having to help unload ten full kegs from someone's van. A poorly lit dance floor and a horde of intoxicated and horny students. You're going to show up at the house only to wait in a freezing line for a half hour just to get in. You'll drink beer in our basement as quickly as we can hand it to you and then crowd the dance floor to jostle about frenetically to the same tired rap songs we've been recycling *ad nauseam* for the past six months. At some point you'll ask to stash your coat and purse in one of our rooms, and at a completely different point you'll have that same coat and purse rifled through. I'm going to throw your boyfriend out the back door and dump a beer on his head. If you're not careful with your punch consumption, you'll trip and fall down our basement stairs right in front of that girl you've been trying to impress all night. I won't let you escape until you've finished *all* of your Room M shots, and I'll lie to your friends and tell them you left for Tri-Kap hours ago. By this point your coat will likely have be stolen and you'll wake up with a new one two sizes too small or large and designed for the opposite gender. This night will have no meaning for anyone involved. It may not even register as a real memory.

As with many dance parties, the first three hours of this particular evening were spent "running table" on the far side of Varsity with Rats. On party nights we would get on Varsity early and play as many games of Ship as possible before getting knocked off. Playing Pong games gave me a sense of purpose during these otherwise direction-less early hours and served to prepare me mentally for any adventures Balls might embark on later that night. Often this backfired and by the time I had finally lost a game the party had ended or worse,

I just got too darn drunk to do anything but pass out.

Our first game that night, against Thalen and Pigs, was a challenging one. Each had a distinct style of play that marked them as superb players.

Thalen possessed the most casual of strokes and didn't so much swing through the ball as he intercepted it perfectly with his paddle, a talent that reminds me of the arcade Pong game of the seventies. Despite the apathy with which he engaged his body and his never changing blank expression, Thalen's shots were among the most accurate in the house. Thalen was also one of those rare players whose Pong ability was almost entirely unaffected by the quantity of beer he consumed. Many times I had seen him too drunk to stand erect, completely unable to string words together cohesively, yet still fully able to hit cups and sink boats. Quite an admirable and useful skill for a Ship Professional. He also talked endlessly. Recanting stories to no one in particular, telling jokes without punchlines, and hitting on women around him continuously.

Pigs, on the other hand, became so intense and focused during a game that he hardly spoke at all. The only comments he muttered were words of self-encouragement or abasement. Intermittently he would mutter aloud, "Get it together Pigs!" or "Hit a fucking shot, man!" To his partner he mainly volunteered criticisms, particularly for events where no one was at fault. These quirks, only on exhibit during a Ship game, were the probable cause behind so many Ship tournament victories; put simply, he wanted it more than anyone else out there.

Pigs and Thalen got off to an early lead amid a flurry of back-boat hits that rendered them sinkable. When this happens you can theoretically lose in a few shots. We would have been down big if Rats hadn't managed to land a sink on his trademark opening two-boat drop shot, a feat he had an impressive success rate on.

At around this time others began showing their faces in the basement. Beetle and Winston were the first two down and immediately called next on our game. Moments later Davis strolled through the basement doors, smiled when he saw our collection of professionals, and called "double next." By the time our game had reached its final moments (they had a full and a half left on their five-boat, while we had our full two-boat left) the table was four deep and two more tables on the JV side of the basement had been set up as well. If I lost now I was unlikely to secure another game on Varsity while the party still raged and I would have to settle for playing on JV or abandon Ship completely for the evening—something I was not yet prepared to do. The mounting pressure climaxed as our teams traded ridiculously close shots on the remaining two boats. Brothers had now collected along the side benches of this epic match-up, oohhing and ahhhing at every critical miss. Games on Varsity often turn into spectator sport. It was here, under the watchful eyes of the house, that I could prove my true worth as a brother.

This heightened threat of losing Varsity inspired my best shot of the game, one that dropped *plunk!* into the back cup of Pigs and Thalen's five-boat. My heart rate slowed. There would be another game after all.

There was little time to cherish victory as Winston and Beetle were waiting nearby with a full rack of keg beer. This next game was set up immediately and with few words. It wasn't long before Rats and I were four games deep and absolutely shitfaced.

The basement was already crowded with brothers by the time the first strangers began arriving in small groups that would pause at the bottom of the stairs when greeted with the unwelcoming sight of three Ship tables mid-game. Often these visitors immediately turned and exited but gradually the crowd began to accumulate to the point where it clearly surpassed the maximum occupancy limit imposed by the Hanover fire marshal.

After our fourth victory Rats said: "I'm off this next game, Balls."

This puzzled me. I never voluntarily stepped off after winning a game and it was rare to go on a Varsity tear like we were while a party unfolded around us. I raised this perfectly logical concern to him with a series of slurred, mispronounced words.

"Do you want to remember this night?" said Rats.

This was a compelling argument. We could both handle a few more beers but seven apiece over the next half hour was pushing it.

"Course I do," I slurred. "I'm real close to being blacked out right now."

"Let's blaze, then chill behind the bar and sober up."

The plan was decent enough so we begrudgingly relinquished our rights to Varsity and began pushing our way through what was at this point a dense crowd that clogged the basement and stairway.

"Rats, Balls!" a voice cried from behind the bar. We paused momentarily and through the crowd noise next heard: "Get over here."

After swimming our way through dozens of people, we found ourselves behind the bar witnessing two of our brethren in the midst of an unsuccessful attempt to rouse some kid who had passed out against one of our back benches. Brother Gunter snapped his fingers in front of his face but it remained unresponsive. This was enough to momentarily sober us up.

"Nope, nothing," Gunter said, "This kid might as well be dead."

"A freshman?" I asked.

"Freshman pussy," Rats corrected, studying the hopelessly incapacitated first-year. "Find out if he has any friends and make *them* take care of him. We need this asshole out of the house." He then headed upstairs.

Rats was right, we definitely needed him gone. Safety and Security made three arranged "walkthroughs" during our parties. If they observed this half-dead freshman, the party would likely end and we could face probation. While Rats was content with putting this all on Gunter's shoulders, I had to make sure it was handled somewhat responsibly.

"Don't uh... you know, let him die." I told Gunter after he had collected a few of the drunk kid's friends.

"Thanks, Balls."

Okay, that was good enough. I followed Rats upstairs.

Bounding up the stairs two at a time, I passed Beetle and a sophomore girl perched on a windowsill on the first floor that overlooked the back of the house. I recognized this girl as a basement regular who had somehow over the past year acquired the demonstrative nickname "Land Monster." I had seen the two in the basement earlier; Beetle had been at the bar when she strolled in with a few sorority sisters. Like most of us already in the basement, she appeared to be trashed and within five minutes she had attached herself to Beetle and I saw them eventually stagger out of the basement together. That was during the beginning of my last Ship game. They hadn't made it very far.

But I didn't have time to dwell on this budding romance for long. Rats was not above starting the session without me. So I continued my climb but became distracted yet again, this time at the windowsill between the second and third floors. From this spot I could see almost the entirety of the house's back parking lot and the front grounds and sand based volleyball court of the Choates dorm cluster that was almost directly behind the house. A small group of students I didn't recognize was huddled between a line of cars but I couldn't quite tell what they were doing just standing there. At that instant Gunter came running out at them from what I assumed was the back of the house, waving his arms wildly and screaming frantically. I raised the window in time to hear him yell:

"Pick him up!"

The huddled strangers parted as Gunter approached, revealing a body lying face down in the asphalt and submerged, it would appear from my vantage point, in a wide puddle formed in one of the many craters spread out in our lot. Gunter knelt immediately and grasped the kid's shoulders to raise him up out of the muck while his friends, who strangely had not yet come to his aid, stooped down as well to help lift the immobile organic object, who I could see from the clothes was our basement pass-out artist, sputtering and spewing water erratically from his face as he was lifted. With the kid propped upright and his arms draped around the shoulders of two friends, the group sauntered off in the direction of the Choates—not walking in anything close to a geometric straight line. Gunter watched them walk off, shook his head sadly, and turned to jog back to house.

Shutting the window, I continued up towards the third floor bedrooms.

Rats lived in the third floor Room H suite, which was identical to all other singles in the house with the one exception of coming equipped with a water bed and a flat screen television instead of a full sized bed and nothing. As I approached his closed door I heard some arguing voices down the hall in Room M, which I naturally decided to investigate.

Brothers Halifax and Woland, along with a pledge, were standing in the center of Room M arguing over a strikingly empty green recycling bin that sat between them on the cluttered coffee table. I found the emptiness of said container particularly distressing given that its sole function was to provide a receptacle for the house punch, charmingly named *Sketch*—a heavenly concoction of Kool Aid, grain alcohol, cheap vodka and shower water. The danger with *Sketch* was that you almost couldn't detect the taste of alcohol—this gave you a false sense of courage with regards to how many glasses of *Sketch* you thought it safe to drink. We loved it primarily because women lapped up the stuff and much preferred it to beer, and its hidden strength tended to bring out notable performances from the brothers who weren't careful in their consumption. The three Chi Gams were arguing about the order in which to mix the ingredients.

"Dude. I'm telling you, it's Kool Aid, water, then alcohol," Woland was saying "I've made punch a million goddamn times, dude. I think I know how to do this."

"Put the water in there first and your punch is going to be weak as fuck," Halifax countered.

The pledge took medium ground. "It's stupid to be arguing about this right now. Why don't we fill it up halfway with water, add the powder and booze, then sample it. If we need more water, we add it."

"Fine, whatever." Woland said, "Let's just do that."

He grabbed the bin with his left hand, squeezed past me saying "watch out, dude" and headed for the third floor bathroom with Halifax and the pledge right behind. Seconds later the shower turned on. I remained in the doorway and focused my attention on the box of wine dangling in a trap-like fashion from the water pipe that passed above the door frame. While wine poured from the box to my mouth and therefore onto my shirt, Beetle opened his own closed door down the hall (Room I) and emerged with an incredulous look on his face. He saw me standing outside of room M and walked over.

"Land Monster is nuts bro, I gotta get rid of her. She won't go away."

I capped the wine and rubbed in the red stain on my shirt. "Ditch her dude; she'll get bored and wander off eventually."

"Excellent idea. What are you up to, anyway?"

"Overseeing the production of punch, you could say," I said.

Halifax and Woland staggered past us carrying the now full container of Sketch.

"This should be enough to black-out everyone in the basement. Careful with that end, Halifax. You got it?" Woland asked as they navigated the punch over one of room M's couches.

"I got it," Halifax confirmed.

But he didn't quite have it. The bin slipped from his fingertips and ten gallons of punch overflowed onto the floor of Room M.

"Shit!" Woland exclaimed.

The Room M carpet was now a marshy sea of sticky red aphrodisiac.

"You fucking monkeys," Beetle laughed.

The pledge rushed out of the room towards the cleaning supplies closet.

"Dude, you were moving too fast," Halifax said. "You know I'm stoned; this is blatantly your fault."

"My fault, asshole? Are you fucking shitting me right now? Go get something to clean this shit up," said Woland, taking a few careful steps around the room to survey the damage. Our poor pledge, meanwhile, had returned and was futilely trying to soak up the punch with a handful of paper towels.

❄

In the Meetings Room a Deejay was playing hip-hop for dancing partiers and a line of students had formed along the shaft of the "cock and balls" leading up to the front door. About two hundred or so people were crammed into the two front rooms while blaring Nas lyrics drowned out all extraneous sounds around them. I could sporadically recognize a few people among the crowd, but it seemed to me that most of our party attendees were not normally in our house unless we were throwing a party.

The line forming outside spilled onto the lawn and into a large unruly group of students, clearly furious that they were stuck out in the cold while the party raged indoors. Closer to the door the mob got more aggressive and actually tried to shove their way in anytime the door cracked even an inch. Brother Cassius Conspicuous was single handedly keeping this growing mass from overrunning the house.

"Dartmouth ID's! Everyone, I need to see some Dartmouth identification," Cassius instructed the line loudly, struggling to be heard over the music and also not quite pronouncing each word clearly. Noticing me he cackled and said, "Balls, my man! What's going on?"

"Ran Varsity for three hours. Some kid almost drowned in our parking lot. Beetle is giving the business to Land Monster. Tweedle Dee and Tweedle Dum dumped a whole batch of Sketch onto the Room M carpet. You know, standard shit."

"Nice bro, feeling that old stroke again? Who did you play with?" he asked, either ignoring or missing the part where we had almost killed some freshman and then ruined the most important bedroom in the house.

"Rats."

He nodded in approval as I grabbed the list of assigned duties from the bulletin board hanging next to the door.

"Who else is supposed to be on door right now?" I asked. Working door at one of our parties really did require two relatively sober brothers at all times. Right now neither one of us completely fit the bill.

"Big Wig was a no show. Oiling down a hippopotamus somewhere I suspect," Cassius said. He raised one eyebrow and took another swig from a bottle of Southern Comfort he was clutching like a newborn.

"Wiggy does like fat chicks," I agreed, taking the ID of the first kid in line. "Who argued the famous '*Dartmouth College Case*' before the Supreme Court?" I asked the confused owner of the card.

I examined the faded portrait on his Dartmouth issued ID. The poor kid looked like he had gained about fifty pounds since the picture had been taken.

"Can you just let me in man? I've been waiting for like an hour. My friends are in there."

"*It is, as I have said, Sir, a small college…and yet, there are those who love it.* Do you even go to this school? Daniel Webster, never fucking heard of him? Come on dude, that was an easy one."

"Daniel Webster was a cocksucker!" someone from the back of the line quipped. "That son of a bitch supported the fugitive slave act!"

"Yeah, but that was more a political decision rather than an ideological position, *asshole*," said some other guy. Both voices were slurred.

As this drunken discussion reached its conclusion I handed the kid his ID and let him inside. In response the line immediately began pushing forward in an attempt to breach the line of defense that Cassius and I had established

"Simmer down! " I yelled at the impatient and certainly freezing line of hopeful partygoers. "You'll all get in eventually…well except you. You might want to try the milk and cookies party down the street."

While working door at one of our parties there are sort of a set of unspoken rules about who gets in right away and who waits. If you are a freshman or sophomore male or unaffiliated upperclassman, you will wait. If you are not a well known member of a popular frat or friends with the doorman or can drop a good name—you will wait. Sometimes a group of ten Theta Delts or ADs would show up, and they usually just walk right in after exchanging pleasantries with the doorman. Common courtesy between frats I guess. We didn't wait much when we went to their parties either. If you are a girl or better yet in a group of girls (even sometimes with a few guys mixed in) you will get in rather quickly. It all depends on the speed with which people leave the house really, because we are always at capacity during parties. If you are a brother you will approach the door as if the line doesn't exist.

While I sorted through the crowd to figure out who was getting in and who wasn't, Cassius was completely absorbed in something happening a good distance away.

"See that kid over there?"

Cassius was jutting his finger out at lone figure standing awkwardly on our front lawn.

"He tried to get in about fifteen minutes ago. Since then he's just been standing there. He's a townie and I'm sure he's up to something. Watch out for him, Balls; he's a sneaky little guy." Cassius raised two fingers to his eyes, pointed them at the kid and assumed a cat-like stance.

Townie! My heart skipped a beat and I began watching the sillouette as closely as Cassius was. No townies would be getting into the house on my watch.

"Look at him standing there," Cassius said a few minutes later. He had yet to take his eyes from the townie. "Oh no he doesn't!" he stammered angrily a second or two later. The townie had begun slinking his way towards the side of the house nonchalantly. Cassius dropped the bottle and sprinted off in the direction of the townie. He tackled him on the grass of the lawn and rained a flurry of blows on the writhing body. Soon the two were rolling around in the grass with neither gaining an advantage,

You can't really miss out on the chance to stomp out some townie, I said to myself while smirking and stroking a non-existent beard. Rushing into the fray, I began generously applying the tips of my winter boots to the townie's ribs while the line leaked into the house. Over the next minute or so, for no particular reason, we threw him quite a beating.

❄

Flash forward an hour or two, and I'm filling beers behind the bar in the basement. Cassius had been remanded to an upstairs bedroom for fear his assault may be reported to the authorities. About fifty students directly in front of me were actively trying to get beers—literally pushing and shoving others out of the way to get to the front. People barely recognizable as someone I may have talked to once before would call me Balls and ask to be hooked up. Acquaintances pretended like they were my oldest and closest confidants. Mutual relationships were formally announced. Applying these tactics to acquire beer is a necessity for guys in unfamiliar basement territory. Girls need only a limited display of flirtatious behavior and relative proximity to the bar to get a beer. This strategy works well. Two thirds of my beers were going to women.

"Remember me?"

It was the *townie*. I guess we had managed to avoid the face region because he didn't look too bad and was even donning a wristband indicating he was over twenty-one.

"How the fuck did you get in?" I said, making a deliberate show of handing out beers to people in his direct vicinity.

"Door guy let me in. So how about a beer?"

"You have to be kidding me. Dude, get the fuck out of here."

"Balls—thirty beers."

Pigs had arrived behind the bar with a rack in one hand to fill a Ship game. Thereafter every beer I filled from the keg was handed to Pigs and subsequently arranged on his carrying rack to the great annoyance of everyone waiting.

"This house is a joke! You can't even get a beer," the townie complained to no one in particular.

At that moment the light in the basement flipped off and on—a signal that we were being invaded by campus security.

We were allowed only four kegs for the night and each one had to be tagged and displayed visibly behind the bar. If you have more than the allowed number of kegs or if the kegs you had weren't properly tagged, then probation was in your immediate future. We had our four "registered" kegs on display behind the bar and after a cursory glance the officers were on their way. What they didn't know was that we had six more kegs hidden in a back room.

"I bet they have more kegs!"

I actually don't fully remember what the townie said here but it's something that drew the attention of S&S. I do remember that what he said made me realize this intruder was no stranger to fraternity basements, townie or not.

"Don't listen to that clown. He's not even a Dartmouth student," I reassured the interested officers. "In fact, I personally barred him from entry at the door not more than an hour ago so I must assume he broke in somehow. Why don't you check to see if he has a Dartmouth ID?"

They did and he didn't, and then he was seized and marched off towards the basement stairs, and then up and out of the house. I remember the visual of this only vaguely but his shouts still echo in my head. "You should be arresting them!" he proclaimed while being dragged out. "I haven't done anything and they… they beat me. They beat me viciously!"

❄

"Balls!" a female voice behind me exclaimed.

Zoey was frantically trying to get my attention from the sidelines of Junior-Varsity.

"What's up?" I said cheerfully. "Enjoying the festivities?"

"The party's awesome," she assured me. "You guys rock!"

"I hope you're not waiting to play on this table." I said. Four brothers were completely engrossed in a Ship game.

"We have next!"

That made me laugh. "Everyone and their mother thinks they have next on that table."

"We'll play, just wait and see. We both know very well that you Chi-Gams can't resist my charm."

Her charm—easily resisted. That well formed freshman body still putting up an impressive resistance against the ravages of first-year…much more effective bargaining tool.

"Do you know my partner?"

I inspected her female friend who was squatting on the same bench and clinging to a beer.

"I don't think so."

"This is Sarah. Sarah—this is... you know, Balls, I don't even know your first name."

"It's Chris, but Balls is fine."

Sarah was tiny and youthful looking with short cropped black hair, a pleasantly plump face and nice boobs. She laughed and immediately poked fun at my nick-name.

"Does that mean you have like…the biggest package in the house?"

"Second biggest," I clarified. "There's actually a guy nicknamed Donkey-Dick"

"Balls," Zoey repeated to herself. "I've always liked it personally, but it does give me this creepy vision of you sitting on your own elephantitis-ridden testicles or something"

"Charming." A rare pang of serious attraction gripped me. Maybe this was a girl worth serious effort after all—lost Dome be damned.

The remainder of the party was spent entirely with these two girls on account of Zoey. I was able to toss my weight around to get us a Pong table and later we went to an upstairs bedroom to chill out and smoke up. It was pushing four before they decided to head home. I had been consciously limiting my alcohol since the Ship games earlier and had substantially sobered up by this point, though I would still classify myself as drunk, just not *Balls-drunk*. If in the off-chance Zoey was interested in hooking up, I needed every ounce of my mental and physical faculties available to seal the deal. They split up to look for their coats while I excused myself to use the bathroom and boot if need be. I told them to meet me downstairs in five minutes.

As per usual following a dance party, the second floor bathroom was in a deplorable state when I entered in search of an amenable vomiting location. Even this room wasn't safe from the endless empty and half filled plastic cups that now coated the house like post-armistice day ticker tape. The sink counter had been assaulted by at least one vomiter—this lasagna-like boot was splotched out abstractly across the remaining length of countertop. The toilet stalls fared no better. The first had been duct taped shut by either a strangely conscientious or utterly repulsed house resident and I wondered what could be so horrific within to cause this immediate and incomplete reaction, given the unsettling appearance of the other two available stalls, whose porcelain bowls were no longer displaying much in the way of porcelain. Using one of the toilets to boot was out of the question so I turned my attention to the garbage can that was normally positioned just in front of the bathroom's open back window. I saw immediately that the can had been cordoned off with a strip of yellow police caution-tape that ran diagonally across a narrow stretch of the room to the windowsill, effectively blocking off a four foot area in the corner. A pair of what appeared to be female legs were sticking out from behind the can and taking a few steps forward I could identify Land Monster's contorted body passed out on the mungy tiled floor in a position that made it look like she had spontaneously collapsed there while admiring herself in the mirror. I stuck my head out above the caution-tape, took a long look at her, and was able to ascertain that she was breathing at least and my head now directly over the can, which was just a foot away from Land Monster's head, I released a controlled boot, producing, to her direct benefit, very little in the way of splatter. I then exited the bathroom. Probably Land Monster's best option at this point was to stay put right there on the bathroom floor, sleep off the nightmare of the previous night, and wake up slightly surprised, no doubt a bit embarrassed, but at least relieved to be apparently unharmed, alone and not far from an exit. It was time to pay Beetle a visit.

Beetle's door was locked but after a series of persistent knocks I heard him propel himself out of his desk chair within and the door soon cracked an inch or two open.

"What's poppin'?" he said through the crack.

"I can hear the porn out in the hallway."

"I thought you of all people would be familiar with the concept of blue-balls. What are you still doing here anyway? Sounds like Pong is done for the night."

"I'm on my way out... thought you might appreciate some background information when the authorities show up to question you."

The sprinkler pipe that ran along the hallway just outside of Beetle's room had been used as a communal coat rack throughout most the party and even now, the party essentially over, a dozen or so abandoned coats remained and with the dimmed hallway lights the hanging outerwear gave the appearance of otherworldly life forms drooping majestically from the corridor ceiling. I pulled the closest Northface down, held it up against my body, determined it was too small and re-fastened it to the pipe before snatching at another. This second fleece was a near perfect fit. Beetle chuckled.

"Stealing coats again, are we?"

"This is a communal set-up, my friend. What's mine is yours and vice versa. You know the drill. Someone gets cold, needs a coat and so they stole mine. Now I'm going to be cold so this dude is shit out of luck. When he's cold, he's free to steal another. No shortage of winter coats at this school."

"I've heard this line of reasoning from coat-thieves before."

"You know Land Monster is passed out on the bathroom floor downstairs."

"What man, are you serious?"

"That's how it looks at least. Wide open window, chilly New Hampshire evening... maybe you want to drape one of these bad boys over her." I held up a coat like a matador for him.

"Or *you* could you know... Fuck, I should probably at least try to wake her up and send her home."

"That *might* be a good idea."

"Kill myself."

❄

The house had long since been deserted, but music was still blasting from the basement and first floor. In the foyer, at the bottom of the stairs, an intoxicated Thalen atop a kid-sized BMX bike was circling the room. Then I observed that he was actually chasing my two freshmen girls. They were laughing and yelling, using their coats to lash out at Thalen as he zoomed past them. I had no idea where he got the bike from but I was even more curious as to which girl he was going to try to take upstairs to his room.

On what would prove to be his final lap, the two freshmen girls still giggling and taunting him, Thalen lost control of the bike and veered down the basement steps, making it about halfway before sliding off the bike and down the rest of stairs so that he was crumpled in a ball atop a pile of empty cups at the foot of the basement. He slowly got up, apparently unharmed, carried the bike back upstairs and set it down in front of me.

"Dude, you totally have to try that."

Thalen would not get the best of Balls in front of Zoey!

I repeated the insane stunt and took a spill that felt like it resulted in several broken bones. I was stunned but otherwise intact and able to drag the bike back upstairs, while my three compatriots congratulated my efforts.

"My turn," came a muffled voice from beneath a pile of abandoned coats. A previously unknown figure emerged and strutted over to where we stood. I had never seen this coat-person before in my life. One look at Thalen told me he didn't know who it was either.

"Dude," Thalen said, "What the hell were you doing buried under all those coats?"

"Hanging the fuck out," the mysterious stranger answered emphatically. He mounted the bike, aimed it towards the stairs and took off.

The kid hit the first stairs at a much faster speed than either of us had and on the second or third step he did a front flip over the handlebars. After a few yelps and rolls his leg caught the railing and he lay motionless, sprawled out on the stairs with the bike resting at the entrance to the basement with its wheels still spinning. His limbs were entangled impossibly in the railing. After a few moments with zero movement from the body we rushed quickly over to his aide.

"Thalen," I said, inspecting the body. "He looks pretty badly injured."

"Is he conscious?" one of the girls asked.

"Hmm...maybe." I kicked him once or twice and the body moaned in pain. "He's lucky he's this drunk."

"He's lucky to be alive."

"We could dump him in the Bones Gate parking lot." I suggested seriously.

"Maybe check to see if he's paralyzed first," Zoey said while stooping down as if she planned to check vital signs.

"Wait...he's moving!"

This mystery guest sprang up, dashed up the stairs and fled the house at top speed as if we didn't even exist. This was the official end to the bicycle riding festivities for the evening. Thalen managed to take Sarah upstairs to his room and I offered to walk Zoey back to her dorm, figuring hers was pretty close to mine and a "walk home" left open additional possibilities.

We stopped outside the entrance to her dorm to exchange goodbyes and then she said something completely unexpected. "Hey, do you know anything about TVs?"

"A little, I guess."

"We've got one upstairs that conked out on us. One of those stupid VCR/TV two-in-ones. A tape is stuck in the VCR. I know it's late but I've already got you here. Do you mind coming in to take a quick look?"

"Sure, why not."

We entered her dorm together—this was actually the same dorm I lived in freshmen year, Wheeler Hall. The lobby was darkly serene, its air vibrating with the soft humming of nearby vending machines, as Zoey led me to her room on the second floor. Without saying a word she unlocked the door and let us in.

"The TV's right over there," she said, walking over to her closet cubby hole. She began shedding layers of clothing as I stooped down to investigate the television.

"Looks like the tape came loose and is tangled up inside the machine," I said. "I'm not sure I'm going to be able to fix it."

"Oooh, that sucks. Nothing you can do then?"

"I don't think so...I could try but I'd probably just end up breaking it. If you want I can come back when I'm sober and give it a shot."

"That would be cool."

I noticed that a Pong paddle sat on the desk next to the dysfunctional television. She had painted it with a gradating series of purples with what appeared to be the New York City skyline in black silhouette. Gold sparkles spelled her name near the top of the paddle on the reverse side. I knew this must be a meaningful memento for Zoey, but painting paddles was something done almost exclusively by sorority pledges and Zoey was still a freshman.

"This is very beautiful." I said, picking up the painted paddle. "I didn't know you were from New York."

"Born and raised."

"Me too."

She had plopped herself down on one of the two beds and was very gingerly removing her shoes. I sat down next to her, took her hand in mine and pressed it against the paddle. Her tiny fingers were entirely contained within the paddle's boundaries.

"It's a shame you can't grip a paddle like this," I said softly with my hand covering hers and my fingertips tightening up around the edges of the paddle. "It's how the game was meant to be played."

She retracted her fingers at once, gripped the bottom of the paddle, and pulled it out of my grasp.

"Oh, I get by just fine like this."

I leaned in to kiss her but she pulled away quickly.

"Balls, I can't."

"Are you sure?"

"You're really sweet Balls but I'm not going to hook up with you tonight."

"Something I said?"

"It's not that...I don't want to be...that girl you, know? The one you Chi-Gams joke about during your meetings or treat like a slab of meat at an auction."

"That wouldn't happen." I said.

"I don't think *you* would do that... but you know how things are."

I wanted say something. I wanted to tell her that not only *could* I do it but that I *had* done it. But I said nothing and instead lowered my head.

"And...I have a boyfriend."

"You have a boyfriend." I repeated.

"Back home, yes. We're attempting the long distance thing. I know...probably not going to work and we're allowing each other some space but I don't know...I want to explore other people I do but I also really care about him."

Here Gonzo and I had been vying for her affections without even considering whether she was available or interested. What did it matter to Zoey that Gonzo and I had battled for the rights to court her?

"Then this was a mistake. I'm sorry."

"Don't be. I am flattered, Balls, and honestly I think you're adorable. I shouldn't have asked you up. It's late and we both need sleep but thanks for a really fun night tonight."

I never did fix that television and that was also the end of my pursuit of Zoey. The sun was rising as I made my confused way back to my tiny dorm just behind the house, and I smiled when I felt the bulge of a Pong ball in my right pocket.

Chapter 10: This is Sacred

"For many years, CFS houses have served as the primary alcohol dispensaries on campus. Since most students are below the legal drinking age of 21, this suggests that flagrant violation of New Hampshire law is routine. Even more disturbing is the range of activities within CFS houses that encourage excessive alcohol use. They include drinking games such as "beer pong" and the widespread acceptance of the repugnant practice of "booting and rallying"—consuming excessive amounts of alcohol, vomiting deliberately or involuntarily and then consuming still more."
– Excerpt from the Summary of the Recommendations Submitted to the Board of Trustees by the Committee on the Student Life Initiative

During what should have been my last winter term on campus, all of our Pong tables mysteriously vanished in a single night.

Kouge's long standing Jagermeister table, a staple of the basement since my pledge term, was unscrewed from its base on Varsity with power tools and along with four others carried right out of the back door of the house. We eventually discovered that the culprit had been Bones Gate—that charming dump across the street that loved to antagonize us. The tables were shredded into strips with a power saw and the wood stacked behind their house for us to plainly see. This tragic event finally afforded me the opportunity to paint my own table. Halifax joined in this enterprise.

Our inspiration was the logo that graced each and every thirty pack of beer that entered our house, well over one hundred cases per week. It was a design all too familiar to the entire campus. Always smooth and never bitter, that was our Keystone. Beetle procured the raw wood for our new tables from the local lumber yard that supplied them to the campus and over the next three weeks, Halifax and I put something like fifty man-hours of work between us into priming, stenciling and painting the design. When finally completed, the general consensus was that this was the single nicest table anyone had ever seen, but for us this was more than a Pong table. This piece of wood, we joked, had become our culminating experience in Hanover, surely worth a credit or two, and would be a permanent mark left on Chi-Gam when we were gone. The names Halifax and Balls immortalized on Varsity for as long as the table held out.

Halifax was an odd character. At Dartmouth he was frozen in carbonite and seemingly could avoid reprimand for any wrongdoing. He was constantly finding himself before Dartmouth's Deans for a variety of offenses, which have included vandalism, trespassing, assault and theft. But each time he was able to construct a strong enough legal defense to cast doubt on the college's presumptive damning evidence. He antagonized the school continuously and the school in turn went out of their way to antagonize him. He was notorious in the house for his devotion to the game of Ship, his questionable set of morals, propensity to engage in conflicts with outsiders and overall brash demeanor. He was also one of the most fiercely loyal individuals I have ever met. The new class we pledged that winter term didn't quite know what to make of him. He planned to run for the office of pledge trainer when he became eligible the following year but I wouldn't describe him as a hazing aficionado by any means; he didn't get off on the kind of psychological power trip that many CFS members become consumed by. He was even eventually elected as pledge trainer and succeeded in doing away with "Hell Night," which nobody was too upset to see gone. He was, however, very concerned with transforming the pledges into what he considered to be the Chi-Gam ideal image—the consummate Ship Professional.

Among our incoming class was one kid in particular who we could plainly see did not take his obligations as a pledge seriously and his attitude threatened to infect the rest of his class. Pledge term at Dartmouth was not really something that took a *tremendous* amount of effort; still, this pledge completed few of our requirements and spent almost no free time in the house. Worst of all, Pledge Korver almost never played Ship.

One night, coming back from Thayer after picking up dinner in preparation for a night of Ship, Halifax and I spotted Korver walking down the pedestrian path that led from the Thayer dining hall to frat row. He was difficult to miss, dressed as he was in a full-body, fuzzy pink bunny suit that he had been awarded at the previous Meetings for his ongoing lack of participation in pledge events. Our leverage to force him to complete his responsibilities was limited by the size of his pledge class (we were looking at fifteen total pledges) and the ugly fact that earlier a baseball pledge baffled us all by abruptly de-pledging mid-term. These fifteen kids were a random collection of sophomores who had barely known each other or the house before pledging so the entire brotherhood was a little anxious about the implications of so small a class for the future of the house. We literally couldn't afford to lose any more pledges.

Halifax pulled the car we had borrowed alongside Korver, lowered the window, and called him over.

"Need a ride, dude?" he asked, exhaling smoke directly into Korver's face through the open window.

"Going back to the house?" Pledge Korver inquired while squinting and waving his hand in front of his face to disperse the smoke.

"Sure, you?"

"Cleanings are in twenty minutes."

"Right, so you'd better come with us," Halifax said in a semi-threatening tone.

"No room in the car."

Korver was right. We had three other pledges in the back seat.

"Then I'll make room," Halifax said.

He hopped out of the driver's seat and threw his cigarette to the ground. He then walked to the trunk and popped it open.

"Get in." he ordered.

"No, thanks. I'll walk."

It was maybe a six minute walk to the house.

"Get in," Halifax repeated. "This is not an option, mother-fucker."

"You're serious?"

"As cancer, asshole. Get in the fucking trunk."

Korver gave me a skeptical look. "Better do what he says," I advised.

Grudgingly, he lifted one foot half into the trunk and then paused as if reconsidering the decision. Halifax scowled, grabbed his other leg and heaved him in.

"This is ridic—" Korver started to protest but the trunk had been slammed shut by Halifax before he could finish the sentence.

Halifax snorted, "The trunk is where he belongs."

"You're going to make a wonderful pledge trainer," I told him.

"I'm not gonna' get elected, you know those assholes. Standard house bullshit. I'd do a hell of a job though."

I didn't doubt it. We got back in the car and began the drive to Chi-Gam. The three pledges were soon laughing in the backseat.

"What are you fuckers giggling at?" Halifax barked.

What looked like a single pink sock was protruding from the back of the trunk and fluttering in the wind.

"I can't see shit, what is that?" Halifax demanded to know, glancing back two or three times in an effort to make out what the pledges and I could see was obviously part of Korver's pledge gear.

"It's his bunny ears."

Halifax laughed.

"Good. We know he's not going anywhere." He adjusted the rear view mirror so that he could see the faces of the pledges in back and said, "Hey, I'll let you guys in on a little secret. When I'm pledge trainer I'll take you fuckers paint balling except you don't get guns and I get to dress you like woodland creatures. You're a deer, you're a rabbit, and you're a moose. Then I let all you fuckers loose and hunt your ass down. How's that for a pledge activity?"

Halifax cackled as he pulled the car into the Chi Gam parking lot.

Then Halifax and I were in the basement wrapping up a one-on-one game on our Keystone Table while a group of pledges cleaned the basement mess around us.

Pledges cleaned the house twice a week and we had this system down to a science. For basement duties first all Pong tables, Varsity excluded, are broken down and set on the side benches against the wall. Any full trash bags are taken out to the huge dumpster in the corner of our parking lot. New linings are put in. The floor, often covered in hundreds of beer cans and empty cups, comes next. This trash is disposed of by two or three pledges with shovels who corral the empty cups and cans into corners and use the leverage of the walls to shovel huge piles of debris into nearby garbage cans. Two other pledges would dump the full cups of beer that lined the bar, side benches, and just about every other flat surface, into mop buckets to be taken out separately from the trash as the added weight of the liquid made taking out the full plastic bags (already stuffed with cans, cups and folded thirty pack boxes) that much more difficult. After the trash is disposed of, the mopping of the floor mung begins and continues until the tile underneath the grime is visible, albeit covered in scattered mop-streaks of brown. Cleaning solution, which we purchase in bulk, is liberally applied to just about everything in sight.

Korver was on basement duty that night. We didn't bother aiming our eliminated cups for the now empty trash cans and the pledges had no choice but to continuously retrace their steps over cleaned territory to account for the random trash we were routinely tossing to the ground. When the game ended, I grabbed the two-thirds full case from the side bench and thumped it on the table to indicate another game would be set up and played instantly. Korver and another pledge were affixing the plastic linings of the two last cans of the basement beside Varsity. The rest of the basement crew pledges were gathering their things and getting ready to head upstairs.

Halifax quite suddenly side armed his paddle in Korver's direction in the manner you might throw a curve-ball. Korver full on body flinched as the paddle hooked left to avoid him at the last second and clattered harmlessly against the wall.

"Korver, you're playing me and Balls. Shiva, you're in too, buddy."

The second pledge shrugged, stooped down to pick up the thrown paddle and approached the table where I was now pulling beers out of the Keystone case and distributing them equally to the two playing sides. Korver hadn't yet moved from his flinched position.

"I'll play, but we should split up teams. You and Balls is totally unfair."

It was very surprising to hear Korver say this and I would have gone for his suggestion in a second. Discouraging the pledges by completely dismantling them in Ship wasn't going to teach them any lesson other than to avoid Varsity Pong with upperclassmen at all costs.

"We're not splitting up teams," Halifax said. "You're playing me and Balls, get over it."

We finished filling the beers, measured the cups into their proper spots, and began the lopsided game. This was like shooting fish in a barrel. The pledges were having a hard time returning our deep lobs and their own return shots were short layups that frequently resulted in deadly hits and sinks. We had all boats sinkable in no time and it wasn't long after that before their four boat went down to a well timed chop-shot by Halifax.

"Korver, tell me something," Halifax said while the pledges drank their beers.

"Is this the first game of Ship you've played this term?"

"Yes, Halifax," Korver said between sips. "This is my first game of Ship...are you fucking kidding me?"

"To be fair, I've never seen you playing Ship either," I commented.

"Just because you two don't let me play on the big boy table doesn't mean I've never played a game."

"You're getting beat like you've never played a game." Halifax said.

"That's because I'm not playing with Peplinski."

"Careful," I told him. This was not the first time that night he had mentioned Peplinski—the pledge who had quit on us only two weeks into the term.

"I'm just saying, if Peplinski were here we'd be kicking your ass right now," Korver said with a chuckle.

"Say that name again and I'm going to lose my shit,"

"You mean Peplinski?"

I could see that Halifax was fuming. Obviously something had to be done here, but even then I recognized that our anger wouldn't last past the night. Waiting until Meetings to try to punish Korver was pointless; this was something that needed to be dealt with right away. Now this behavior was pretty harmless and even though Korver was seriously pissing us off and being totally disrespectful to the house in the process, it would be pretty difficult to convince the brotherhood to discipline Korver at Meetings for such a petty insult. Halifax, simultaneously coming to the same conclusion, began slowly walking past the Pong table towards our victim; I flanked him on the opposite side.

Korver raised his hands up in protest. "What are you guys doing? I was just joking around."

"It's too late, asshole," Halifax said.

We closed in on him; the other pledge kept his silence and took a few steps back to completely absolve himself from whatever was about to occur. Halifax seized Korver by his arms, and with my help, dragged him from the basement up to the privacy of the Brothers Room. The danger of the situation was that neither of us had a clue as to what we were going to do at this point. The worst idea could instantly work us up into a deranged frenzy. Korver, not knowing whether he should resist or not, decided to play along for the time being.

"Let's give this fucker a Swirley Whirley!"

I think this was my suggestion, but I can't be completely sure. Either way we both burst into devious laughter. Korver merely grimaced and looked to his pledge brother, who had quietly followed us upstairs, for help. The mute pledge shrugged his shoulders.

We dragged Korver over to the Brothers Room's handicap accessible bathroom that the school had recently forced us to install. All parties were immediately taken aback at its hideous state. The toilet bowl that Korver's head was about to be plunged into was covered in numerous brown speckles of dung and dried piss that were caked around the seat and base of the toilet, rendering it completely unusable for anything but urination. A puddle in a two-foot radius surrounding the porcelain base told me that most of the brothers who had recently utilized the bathroom had been too drunk to aim properly. The sink, just opposite the toilet, bore the apparent traces of a recent gunshot wound cleaning, covered in drops of dried blood that were spread out in a fan like pattern, decorating the floor, walls, and sides of the toilet in avant garde gore.

"Don't do this," Korver pleaded.

We ignored him; we no longer had any other option. Even if we had second thoughts about what we were about to do, such a big deal had been made about Korver's punishment that we would invariably have to proceed. No longer were we defending the house itself, we were defending our own gross attachment to it.

Korver resisted us as much as he could. He tried to fight us off with his hands, but we soon had him backed in a corner and were able to grab hold of him. Halifax maintained a grip on his arms and midsection while I grabbed his legs and attempted to hoist him into the air. Halifax was forcing Korver's head into the bowl; the pledge's hands gripped the filthy edge of the toilet seat in an attempt to keep the top of his head out of the dirty toilet water. With his legs arched in the air, I slid my hands down his waist to put more pressure on his torso, hoping to break the grip he had on the seat. We struggled in this way for many long seconds; periodically Halifax would laugh fiendishly and take a swipe at Korver's hands with one of his free arms, trying to break his grip. When Korver did lose hold of the seat and we seemed nearly about to submerge him, he miraculously regained his grasp and opposed us as fervently as before.

The three of us struggled on in complete silence. Even Korver had given up on his pleas of mercy and instead concentrated full time on keeping his head shit water free. It was the kind of silent battle that reflected the utter hatred the two sides had for each other. While none of us would speak of this encounter ever again, every conversation I have ever had with Korver since this has reflected the resentment this memory has left him with. I've never apologized. When it became clear the standoff would not be broken, we lowered Korver to his feet, explaining that he was a pledge and he had behaved unacceptably. It took me a moment to even remember what he had done.

"Apparently it takes three drunk Chi-Gams to Swirley Whirley a pledge," Halifax said. "Make a note of that!"

The Two pledges scattered as Halifax and I collapsed on the leather couches of the Brothers Room. Halifax began rolling a joint with a pack of Zig-Zig's laying on the coffee table. I lit a cigarette and watched him as I scanned the two hundred or so channels that made up our cable system. The Stalingrad sniper movie *Enemy at the Gates* was just starting so I threw it on. Halifax began explaining to me how two-man sniper teams would wait for days to take the right shot; patience proved to be the most coveted attribute of a long range marksman. My hands shaking, cigarette ash spilling on the floor, I told him I would be his spotter, he could pull the trigger. After the joint, we played a three-game one-on-one series on Varsity. The Swirley Whirley incident had practically been forgotten.

In the basement one evening—Beetle, Winston, Rats, and I played a game of Ship together on Varsity. It was late in our senior spring, and the conversation had turned to graduation. Along with the rest of our class, the three of them would receive diplomas in a week. I had three terms left (on account of my parkhursting) and had once again enrolled in summer classes to make up for lost time.

"Can you imagine not doing this?" I asked the group once our game had been set up and teams decided. Winston and I were squaring off against Rats and Beetle.

"Beating you at Ship?"

Rats served for the first volley of the game and I, holding the opposing paddle, predictably aimed for the three-boat in the hopes of making it sinkable on our first shot.

"Ship is our life up here… how can I can live without it?"

I had missed short and wide, allowing Beetle to tap my shot gently into the third cup of our five-boat. The ball ricocheted off the lip of the cup, taking an unsavable nose dive off the edge of the table but I was able to instinctively lean over and snatch it out of midair before it could escape into the vastness of the basement. I lifted the cup to my lips and waited for a response.

"Playing Ship every weekend for the rest of our lives is not realistic," said Winston.

"I'll tell you what's going to happen," Beetle continued. "We're going to get jobs, get married, have kids, grow old, and get over Ship. That's the way of the world, dogg."

"I want you to listen to me Beetle. Come find me in ten years and I can guarantee that I will have a Ship room in my house. Permanent table—measured to the exact specifications of Varsity. I'll invite you guys to dinner, but instead of hitting the parlor for a scotch and cigar after we eat, we retire to the Ship room for a nightcap of Pong. Our wives, of course, are invited to play with us. I'll tell you right now, Ship ability is near the top of my list for desired qualities in a potential partner."

"Balls, you sound like a mental patient," said Beetle.

"And that whole fantasy presumes that at some point you'll actually own a house, which is a scenario I find pretty unlikely," Rats said.

"Will you even be able to afford a Pong table on a fast food salary?" Winston asked with a laugh.

"You guys are dicks."

We were in the middle of an intense rally so the conversation came to a halt as we all focused on the game. The point ended with me hitting their four-boat but Beetle managed to knock it back over to our side on a miraculous, off table, stooping shot—saving the hit.

"Nice save."

"For me that was an easy one, and Knight, when it comes to life we all have to grow up eventually. That time is rapidly approaching...at least for us."

"Who's to say I can't make Ship a part of my life on the outside?"

"It's fucking Beer Pong, you'll outgrow it," Rats said. "Everyone does. Now are you going to serve or what?"

I had been cradling the ball and paddle for sometime.

"Fuck that. If I want to play Ship, I will. When the time comes when I don't want to play Ship anymore, I'll stop. Not a moment before or after."

I finally handed Winston the paddle who served the next point, a decent one too, but Rats landed an impressive underhand swat that sunk a full cup on our now badly damaged five-boat.

"You'll play Ship for exactly as long as it's convenient for you to play Ship."

I scowled and pounded the first half of the lost beer before handing the half-filled cup to Winston to finish.

"What are you going to do when you finally get out of here?" Winston asked next as the last drop of Keystone from the second half of the beer rolled down his throat.

"You know, I haven't a clue."

"I always saw you doing something with video games." Beetle said. "I tell people 'If you want to hear Knight say something intelligent, ask him about Playstation.'"

"I'm not a programmer or an artist or an established writer and I have no interest in the corporate or marketing side of gaming. I want to design and write games yet I have practically no applicable skills and would certainly have to work in testing until I could convince someone I'm too smart to be working in testing. I'm going to have a fucking government degree."

"A government degree from *Dartmouth*...You can do pretty much whatever you want."

"The whole thing is off. It just doesn't feel right. I shouldn't be in despair about my future right on the verge of an Ivy League degree."

"Despair about your future? Dude, you're twenty-one fucking years old. If you're being serious then you need intensive therapy." Beetle shook his head in disbelief. "You're more self-hating than most Jews I know... and trust me, I know a lot of Jews."

"So...you're saying Balls," Rats began saying, "that you have no prospects, zero motivation and don't have a clue what to do with your life."

"That about covers it."

"Hard times, Balls. *Hard* times," Beetle said, shaking his head sadly.

"I figured this out a long time ago," Rats declared smugly. "You're going to move to Brooklyn, become a film professor and get high every night—just like your old man. Ha Ha Nghaa!"

"Kill myself," I muttered.

"Better yet," he bared his teeth to reveal a twisted smile. "You actually told me this once. You're going to be homeless, living in a park in D.C., dispensing free political advice to aspiring politicians. Eventually you'll find the perfect candidate and coach him into the presidency but sadly your suddenly successful protégé forgets his wise homeless master and you end up penniless, disease ridden, and crazed."

"I told you that?"

"After about two blunts, yeah, brah."

"Knight," said Winston in a obnoxiously serious tone, "You must have *some* aspirations for your life."

"I do actually. Not too different from your own I suspect." I said, attempting to match Winston in his severity. "First and foremost, I want to live a happy, healthy and prosperous life. Obviously I should desire wealth and crave to experience all that that entails, but far more important is security—being able to ensure the well being of the people I love. In my professional life I want to be successful, innovative, and creative, while still giving back to my community and positively impacting the lives of others. In the ideal scenario, I would have the flexibility to pursue my various outside interests as well as raise a well-adjusted, happy family. I want to meet a beautiful and intelligent woman to raise my children and in forty years I want to look into my grandchild's face and see something that reminds me of the youthful naïve boy that I once was. I want to die with no regrets and in my sleep, peacefully. Ostensibly, those are my dreams."

"But...what are they really?" Rats asked with a curious grin.

When the Chi-Gams graduated they went to New York, that is, except the ones who were going to continue on to graduate school or who were set up comfortably elsewhere. The NYC contingent by and large worked consulting or financial jobs, entry level salaried positions with investment banks, mutual funds, hedge funds and consulting firms whose names I had never heard before but that were, I was assured, extremely prestigious and lucrative post college positions despite the long hours and general lack of substance. Some of these kids would survive to move up in these firms. Others got the hell out to pursue careers elsewhere or take a business school break to then re-attack the industry with renewed focus. The top thinkers of our generation living on the promise of future wealth and power, showing no inclination whatsoever to pursue fields in which their employers' and stockholders' bank accounts and investment options were not the primary benefactor.

The graduate students were subjected to more work than they had ever done during their four years at Dartmouth. These kids were instantly transformed into real students again. Their unhealthy drinking habits came to an end (or were at least curtailed) once their attachment to the house was severed. The fact that they were all able to do so effortlessly gave me a degree of hope. If I held on a little longer I might be able to make that transition as well.

Rats went on to graduate school, as did Yogi, and a handful of other brothers in the house. Thalen went to work for his father. Winston got a job with a top financial firm and within two years was running his department and making six figures. Pigs and Beetle got top consulting jobs that they both soon quit. Kouge was also in Med School. I rarely saw him by this point, and his sudden interest in the medical field seemed to be the result of a combination of parental pressures and a desire for a life that could be easily managed. Try as I might I couldn't find anything inherently wrong with these choices, but I felt like the few people I identified with were on a life-path that I barely understood, let alone could replicate.

When did they have all this time anyway? My days were spent recovering from the night before, and my nights spent drinking sunken boats. How did the kid I played four games of Ship with the previous night manage a corporate interview and a meeting with his academic advisor the following day? My reality dictated that Ship doesn't allow for this sort of future planning. Behind the scenes my friends actually had complicated lives independent of our basement existences.

And when they graduated they would be instantly propelled into the world of six figures, the world of Orwell's omnipotent *Money God*, typified by an endless pursuit of things. I saw the flowers around me blossoming into complacent consumers, forever waiting for the next upgrade or newest version, never be satisfied with the present, always looking to what lay on the horizon. The shocking thing to me was that everyone around me was okay with this realization, or maybe they had known all along what I thought I was only now just discovering: that the men and women of Dartmouth heralded in the next generation of yuppies, with their newer, smaller and smarter looking things. The palm pilots, plasma screen TVs, camera phones, portable video game systems, Blackberries, and three-hundred dollar a week coke habits. I wanted nothing to do with this world and revolted against it the only way I knew how, by ignoring it entirely and instead immersing myself in what was widely viewed as taboo, underground debauchery.

The last week of what should have been my senior year was a campus wide orgy of Pong-playing, other people hooking up, and drunken shenanigans. Finals had ended but graduation wasn't for another week giving the soon-to-be college graduates ample time to celebrate entering the real world. Hundreds of underclassmen wanting to join in the festivities and wishing to party with the departing seniors one last time, stayed on campus as well. Everyday during this period we would wake up, start to drink, and continue drinking until we passed out later that night. As the week wore on the heavy drinking began to take its toll on my body. Each subsequent day I slept later in the afternoon and woke up in an increasingly debilitating bodily malaise. The only way to cure these physical ills was to begin drinking immediately. Naturally the earlier I started drinking, the more distress I would be in the next day and thus the earlier I would have to start drinking. It was a vicious cycle. It is a very strange thing not being sober for an entire day, or worse a whole week. My friends who had been with me since the beginning were for the most part moving on, but I was stuck and felt no closer to leaving Dartmouth than I had felt two years before. I had chosen a different path—instead of integrating myself into campus life, I had chosen to conquer only the basement.

Now I alone out of my classmates had actually seen my earning power decline since I had been at school. Who could have predicted this vast change in my attitude towards life or the habitual drug use that has made me such an undesirable candidate? I had no practical skills and, as Rats so eloquently pointed out, zero motivation and no prospects. I hadn't made any truly helpful connections and cultivated, along with my education, an intense hatred for corporate America. My method of avoiding this conundrum was by continuously convincing myself that I had to focus on getting out of Dartmouth before I let fear over the future take hold. I fancied that like so many protagonists in fictional accounts of youthful idleness often tackled by the European masters, my vocation and calling in life would present itself at the opportune moment. I simply had to recognize it when it arrived.

❄

Brother Woland stood before us in Room M, obstructing the television and waiting for someone to acknowledge him. Nobody did. He impatiently produced a long sustained "ummmm" to which he finally got the attention of the room.

Woland was a kid who I only got to know after my suspension. He had cultivated a horrible reputation within the house while I was gone and a good deal of brothers flat out disliked him. Truth be told he was a bit of a dick. Both of us had settled into our roles in the house. Me—a well-known drunk, stoner, and Ship player who was prone to blackouts, vomiting and irresponsible behavior and him—arrogant, distant, and solely focused on his own self-promoting, wicked agenda. We soon found that many of our extracurricular activities overlapped and that we actually got along quite well together. Ship Professionals. Check. Chronic marijuana abusers. Check. Disregard for established social norms. Check plus. Every other word out of Woland's mouth was "dude" and I mean this almost as close to a literal sense as you can get with hyperbole—the dude said "dude" all the fucking time. He was an excellent Ship player, always ranked among the best in the house and right then I couldn't be less surprised that Woland stood in front of us. He never lived in the house but was always the first brother scrounging for games on a Wednesday, Friday or Saturday night. His first question was an obvious one.

"Dude—what time you trying to play games?"

These were the words I almost dreaded to hear but came to expect, especially as afternoon made the slow transition to night. Until this point Ship had been on all our minds though nobody wanted to be the first to bring it up. Once you played that first game your fate was sealed and you wouldn't be sober again for the rest of the night.

"What time is it?"

This question was asked as if I had a very specific Pong start-time in mind.

"Five forty-five, dude."

"How about six?"

He laughed, "All right, dude, sounds good. What are teams?"

Halifax sat slouched on one couch and raised his finger half heartedly to signify he intended to be among the game's participants. Gonzo and Gunter were on a second couch and not giving any positive signs of being anxious to participate.

"I'll take Gunter," I said. "You take Halifax."

"Gunter, congratulations dude, you've just been nominated to be our fourth." Woland said.

Gunter remained motionless on the couch and presented his case.

"Guys, I don't want to drink this early. I'll be hammered by ten and blacked out by one. I think I actually want to *remember* tonight."

"Dude, it's a fucking Friday," said Woland.

"He makes a good point," Halifax said, getting to his feet and adjusting his baseball hat. "Friday night, dude."

Gunter knew that this was an unimpeachable argument and probably in his heart of hearts wanted to play anyway so he grunted his consent and stood up along with the rest of us.

"Wooo, peer pressure!" I teased, waving my fingers at him menacingly.

"You guys are assholes."

They killed us in the first game—we didn't even sink a boat. A *shutout.* Looking in disbelief at the lopsided victory (they still had ten cups on their side while we had one, the mine) I demanded a rematch to officially erase this blemish of a loss. Refilling our downed boats was the only way to feel whole again.

Gunter looked less than enthusiastic about the prospect of another game and was moving about rather lethargically on account of the seven beers we had each consumed over the course of twenty minutes. His standing so uncomfortably made me realize how full I was. Any movement made me painfully aware that I might blow any minute.

Five minutes of gut wrenching agony was all it would take to make me feel right as rain again. I had this option before me far too many times to count: To boot or not to boot? This was constantly the question. This near-boot feeling couldn't be endured much longer, and I knew I had to be in the best possible shape for the next game if we wanted any chance of winning. My only option was to step away from the table and force myself to vomit.

Both cans on the sideline were already full to the brim with empty cups and cans. I poured and chugged a full beer and tossed the cup onto the floor, then hunched over one of the cans, gripping the sides as I had done hundreds of times before. A fragrance I cannot describe as appetizing caused my stomach to convulse and some pre-boot surfaced in my mouth. I spat it up quickly and prepared to pull the trigger. Woland looked over at me, apparently not wanting to miss the show I was fixing to put on, but my other two friends didn't give me so much as a glance as they continued filling the game. And who can blame them? This was a sight we were all too accustomed to seeing. I waited until I had Woland's full attention and then, closing my eyes, stuck my finger as far back into my mouth as I could and wiggled it as if I was trying to tickle my tonsils. Before my finger had been in my mouth for five seconds I lurched forward involuntarily and puked up about a cup of vomit into the can. I waited for a few moments to see if any more was going to follow but all I felt was the acidic burn of the bile aftertaste. Few things are worse than preparing yourself mentally for a boot only to be rewarded with a pint of phlegm. Then a most severe disturbance hit my stomach. I threw my head back over the can instinctively and felt a surge rush through my throat. A thick continuous river of vomit flew from my mouth almost completely horizontally like a fire hose and hit the inside rim of the can, splattering the walls of the basement behind it. I puked for what seemed like an eternity and by the end was reduced to tears, once again feebly clutching the sides of the garbage can as I spat up the residue of the expectorated food matter. When I was done I blew my nose over the garbage a few times, wiped my face off with the sleeve of my shirt, stuck a cigarette in my mouth and lit it.

"How was that?" Halifax asked. Though he had pretended to ignore my display he was all too aware of what I was up to in that corner.

"Painful," I answered, clutching my torso and making sure to take frequent drags off the cigarette.

"I almost always boot during my first game," Woland declared, but then glancing at the result of our latest contest he clarified his statement. "Well, that is, if I actually drink any beer."

"We'll see what we can do about that in this next game," Gunter said, showing signs of emotion for the first time. Gunter was drinker first, a Pong player second. He had reluctantly fostered a deep respect for Ship along with the rest of us but rarely became competitive and never seemed to care whether he won or lost.

Woland, meanwhile, had decided this to be an opportune moment to change the subject. "Dudes, want to smoke a bowl before this next game?"

"I can't play stoned, you know that," Halifax said.

"Yeah, dude, I know, but I play really well stoned so it balances out in the long run," Woland replied condescendingly. "What about you, Balls?"

"I need to get this taste out of my mouth," I answered. One final chunk had surfaced in my throat. I quickly spat it up onto the floor.

"Dude, you seen my new bowl?" Woland thrust his hand into his pocket and pulled out a small fish shaped glass bowl. "Just picked it up."

"Nice ," I said while inspecting the piece. "Lefty, huh?" I was fingering the carb and holding the bowl to my lips testing out how it felt.

"Yeah, I really liked this design but they didn't have any righties. The way the carb is positioned it doesn't really matter though."

"That's true," I agreed. He had his sack out so I handed the bowl back. He packed it, took a huge rip and passed it to me to continue the cipher.

Now we were stoned and filling the remainder of the beers for our game while having an utterly ridiculous series of conversations.

"No, dude," Woland said definitively while filling the third cup of his four boat with Keystone Light. "I'll tell you exactly what you would do. You buy a small island in the Caribbean or South Pacific. Then you build mansions on the shore surrounding the entire island for you and your crew. Each mansion links underground to a fucking dope complex in the center of the island. That's where we all chill together. Dude, how tight does that sound?"

We all immediately got into his little fantasy.

"Didn't the Wu-Tang Clan do that?"

"I'm talking about the Caribbean, dude, not Staten Island."

"Hey, we can probably get recognition in the United Nations," Halifax said. "We should name ourselves 'The United *State* of America,' that way when the Secretary General calls on the U.S., me and Balls storm up there and interrupt the US Ambassador and say we thought we had the floor."

"We've got our own enclosed glass box where we're smoking blunts—hot boxing the fucking UN."

"A delivery guy walks into the room out of nowhere and Kofi Annan is like, 'Did you assholes order pizza to the General Assembly again?'"

"Picture me in there, dude. I'd be like: 'God Dammit, Sweden! You're really starting to piss me off over here!'"

Though there was a new cast of characters, the script was much the same. Each year a new class of wet under the ear freshmen was sucked up into the Dartmouth's machine to be chewed up and eventually spit out as grizzled Pong veterans.

The second game went much better for us. We managed to barely win despite Gunter's miserable performance. During the third game I was on fire. Four boats under my belt in less than a half hour. It usually took around five beers for my stroke to loosen up and my shot to hit that line right above Varsity that I knew would guide the ball into the cups. When I did get into a groove it could last for four or five games, until the beer began to seriously hamper my motor skills.

Sometimes when I hit a shot I know I've sunk a boat as soon as I make contact. I don't even attempt to pass the paddle to my partner and when the ball splashes into the cup I say nothing and merely toss the paddle onto the table as if it were the most common occurrence in the world. A surge of euphoria races through my body and I feel stronger and more powerful than I've ever felt in my life. Nothing compares to the feeling of sinking a boat.

Chapter 11: The Legend of Balls

"There is a large disconnect between leadership of the CFS system and at least some of its members. Although CFS leaders say they despise offensive behavior and do their best to stamp it out, they think they have little leverage against the offenders."
–*Excerpt from the Summary of the Recommendations Submitted to the Board of Trustees by the Committee on the Student Life Initiative*

It's somewhat obvious on campus that the easiest way to hook up at Dartmouth is to go out drinking at fraternities. People did date—though it was hard to tell why all these couples had decided to extend their relationships into the sober hours or where they went on dates, or what the point was besides securing regular sex. Let's say my knowledge on the subject is limited and you'll need to turn elsewhere for an examination of Dartmouth College dating culture.

Balls was strangely adverse to pursuing basement hookups during his time at Dartmouth, for the most part choosing to ignore the girls who visited his house. For Balls, Beer Pong trumped everything else but it's hard to say whether this was because at the time he was genuinely uninterested in forming relationships with the opposite sex (or with anyone not in his fraternity for that matter) or if he was just no good at talking to women to begin with and terrified of learning how and so formed his Pong preferred stance on the matter strictly as a defense mechanism.

Balls managed to become very close with one female student during the second half of his college career—basically a female version of himself with superior social skills. And for whatever reason, they never explored anything other than a platonic relationship despite all those drunken nights together. Meanwhile, she would routinely prey upon the brotherhood, plucking out house execs or pledges at random, and hooking up with them in upstairs bedrooms or even the Brothers Room on occasion. She was a devoted Ship player and a constant fixture on Varsity, where the two of them partnered up to blow out teams of underclassmen. Birdie would have been a Chi-Gam for sure if not for her gender.

Instead she pledged a sorority located on the other side of campus, Kappa Kappa Gamma—for Balls the sorority equivalent of Kafka's Castle. Birdie was rarely at Kappa outside of their own Meetings and preferred Ship with Chi-Gams to the games of Shrub surely going on in her basement on a nightly basis.

It was during a game of Ship with Birdie on Varsity when Balls learned that one of her sorority sisters (a newly pledged sophomore named Kathy who had been seen lurking in the basement several times over the past few weeks) had observed his stoic Ship professionalism pent up behind Varsity, actually thought he was really *cute* and wanted to take him as her date to the approaching Kappa formal. Balls laughed out loud at this news. Woe to the girl who accidentally finds Balls attractive!

Now Kathy was pretty attractive herself, but that didn't matter to good ol' Balls, who was oblivious to such obvious details. Still, he did realize that this was probably his only chance of ever attending one of these sorority formal type events. So when Kathy officially invited Balls the next day via blitzmail, he replied in the affirmative. Balls knew for certain that a handful of Chi-Gam hardliners would be operating behind the scenes and at worst this was a rare opportunity to get annihilated outside of the comfort of the house.

Most fraternities and sororities held formal and semi-formal events each term. Semi-formals typically took place in the actual house of the organization who hosted it, while formals were usually planned at outside venues. For both events brothers and sisters invited dates, dressed up in sport coats, dresses, khakis, scarves and ties and drank excessively.

On the night of the formal, Balls picked up Kathy at her dorm, and met her roommate (a fellow Kappa) and her roommate's date for the night. When the four of them arrived at Kappa they found two Pong tables set up in one of their front floor communal rooms, where sixty or so slickly adorned students were mingling in one massive blob. Balls' first inclination, obviously, was to call next on one of these tables because if he was playing Pong it would look like he was socially engaged, but remembering his date, her roommate, and the other chap, Balls realized this would be impossible to pull off without appearing completely obnoxious. Maintaining a conversation with his friends for more than a few hours was barely tolerable, how could he do so with this unknown group? The only reasonable solution was to black himself out early with the open bar and unleash himself upon the unsuspecting guests.

"I'll get drinks," Balls told his group.

Instinctively locating the alcohol supply, Balls filled several glasses of punch in a determined effort to appear busy in the midst of a debilitating panic attack. *I don't know anybody, and I'm exposed.* He anxiously made a mental note of the familiar faces in the room. Two or three junior Chi-Gam ball players were trading stories and laughing loudly behind one Pong table, their dates nowhere to be seen. On that table Woland was playing Pong with his girlfriend (a Kappa obviously) against Halifax and Birdie. Balls tried to get their attention but they were engrossed in their game and didn't appear to notice him. He scowled and returned to the group.

The next thirty to forty minutes were spent dispatching cups of punch and champagne while Kathy, her roommate, and her roommate's date talked around him. Balls was drinking two or three times faster than everyone else, and suspected his blatant alcoholism was a clear indicator to the group of his underdeveloped social skills. The conversation focused on a number of pretty standard, mundane topics at which Balls feigned what he hoped to be an appropriate comment every time he got the feeling one was expected of him, but he could tell they suspected something was wrong and that he didn't quite know how to interact in this setting. A sense of relief hit when an announcement rang out that buses had arrived.

The Kappa formal was being held at a venue called Bates Mansion, a colonial-era farmhouse located on a lush fifty acres, often used by CFS houses for off-campus events such as this. Three coach buses had arrived outside to transfer the college kids from the sorority house in Hanover over the Connecticut River to this Vermont farm that would be the site of the evening's festivities. It started to pour while they were in transit, and upon arriving at the property, the formal-goers were herded through the rain to the ten thousand square foot mansion where inside cocktails and hors d'oeuvres were served across several rooms on the first floor.

The group mingled and drank cocktails as quickly as the bartenders could refill their glasses. A makeshift tent was being constructed just outside to shield the banquet tables and dance floor from the torrential downpour that had started. Balls and company were ushered out of the mansion and into this tent once it had been completed and ended up at a table with Kathy's sophomore friends—all complete strangers to Balls. Not that Kathy and her friends weren't making an attempt to include him—they were, but Balls was being asked questions he couldn't possibly have any earthy answers for—questions which boiled down to: t*ells us, Balls, what kind of person are you*? He was shocked that this wasn't already known—*did Kathy really have no inkling of who I was?* Balls found that very hard to believe and frankly a bit distasteful.

Still drinking, and feeling utterly alone despite the wealth of activity around him, Balls made another attempt to locate stray Chi-Gams to rescue him from the situation. He caught sight of Woland's girlfriend sitting with some of her friends at a table across the room but Woland and Halifax were nowhere in sight. Balls did, however, spy Birdie perched at the bar placing an order so he excused himself from the table to join her. Her back was turned so she didn't notice as Balls snuck up from behind and tapped her on the shoulder.

"Birdie!" he exclaimed, throwing his arms around her neck. "Boy am I glad to see you."

"Whiskey shots?"

"Certainly. Set em' up."

They downed several rounds of shots and discussed their current predicament.

"You've already abandoned your date, Mr. Knight. May I ask why?"

"Seems you have too."

"Actually, I sort of hate these kind of things…"

"You aren't alone there."

"Kathy actually likes you as hard as that is to believe. Give her a chance. You know, you could totally fuck her tonight if you wanted to."

"'If I wanted to' being the key qualifier. Spoiler alert: I don't."

"Well, that makes sense. A girl suddenly shows interest and you don't have a clue what to do. Don't you worry, Balls. It'll all be over soon. You'll be back to the safety of Chi-Gam and playing Ship before you know it,"

"You know, you're so right, Birdie. In fact I see us as Pong partners sometime in the very near future."

"Let's survive tonight, then we'll talk Ship."

"Deal. Any idea where Halifax and Woland are by the way?"

"Hmm...I think I saw them leave the tent together fifteen minutes ago. If I had to guess I'd say they were probably finding a nice secluded smoke spot."

"I better go after them."

"That's a terrible idea."

"Possibly the worst idea I've ever had."

Outside the rain had slowed to a light drizzle, the sky was just beginning to grow dark, and the frigid New Hampshire air brought goose bumps to Balls' skin. He knew Woland and Halifax were around somewhere and though he also realized smoking would not help him in the slightest at this point, he *needed* whatever he could get his hands on.

Halifax's unmistakable laughter was heard as Balls reached the end of a long gravel driveway and approached the edge of an expansive pasture. While scaling the waist-high wooden fence in front of him, he noticed a small shed about fifty yards down, partially hidden among a grouping of bushes. A flickering lighter illuminated one of the unseen sides of the shed. This was exactly the sign Balls had been looking for.

Halifax and Woland were huddling for warmth and shielding themselves from drizzle behind the tiny shed. With them was a Heorot and two Theta Delt '04s whom Balls recognized but wasn't particularly friendly with. The five of them were passing around a small spoon shaped glass bowl as Balls approached. They expressed some surprise that he had been operating solo thus far tonight and welcomed him into the circle.

"So, how did *you* end up here," said one of the Theta Delts as he passed the bowl, appearing to be just as surprised to be at a Kappa formal as Balls was.

"I'm here with a girl," Balls reassured him.

The Theta Delt cocked his head at an angle as if confused.

"This girl, Kathy," Balls explained. "Sophomore or something I think."

"Oh, Kathy? I know that chick." said the Theta Delt. "She's pretty cute, dude, but I meant like... how did you find us back *here*, behind this shed."

"I was looking for a lighter."

For the next twenty minutes or so they passed the bowl back and forth, not giving the formal or their dates a second thought. Balls hadn't seen his date in over an hour. Common decency told him it was time to track her down and repair whatever damage had been done by his inconspicuous absences.

Kathy was sitting alone at their table when Balls returned, finishing up her second helping of stuffed chicken breast and steamed vegetables. Her face brightened up when she saw him and even in his advanced state of highness,

Balls really did feel sorry for her sitting all by herself at her own formal. Why had he agreed to come if his plan had been to completely ignore his date? Balls, overcome by a sense of pity and downright depression, then asked her if she wanted to dance, to which she happily agreed. They both stumbled a bit on their way to the dance floor, and it occurred to Balls that while Kathy had only made two trips to the buffet, she had in all probability made many more to the open bar.

They were a mess on the dance floor and clumsily tried to keep on their feet while bumping into other couples, who were giving their strange dance moves skeptical glances. The pair needed to be on the first bus back to Hanover, so as soon as there were positive signs of the formal winding down, Balls hastily pulled her back to the table to collect their things. At around this time the alcohol Kathy had consumed fully hit her system, and she basically had to be carried onto the first bus by Balls. Other formal goers anxious to depart had begun streaming on as well.

As they took a seat in the back-row, Kathy let her head collapse against Balls' shoulder and then whispered something in his ear that nobody has ever said to him before.

"You're mine to hook up with."

Balls doesn't quite understand how this perfectly reasonable individual in front of him could be so blind to the way things really were. Balls is a problem to be figured out, a liability to be accounted for—he isn't something you showed off to your friends. Balls knows this. He is also aware that the bus hasn't given any positive signs of an approaching departure, and the bus driver is outside chatting by the curb with one of the other drivers. The way out of something like this, Balls remembers, is to act totally unpredictable. This realization inspires Balls to stand up in the aisle and make a peculiar declaration:

"I'm commandeering this bus!"

Balls wins a few cheap laughs with this odd threat, but the passengers soon resume their post-formal conversations. This is no joke though because Balls lurches for the driver's chair. He plops himself down and pulls the lever that closes the bus doors. This raises some concern with the couples. He then attempts to pull the bus into gear but almost immediately four or five guys have Balls restrained but he keeps kicking and fighting anyway, more at the steering wheel and dashboard than at his assailants. By the time Balls had been subdued and is being forcibly dragged to the back of the bus, an exorcism has occurred.

Balls was gone, and now I cowered in shame in the back row next to Kathy as the bus doors opened and the irate bus driver stormed aboard.

"Un-fucking believable, you spoiled fucking college kids," he grunted in disgust amid a flurry of giggles and laughs.

Back in Hanover, Kathy and I stumbled off the bus together and successfully navigated our way to her dorm without either of us being seen by campus security. She had her arm around my shoulder as we tripped our way up the stairs to her dorm room. I could tell that she was expecting me to follow her in but I gleefully ignored the obvious signals and instead braced myself against the door frame to say goodbye. I had successfully survived the formal and now it was time for more pressing matters. As soon as the door was closed, I abandoned her and made a beeline for Varsity to call next on a Ship game.

A month later I was approached at random by a student I didn't know while walking across campus. He asked if I was the kid who had tried to hijack the Kappa bus at their last formal. I told him that I didn't think so and he said "too bad because that was one crazy ass dude" and it only occurred to me somewhat as an afterthought as he walked off laughing to himself that I was in fact the "crazy ass dude" he was referring to.

❄

Do you remember what you did last night?

I hate this question because the answer is more times than not, no. Enjoy these moments of *schadenfreude* as you recount my drunken exploits from the previous evening because they are not revelatory for me in any way. These are just the latest handful of helpless moments I have endured while imprisoned here in this frozen gulag of a place from a series of increasingly helpless moments. There is no cerebral connection to the events you describe, and since I've already admitted that I don't remember a darn thing and owe you nothing further, I'm just riding this out and hoping things don't escalate. I'm also hoping that my memory doesn't slowly fizzle back into focus just as the climax is being reached so that I can see the atrocities I am about to commit before you even tell me I've committed them. This world of blackouts is one in which Balls reigns supreme. Yes, he has done the terrible things you are describing but no, he isn't here to take your call right now.

A six foot four baseball player confronts Balls in the basement and squares him up against one of the wooden support beams. There has never been a human being who has wanted to punch Balls in the face more than this person standing before him. The highly suggestible Balls is blisteringly drunk and not at all aware that the person he has recently been convinced to openly insult in the basement is in fact dating this mammoth of a man. Balls says "Oh, did I fuck up?" Looming menacingly over him, the athlete thinks long and carefully about his next move before deciding to walk away. He has come to the conclusion that it is better to accept the fact that his intoxicated fraternity brothers will on occasion verbally assault his girlfriend in the house rather than take the risk of seriously injuring this obviously mess of an individual (but still brother) by pummeling him in public sight. The phrase "nice thunder-thighs" obviously not being an appropriate compliment for use in face-to-face interactions. I am not good with women.

It had become routine for me to be accosted in the basement, some drunk and blathering freshman screaming out "Balls!" and then embracing me. Often I was convinced I had never seen this person before but to these unfamiliar Balls enthusiasts it was as if I was a living legend. While drinking I treated them like members of my own personal fan club but during those rare sober hours, I secluded myself almost entirely in the upstairs bedrooms of the house... as if I didn't want any outsiders to know there was a non-intoxicated version of Balls. For Pong games I was sought after as a partner by dozens of people a night and sometimes (to my delight of course) called the Pong Master behind my back. My skill level had plateaued, yes, and while I was one of the better players in the house I hardly deserved legendary status. My principal accomplishments were the high standards of conduct I expected of a game, my encyclopedic knowledge of the rules of Ship and the sheer quantity of games I played, almost certainly the most Ship games played out of anyone I have ever known outside of the Pong Master, who had many more years to his record. Unlike most elite players, I was not a Pong snob. I would partner up with anyone in the basement regardless of his or her reputation as players, and would accept any challenge, even occasionally allowing a couple of freshmen to break their Varsity cherry on my watch. I was the final piece of the puzzle for many three-person groups who were struggling to find a fourth and it was not uncommon for me to arrange the teams so that I was at a great disadvantage. The challenge for me was part of the thrill.

A younger tennis player has embarked on a quest to play two hundred Ship games in a single term. To mark his progress he has his opponents sign their name in a notebook he carries with him at all times in the basement. Balls sees this unfold over the course of a term and smirks from a distance. He doesn't need signatures in a fucking book as proof of his dedication to the game. He goes out there each and every night and earns it.

Sometimes I try to estimate the number of Ship games I have played over my career. If we assume during my peak years (lasting perhaps nine terms) that I played on average 2.5 games per night (a fair assumption I think considering that I would often play 5-10 games in a single day/night and played Ship at least five nights a week) then I would have played 175 games per ten-week term or 1,575 games over that ninety-week stretch, which would amount to approximately 7,875 cups of beer consumed during Pong alone in those three years as a full time student. I think this is an estimate on the low side. When put in these terms the scale of it all was frightening to think about.

Gonzo and Balls are the three-time defending Pledge Olympics champions, despite neither one of them actually being a pledge. They are especially adept at the basement obstacle course, an event requiring them to steer a shopping cart through a gauntlet of beer stations—one in the cart and one pushing—chugging several cups of beer at each station. They are the only brothers in recent memory that make a point of competing against the pledges on each and every Olympics night and the poor bastards don't stand a chance.

For four years I had been gradually losing my identity and by now it had all but eroded away. The friends who knew me before I had become Balls were gone and when they left, all traces of that previous person disappeared with them so that all that was left was Balls. This is how I introduced myself in the basement. Half of the people I knew didn't even know my first name and I told people that I was majoring in Ship. I played Pong so I wouldn't have to engage in conversations of substance, and got stoned when I was too drunk to play Pong. Either way I could be antisocial without actually seeming antisocial and yet for the first time I felt like I had "made it" within my fraternity. I had a social skill and it was Ship. Balls was well known, well liked and considered an all around fun person to be around. But perhaps I give myself too much credit because while I was notorious inside Chi Gamma Epsilon, I was virtually unknown outside of our basement.

Balls is growing frustrated with the slow progress of a game of Ship being played on a Junior Varsity table by four freshman guys. He takes advantage of a momentary lull in the action to remove a cup from one side of the table and withdraws to the trough where he replaces about half the beer in the cup with his own urine. He then casually walks back to the table and reinserts the pee-cup just as the temporarily distracted players are getting ready to resume the game—a trick he learned from Kouge years before. Balls then takes a seat on the side benches to see who is the lucky individual who gets to sample the Balls Beer.

I was living a life without substance or consequences.

❄

I was not the only one on campus in this position. While I was the most visible super senior in Chi-Gam, I knew a few here and there in almost every fraternity on campus.

Being a super-senior meant I had one of the highest housing priority numbers on campus and a few of the '04s who were now in their final year convinced me to apply for one of the coveted senior apartments for my last two terms at school—the only college residential option that gave students private access to a full kitchen. These apartments were located on the edge of campus near the engineering school and had been newly furnished with rock-hard fireproof furniture that ironically Gunter ignited while ironing a shirt for a corporate interview. This became one of many items we would be expected to replace at the end of the year. The full kitchen was also brand new, but within a week the microwave looked like the aftermath of an ecological disaster after Halifax decided to nuke a saran-wrapped burrito inside, igniting the cardboard plate he had constructed from the top of a Keystone case we had confiscated from the house. The sink was soon clogged with blackish-orange crud that seemed to replicate of its own accord, although surprisingly, there were no pests. Within a week or two the place was covered in layers of cigarette ash, blunt guts, empty boxes of food, and Ramen Noodles and EasyMac residue.

It was just the four of us living there at first; we each had our own bedroom but shared a bathroom, living room, and kitchen. My quad-mates were Gunter, and two of his '04 pledge brothers, Cuddles and Hurls. This should have been my most comfortable living arrangement so far at Dartmouth and promised to be totally conducive to academic success, not to mention a long enough walk from the house to discourage a large number of spur-of-the-moment Ship games... if not for the fact that two weeks into the term we were blessed with an additional two roommates. Three weeks later and the head count jumped to eight.

The first to move in, Halifax, had been hospitalized after the sudden onset of a jaw and throat infection during the first week and a half of the term and thus he entirely missed the signup period for classes. The school's response was to put him on administrative leave and when he returned to his single he found an eviction notice posted to his door. His belongings had been bagged up and moved downstairs to the dorm's basement storage facility. Now homeless, he showed up at our door with these bulging plastic bags and resolved that he wouldn't be going home for the term. Since Halifax had until that point spent all his free time not devoted to Ship at our apartment anyway, the new living arrangement wasn't inconvenient in any noticeable way. In fact it was a bit a relief having him there since it no longer made any sense for him to extradite the television we had stolen for the apartment from amongst the items he had been storing at the house while hospitalized.

Satchel Mathis was the next roommate to join our troupe. Our sudden and unexpected friendship, materializing in both our last months at Dartmouth, exemplified in splendid fashion what we all cherished so much about the house. You never knew what brother, at what time, could become a partner in crime. For example, during the previous three years I had known who Mathis was, saw him on a weekly basis at Meetings and occasionally got high with him. We never made special arrangements to hang out but when around each other we genuinely got along. Within a week of our class graduating we identified each other as the only two '03 undergraduates left in the house. A month later him, Halifax and I were inseparable. Rather than make the long trek across campus to our apartment (where he too spent the vast bulk of his free time) multiple times a day, he decided to move in as well. His presence was even less of a headache than Halifax's given that technically he had his own single on the other side of campus and tended to keep most of his shit in his car anyway. Plus he smoked us up nearly every day.

And as ever Chi-Gam was the epicenter of my existence. But things were different. Meetings were still fun but lacked that sense of thrill I felt when I was younger. Now it just seemed like everyone was going through the motions of holding Meetings. I still did the *Balls Quick Six* every single Wednesday, always upon request, but even that was essentially a completely dissociative enterprise. It had to be. I started to notice that each successive year the classes seemed to hang out less and less. Four years ago the basement would be packed by eight on a Friday or Saturday, but now it was just me and the other surviving professionals. But at other times I was alone, sitting impatiently on the couch in the Brothers Room, waiting for a game of Pong to materialize. The revolving door of Pong players seemed to be slowing down. Maybe my appetite for Ship had become insatiable but it seemed as if nobody were around

❄

Satchel Mathis and James Halifax sat in waiting room silence on a dreary, weather-worn loveseat that rocked slightly on its sloped legs. Both stared at a static spouting television with an animal ferocity. The living room of this off-campus apartment belonged to a recently discovered attractive friend of Birdie's. The game was now afoot. Upstairs a shower could be heard running. My two friends, a look of stoned determination on their faces, hadn't said anything in minutes.

"What the fuck?" said Satchel suddenly.

"What the fuck, what?" Halifax countered.

Satchel's eyes lit up.

"Dude...are you fucking shitting me right now?" Satchel said.

The water upstairs cut off abruptly.

"Well, clearly one of us is going to fuck this girl," Halifax replied, measuring his words carefully around the sound of a closing door.

"Oh, for Christ's sake!" Satchel exclaimed. "Obviously!"

Footsteps could be heard on the floor above.

"Well, I just assumed... you know I need a slump buster!"

"I know that, dude. You *do* need a slump buster. But you know me. This isn't the one." Satchel laughed.

"Let's shoot for it."

"Ro, sham, bo?"

"Two out of three?"

"Obviously."

Rock, paper, scissors. A practical solution to almost every man-made problem. Halifax took two of three.

"Sweet," he said in a muted, celebratory tone.

"You're really chapping my ass here, Halifax, but you got me tonight," said Satchel Mathis, grinning and slapping his hands together emphatically. "Treat yourself out... but know this." He stood up to leave. "I will fuck that girl."

The next night he did just that.

Satchel's guiding philosophical principle was that the whole great big mess of the world around us was actually just some astonishingly cruel joke. A hoax perpetrated by a non-existent god. If you didn't think this was funny, he used to say, then the chances are the joke was on you. If something succeeded in piquing and holding his interest he would become a connoisseur nearly overnight. One term he became a tobacco enthusiast; at all times he would have up to ten different packs of cigarettes on him, cloves, milds, menthols, ultra-lights, even Capris. He distributed them unselfishly among his friends; before leaving a room I remember him on many occasions tossing a handful of various cigarettes to a crowd of brothers chanting, "Treat yourselves!" Every term he seemed to have cultivated a new hobby. For a while he substituted different blunt brands for the cigarettes. During this phase he would normally be carrying backwoods, several flavors of phillies, an assortment of alcohol soaked blunt wraps and of course at least one or two of his favorite Dutch Master makes. Another term he purchased a subscription to High Times magazine and became a botanist, secretly growing several cannabis plants in his dorm closet. The idea that at any second a microscopic meteorite might pass through his brain, killing him instantly and without warning, fascinated him. Hundreds of twisted and perverse movies and images found a home on his hard drive. He collected an entire series of them called "faces of death." Among these were grisly animal attacks, accidental suicides, bum fights, and the occasionally bestiality clip. He was never more than five feet from his laptop and kept it hooked up to the Internet at all times to research interesting facts or settle any arguments that arose. The sexual exploits of the man were matched perhaps only by Thalen, the difference being that Thalen was a hunter, Satchel the prey. He was the only guy on campus I knew who routinely received booty calls and at any given time he could be expected to be fucking three or four women. We called him a man-whore; either he had ridiculous stamina, un-believable pillow talk or an enormous cock. I tended to believe all three.

One late afternoon at the senior apartments, Satchel was getting ready to roll a blunt. He had already ground up a significant quantity of weed and now removed an opened pack of Honey-Berry Backwoods from a brown paper lunch bag that served as a carrying case for all of his weed related belongings (inside there were typically a half-dozen types of cigars, a grinder, rolling papers, several rolled up balls of paper containing shake and upwards to one ounce of high-grade, indoor-grown, hydroponic marijuana), and slid one of the cigars from the package which he then ran lengthwise under his nose while sniffing loudly. After unraveling and emptying the guts of the blunt onto my carpet, he licked the inside of the tobacco leaf, filled it with most of the weed that had recently been ground up and re-rolled the leaf, applying substantial pressure where the two ends of the leaf overlapped. After the blunt was prepared and lit he said:

"So…I was fucking this girl last night, right?"

Satchel took a couple of long pulls and exhaled a large cloud of smoke into the room. He sat back on our couch, holding the blunt at arm's length like a cigarette.

"And we're really going at it; I'm fucking the shit out of her. So I flip her over and fuck her doggy style for a while and when I'm ready to cum I pull out my schlong to shoot it on her ass and I shit you not, dude, the jizz flies across the room and hits the goddamn wall."

Satchel's laughter is contagious so when he says this and starts convulsing rapidly and laughing so hard that the weed in his lap is vibrating over the side of the surface he was using to roll the blunt on, it is hard not to do likewise.

"So she says, 'Pretty impressive, Satchel. Why don't you sign your name?' I mean for Christ's sake! Can you believe that shit?"

He burst into another round of laughter.

"I've been calling it 'The Shot Heard around the World.'" Satchel shook his head in disbelief, "I'm just trying to wrap my fucking head around the fact that this chick wanted me to notarize a goddamn jizz stain on the wall!"

"Anyone else's name up there, dude?" Halifax asked.

"Oh, for fuck's sake. There's probably signed cum stains all over that fucking place!"

President Boomer stood in front of the meetings room fireplace waiting for the entire brotherhood to assemble for an impromptu meeting. This was a real meeting during daylight hours and most everyone there was sober. The president shuffled his feet, mentally reviewing his planned words while waiting for a handful of independent conversations to come to an end. I sat next to Halifax on a windowsill with a smoke and a beer, intently monitoring the mood of the room and periodically sending sympathetic looks the president's way. When the room finally settled down Boomer began his speech.

"Alright guys, there are a couple of things to discuss tonight so let me say what I have to say, and we can start running tables. Now, first of all—what you assholes do in your free time is your own business. I'm not going to stand here and tell you that you can't drink during the week. That would be fucking retarded. I'm not going to tell you not to do drugs; that's your own damn business. But you can't do anything to jeopardize the house. Your actions affect the rest of us. If you want to do drugs, do it in your goddamn room, not in the public spaces of the house. We don't need or want that image. After all, that's what Bones Gate is here for."

"What about Randall?" A ball player said, leaning over an empty cup in his hand to spit out a chunk of tobacco juice that had been collecting in his gums.

"I'm getting there, Suds," said Boomer. "Now I know some of you guys are friends with him...and that's fine. I'm not here to tell you who you can and can't be friends with. But at the same time we can't have this kid in the house…under no conditions. He's not a student, he sells drugs, and he puts us all in danger. I don't care what kind of transactions go on between you and him outside of the house, but he can't do business here. Period. That now said I'm reinstating the Judicial Committee. I know, groan all you want, but we need some accountability. Break a house rule and suffer the repercussions. Cleaning duties, fines or for a serious offense—house separation."

You could hear a pin drop as the entire brotherhood began reliving all the stupid shit they had done over the years—the concept of the house holding its members accountable for blacked out shenanigans was an immediately scary thought.

"Look, I know we all do dumb shit," President Boomer said. "I do stupid shit too. I'm not trying to punish drunkenness, but the house needs to be respected. You break a window, you pay for it. It's as simple as that. Okay, that's it guys, let's play Pong."

Back at the senior apartments later that night, Halifax, Mathis and I sat on couches while an animated Randall stood in the center of the room gesticulating wildly and laughing.

"Ever notice at a ball game the announcer over the loudspeaker says to the crowd… 'HEEEEEY YO!!' and everyone in the crowd screams back… 'YEEEEE YO'!!!"

Randall's stuff had somehow been moved into our apartment without any of us realizing it or putting up any objection. He said he'd crash with us for at most a week.

"Hanover Po-Po is on my ass, so I'm just gonna' chill here and be incognito."

I failed to see how that would be possible, dressed as he was, in a Sean John, orange velour jumpsuit. Sensing my skepticism he elaborated:

"These are just my lounging clothes."

At some point during that fall term this kid, who everyone assumed to be a townie by his mannerisms, fashion sense and decidedly non-Dartmouth speech pattern, began hanging out at various houses on campus almost every night there was any activity. This small time hustler surely saw the recreational drug habits of the campus as a way to make a quick buck, and made little attempt to hide the particulars of his business from anyone. Transactions and drug use happened out in the open. In general during this time coke usage seemed to have skyrocketed on campus and became noticeable in public areas of a whole slew of frats. You'd see brothers breaking up lines on the bar or a Pong table. Everyone seemed to have come down with the same nose cold every night. These had become the walking dead among us. Randall was our "patient zero" and the disease spread out across The Green like an infection.

For my own peace of mind I felt compelled to find out how Randall had ended up in our apartment in the first place. First I questioned Mathis, who put the blame entirely on Gunter since Randall's clothes, gear and drugs were all stored in his bedroom. Gunter merely shrugged when I pointed this out and said "who cares how it happened, we're all screwed is the important issue." Cuddles and Hurls both assumed Halifax to be at fault, I assume because of the perception that he and Randall were friends. When I accused Halifax he got angry and replied:

"Actually I didn't really have anything to do with it but I always get blamed for this sort of shit. I don't even have a car dude, how would I get his stuff here? It must have been you and Satchel in that shitty blue Explorer of his."

I let the mystery die there.

Within another few days Randall moved in his girlfriend and suddenly there were eight of us staying in this four bedroom quad. Halifax moved out of the apartment and into the Brothers Room shortly after.

"Randall is paranoid or crazy or both. The kid keeps talking about the cops being after him. You think I'm going to sleep at your place?" Halifax told me.

"What would you suggest as the proper course of action?"

"Just ask him to leave," he said with a shrug.

Randall slept all day, transforming our living room into a mausoleum until sometime after dusk. The lights in the apartment were always off, and the shades always closed; no light got in. But then from about six to six there was constant activity. Unfamiliar people came and went, a cloud of smoke about three feet thick came down from the ceiling, and Randall never ceased to break up lines. He spent hours in negotiations with his girlfriend to get her to front him the cash to get out of Hanover since he had abandoned selling after it became increasingly apparent that he was no longer welcome in the majority of the frats on campus. All his money was tied up in several ounces of coke he stored in one of the back bedrooms.

Our new houseguest was convinced that either Hanover police, or worse, the DEA, could raid the apartment at any minute. This was a confusing time for us all and school once again disappeared off my radar. The classes I was taking weren't particularly worrisome (no science labs), and so I wasn't too concerned about any repercussions for missing seventy percent of my classes. I scrambled for the tests, wrote my papers the night before, and avoided eye contact with the professors if I saw them around campus. Pretty standard Dartmouth fare for me.

"So Randall, give me your timeline for moving out again."

"John," Randall said bluntly.

"Right, right. I forgot. *John*, so okay, same question."

Randall for the past week or so had been insisting that we call him John. He figured the police had gotten wind of a drug dealer on campus named Randall so he asked everyone to call him John, the most common name out there according to him. I didn't quite see the point in continuing this charade when only we were around (we all knew his real name) but I suppose he wanted us to get used to it so we wouldn't slip up when it really mattered.

"That depends. You know anyone who wants yey-piece?"

"Isn't cocaine supposed to sell itself?"

The real conundrum facing us here was Randall's obvious stability issues and our fear over direct confrontation. A fellow Dartmouth student we could deal with easily; he or she would have to conform to the rules of the campus where we were clearly in a position of power. But townies don't conform to the standard Dartmouth hierarchical schematic. *Townies* do whatever the fuck they want and the truth is that I was fucking terrified of what this kid might be capable of. The rest of my roommates were behaving as if they too had sensed things had escalated beyond our control. Cuddles moved out to live with his girlfriend across campus after surprising Randall and his own sweetheart in the midst of an impromptu fellatio session one morning. Hurls, more or less a transient to begin with, basically just decided to avoid the apartment entirely. Everyone expected Halifax to be the one to take action, since he was the assumed culprit. Halifax continued to maintain his innocence and imply that perhaps Mathis (enlisting my help) had been the primary offender. My large gaps of missing time meant I could hardly deny these charges.

Somebody had to step up, I decided, but to do so would require a certain degree of liquid courage—afternoon Ship games were in order. With a few games under my belt I headed for the apartment with one goal on my mind: this invader had to be expelled from our lives at all costs.

What I didn't know at the time was that earlier that afternoon, Gunter, the only original roommate still sleeping at the apartment on a regular basis, had already come to the exact same conclusion after being told in confidence that Satchel had received a call from the Hanover Police requesting (but not quite insisting) that he come in to talk to them. Satchel also confessed to Gunter that he was a notoriously bad liar and in fact almost totally incapable of lying and that if questioned by the Police about Randall's whereabouts, he would have no little choice but to direct them to the apartment. "That is." he told Gunter, "unless he leaves *right* fucking now and then I can tell the cops, '*Hey officers, I don't know where the fuck he is. Are you shitting me?*'"—see with Satchel, as long as he was telling the truth, the truth could be as outlandishly phrased as he liked.

Gunter had no idea why the Hanover police wanted to talk to Satchel—he didn't know if the request was related to Randall or some other trouble Satchel was involved in or even if it was true that the police wanted to talk to him at all—but this late in the game Gunter wasn't taking any sort of chances. He went straight out into the living room and informed Randall, while a blunt was rolled by our guest on the coffee table, that it was fairly likely that the cops were currently on their way to arrest him or would be very shortly and that it would be prudent for him to leave the apartment at his earliest possible convenience—like right *fucking* now.

"Okay, okay. Let me finish rolling this blunt first."

It was actually two blunts that were rolled and smoked before Randall gave any signs of moving from his place on the couch and that was only because his girlfriend had arrived and was banging on the locked door while screaming his name.

"You... really gotta go," said Gunter.

"In a minute. Don't rush me. I'm leaving..."

A screaming match ensued between Randall on one side of the front door and his girlfriend on the other. It was lengthy and went nowhere. She eventually flew off in rage and he returned to the couch where he sat in silence a few feet away from Gunter for almost exactly fifteen minutes before standing up and declaring "Peace, I'm outta' here." He then grabbed his packed bags, which had been placed by Gunter next to the front door and strolled right out of our lives.

It wasn't long after this that I flew into the apartment in a whirl, expecting to find Randall and his girlfriend spooning on a couch. Instead, Halifax sat with a video game controller in his hands and a cigarette dangling from his mouth.

"Where is Randall?"

"Gone," Halifax said, not looking up at me.

"Well, when is he coming back? We gotta solve this issue today."

"He's not coming back, dude. You can thank me for that by the way."

"How the hell did you pull that off?"

"I reminded Satchel that he couldn't tell a lie."

From that point forward the senior apartment was kept locked at all times, although significant damage had already been done both to the physical space and our psychological health. Randall left the campus, and as I hear, vacated the state shortly after.

❄

Waking up one morning, I had absolutely no recollection of the night before. The familiar surroundings of the Brothers Room, along with the hazy hung over state I found myself in, allowed a full sixty seconds of bliss before reality reared its humiliating head.

On the couch next to me, snoring loudly with an Xbox controller in his lap, a fully clothed Halifax was still passed out. Neither of us had intended to spend the night in the house. He roused from his slumber and slowly opened his eyes.

"Awake?"

"Yeah, dude," Halifax lied, his eyes still half closed. "I was checking my eyelids for holes."

He turned away from me to face the couch cushions as if my existence was only something to be momentarily noted.

"Good god, we got wasted last night. What the hell happened to me after that last game?" I genuinely had no inkling of my late night activities.

"Do you mean the one against Gonzo and Queso?"

"We played those two?"

"Twice, dude."

"My head is bumping."

"Do you remember pissing on the house X-Box?"

As a matter of fact I did not.

"I had to tackle your ass," he sat up and chuckled. I could tell he was pleased to be the first person to reveal this to me.

"Does it still work?"

"Well, yeah but...we were all in here playing Halo and you stroll in obviously blacked out. Then you just whip out your cock and start to piss straight up into the air. A nice high arc. You fucker."

"Oh, Jesus," I tried as hard as I could to sound shocked but wasn't.

"We were all yelling at you to stop but you just kept right on pissing, like we weren't even there. When your piss stream got close to the Xbox I had to tackle your ass. So what do you do? You just laid there on the ground and you continued peeing on yourself and we just kept right on playing Halo. It was fucking hilarious"

This was Old Balls. I was now content with getting blacked out drunk and urinating on the most expensive item in the room I passed out in. The drugs were finally gone, and my school work was once again suffering; now it was time to turn my full attention to Ship.

Chapter 12: A Scholarly Tomb

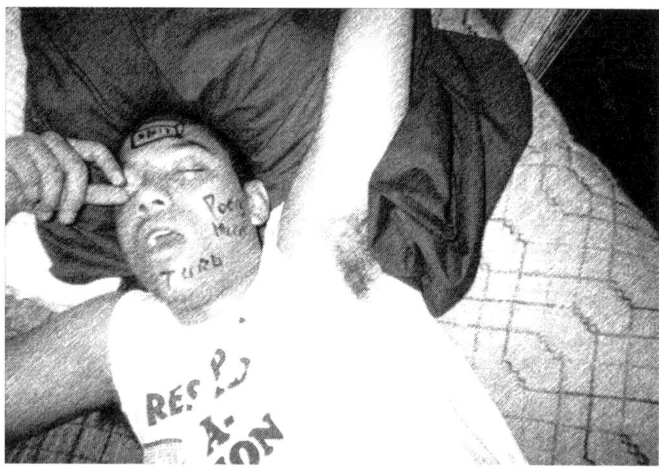

"Dartmouth should be a place where learning is paramount. By this, we mean not just learning by absorbing material in the classroom or mastering skills such as critical reasoning. We also mean learning in the sense of coming to know more about one's self and others, through interactions among students themselves, together with professors, administrators and others."
– *Excerpt from the Summary of the Recommendations Submitted to the Board of Trustees by the Committee on the Student Life Initiative*

re you still in this class?"

This question was posed to me via email by an art history professor who co-taught a cross-curricular elective that was one of my few remaining graduation requirements. I answered: "I think so." Two weeks later I received a second email from this professor, in whose class I thought I was holding a steady C, requesting to meet with me in her office.

On the short walk from Webster Avenue to Carpenter Hall, I started thinking. For a long time I had been convinced that everyone around me was operating under some misguided set of principles and that my own instincts, however absurd they appeared at surface, had set me upon a path to self-enlightenment. I reasoned that if everything I had worked for in my life were destroyed, then my downfall on a Ship table would at least be a noble end. At this point I felt sick to my stomach and hunched over as if to vomit on the sidewalk. This was my last chance at Dartmouth, but I still wasn't attending class with consistency. I resolved right then and there to not drink another drop of alcohol for the rest of the term. *No more Ship!* I would sequester myself in the library until finals were over and thoroughly read and absorb every piece of material listed on my collection of syllabi... even the perennially avoided "recommended reading." But, still bent over in a booting formation, I realized too much time had elapsed. Studying incessantly at this point would only waste an exorbitant amount of time that could be better spent playing Pong. Churning stomach acids caused me to wince as I straightened myself and decided firmly that if this was going to be my final term at Dartmouth, I would enjoy these last few weeks. *I should really be playing Ship right now!*

By the time I had climbed the steps of Carpenter Hall, these thoughts had vanished from my mind.

"I don't know how you expect to pass this course," the professor said curtly after I entered her office and took a seat. "Rarely do I fail a student but your last in-class essay showed almost no effort at all." She handed me a small blue essay book that I vaguely remembered handing in three weeks before. "I gave this back in class a week and a half ago and while it shows you have done the reading, no ideas from class are present in your work."

"I'm a super-senior; I don't really go to class."

She eyed me strangely.

"You're taking a huge chance here. I hope you understand that," she said. "You might want to consider dropping the course."

"That's really not an option if I want to get out of here next term. The final paper is worth forty percent, right?"

She nodded,

"So...I figure I'll start working on it now, put in a ton of work and research, and drop a dime."

This was my brilliant plan that I so eloquently laid out before her.

"Good luck."

It was impossible to stay focused on Ship that night. Barely passing a class was not a new concept and somehow it seemed everything always turned out alright... except for that one time, and that had been a horrible mistake. Finals were rapidly approaching and I sorely needed to ace them. This was going to be a close one.

One class, a history seminar on the Mongol Empire, was an all or nothing sort of deal. The final grade would be almost entirely based on a twenty-five page research paper I had been working on much of the term examining the transference of political institutions from the Mongol-led Golden Horde to the fledgling Russian Empire, at the time called Moscovy. The professor had long ago come to terms with my lack of attendance at her roughly three-hour, twice weekly seminar. She still approved my research topic and helped progress my thesis during the few one-on-one meetings we arranged for office hours. I had done the research but had yet to write the paper. Luckily for me, writing history papers happened to be my specialty.

It would have been an absolute embarrassment if I was in danger of failing my second class, Russian 13, entitled "Vampires, Witches, and Firebirds," which had to be one of the easiest classes I had ever taken at Dartmouth. Yet by this point I needed to actually ace the final exam and paper at the end of the term if I even wanted to pass. The issue here was that while my graded work thus far gave me a legitimate C, attendance was worth a full third of the grade, and by this point in the term I had forgotten where class was even held. About twelve other younger Chi-Gams were also enrolled and if I had just taken the initiative to have one of them sign my name on the attendance sheet passed around every morning in the hundred person lecture room.... Still, just an easy final and a three page fairy-tale due before the end of the term. Shouldn't be a problem.

My third and final course, the art history cross curricular with the overly concerned professor, was the class that worried me the most. I had gotten a D minus on this last test, which meant I had a C, a D minus, and an F (my probable participation grade). To ensure a passing grade I needed to start the final paper a week before it was due which seemed reasonable considering I usually pulled Bs on history papers while writing them in one sitting the night before without actually editing or reading them over before handing them in.

Somewhere along my journey I had irreversibly changed but it was easy to explain away this metamorphosis. It wasn't my fault because you see my genes had given me an addictive personality and my environment a chance to exercise it. Dartmouth had laid infinite options at my feet, but the only path I could discern led directly to Seven Webster. I was on the verge of accepting my lack of ambition and savage complacency as defining character traits, hereditary and too powerful to combat. My flower had withered and died long before it had a chance to blossom.

And then Satchel Mathis was saying: "It's like this gong that goes off in your brain! And that's how you know it's time to pop a Zoloft. After that I'll think about it every five minutes until I finally down one of these little blue boys." He held my prescription bottle in his left hand and flipped one of the tiny bluish pills into the air, acrobatically catching it in his mouth.

"Ahhhhh..." said Mathis.

"I didn't realize you were clinically depressed," I said.

"Oh, for fuck's sake, dude. Look at the world we live in. 9-11, the War on Terror, stolen elections, Iraqi insurgents, the Patriot Act. Shouldn't we all be depressed?"

"When you put it that way..."

Mathis shook the pill bottle in his hand.

"This here is a miracle drug," he said. "Although it does kill your boners. I just pop a Viagra or two to balance it out."

"Where the fuck are you getting Viagra?"

"Dude, anything can be had if you want it badly enough."

"How about E?" I ask.

"Never take Ecstasy and bang, it will never feel the same," Halifax interjected as if he had first hand knowledge of this phenomenon.

"That's horseshit dude, I roll all the time when I fuck." Satchel said laughing.

Somehow this admission failed to surprise me.

❄

On a frenzied night during finals week, Satchel and I parked ourselves in a crowded and unfamiliar computer lab, located in a suspicious part of the library I didn't even know contained computer labs, with a firm resolve to polish off our final papers for the term.

Everything hinged on this night. Every fifteen minutes or so, Satchel and I would take a smoke break on the side of the brand new library addition, Berry Hall, working down a blunt Satchel had prepared inch by inch, and periodically clipping it for "later use" to prolong our high throughout the night. My Vampires, Witches and Firebirds final assignment was written in about an hour—Mathis contributed to the preposterous storyline of this originally penned fairytale almost as much as I did. The tough task was the Mongol history paper—well researched but hastily written. Satchel had nothing at all to contribute on this front and it eventually reached a point where I was almost copy and pasting whole paragraphs from the introduction to the conclusion and changing a few words here or there just to meet the minimum page length requirement.

But as the night drew to a close and the sun began creeping up over the horizon, I finished it, probably with a half hour or so to spare. Satchel was quick to congratulate me.

"Tight, dude! *Tight.* Now send it off!"

I did, via blitzmail, prefacing this excellent accomplishment with:

Dear Professor,
Here is my final paper on the Mongol Empire. I pray you enjoy this scholarly tomb.

I hit send. It wasn't ten seconds before Hurls, working on a term paper of his own next to me in the lab, pointed out I had spelled tome with a B.

❄

Dean Cunningham was probably responsible both for me being accepted and expelled from Dartmouth, indirectly of course, and although I believe she is probably a good person at heart, our interactions were far too ironic to leave out of this comedy of errors.

She called me at the conclusion of my super-senior fall while I was home during Christmas break waiting to receive my grades. This was before the start of the Winter, which would have been my second term in the senior apartments. The first words out of her mouth after I confirmed my identity were: "Your F in Vampires, Witches and Firebirds separates you from the college."

Did I hear that correctly—I had failed the Russian fairy-tales class?

They called it separation but in truth it was expulsion. I immediately thought back on all those lost departed souls—my freshmen year roommate, the feces hermit, Dante, Randall—now *my* number had finally been called and it was time to pay up on all those games of Pong I had played on borrowed time. How could I have let it come to this?

In any event the decision was not yet final so I found myself in a weird limbo. My only chance was what the school called a *Judicial Appeals Hearing* scheduled during the first week of the next term. Neither parent was briefed on the situation. They were convinced that I had reformed my lifestyle after my previous suspension and had no inkling I was so close to separation. I headed back up to school for what they thought was my second to last term, confident that I could get this unjust verdict overturned by the appeals committee.

Cunningham requested to meet with me before the appeal. Not that she really wanted to meet with me, but I suppose this was the standard procedure at the time. I can recall all the agonizing details of this encounter almost verbatim. To this day I wish I had the ability to repossess my body at that exact moment to explain to Cunningham exactly how I felt. As it was, I stumbled through the entire delicate procedure, unconcerned with the enormous ramifications.

I had prepared a letter of appeal for the committee to read before making their decision. Cunningham held this letter in her hand and scanned it very quickly before telling me that it made my point well but didn't exactly allude to the "extenuating circumstances" that would be necessary for a successful verdict.

"Emphasize the depression more," she suggested. "Do you have a note from a specialist?"

My appeals letter had been completed the night before. Winter break had been spent trying to forget the terrible things that were happening to me, not preparing for my defense.

"I haven't seen my therapist in more than a year."

"Have you seen anyone on campus?"

"No."

She squinted her eyes as she stared at me in an attempt to comprehend how exactly I had ended up in the seat before her.

"You're an '03 right?"

I nodded.

"You know, I probably had a hand in your acceptance five years ago."

"You were the Director of Minority Recruitment."

"That's right. Only for that one year though. Before that I was in the admissions office. This was back when the college was just starting to heavily recruit minorities. At the time I saw these students, mostly black males mind you, getting separated before they graduated. The school was letting them in with one hand and tossing them right back out with the other. This was one of the things I wanted to change and I think we've done a pretty good job."

She said this last bit casually but the words stung. Was she mocking me?

"Have you thought about what you're going to do if the appeal doesn't go through?"

Yes, I have. Purchase sniper rifle, ascend Baker Tower, murder freshmen.

"I've been focusing all my energy on this whole appeal process. I'd like to finish up my degree here but when the time comes, I'll start thinking about leaving."

I don't think this answer pleased her because she said, "Well, you might want to think about it now. You might also want to think about how you're going to leave. Do you have a car? You'll need to leave campus within forty-eight hours of the verdict."

"Is it possible to get an extension on that deadline?"

"Well, you'd normally have to be gone by Friday, but I suppose…" she looked up at the ceiling as if calculating some imaginary number, "…we can probably give you until Monday."

"What happens if I don't leave?" I asked indignantly.

"There won't be a police escort if that's what you're hinting at. You're not allowed on campus though. No Winter Carnival and no Green Key. I do, however, see separated students walking around campus from time to time. Don't get caught; that's my advice."

Good luck finding me in the Chi-Gam basement.

"You are going to finish your degree, right?" she asked. When I didn't answer she said, "If the committee asks you what your plans are, it's very important that you tell them you are going to finish your degree. You may have fallen off the bike but you still know how to ride it."

Does she really believe this bullshit coming out of her mouth?

"Umm…right…degree…of course..." was all I could muster. I was no longer thinking about myself or these theoretical future plans I was expected to formulate to even be considered for reinstatement. I was thinking about her and how she'd cease to feel sorry for me the second the clock struck five and it was time to go home.

"What do you think my chances are?"

"It's hard to say, every case is different. It's going to come down to who is on the committee and how they interpret your statement. I told you that I didn't see the extenuating circumstances, but maybe they'll see something I didn't. You never know with these things."

Helpful comment. That was an extraordinarily insightful and helpful fucking comment.

"The fact that I'm so close to graduation must help, no?" I asked. Any hope I had was systematically being drained from my system.

"Well, normally yes…let's see," she studied my transcript looking for some sign of life. Oddly enough I had received all B's and F's. "You have 28 credits…"

" –29," I corrected. "I got a credit for a four on the AP Chemistry exam."

"And you need 35 to graduate... I have to tell you, I've seen the school separate at 34."

"That is absurd."

"How many times can we hear the same story? We're talking about students who have been given not only second chances but also third and sometimes fourth chances. When is enough, enough?"

"I'm confused," I tell her. "What does that have to do with me?"

A few moments of uncomfortable silence followed during which she carefully inspected my file before she glanced at her watch.

"It's time to go upstairs," she eventually said.

In single file, me following behind her with a solemn head bowed down, we walked into the office of Judicial Affairs where I was seated outside a large meeting room, into which Cunningham then disappeared. A few moments later, she poked her head out and told me they were ready for me.

Appeal hearings do not resemble their movie counterparts in any way. College movies from "Animal House" to "Van Wilder" project the same image of a school's nameless academic council being convinced of the ultimately immeasurable potential of the story's hero. The public hearing is documented by campus and local news sources and a large crowd, denied entry to the actual proceedings, waits outside for the verdict, holding signs and reciting sing-along songs like some goddamn hippie anti-war rally. After some heartfelt and heroic words, which amount to "I have bled for four long years at this school. Give me a chance to leave a graduate!" the committee reverses its decision to the cheers of the crowd on the condition that the hero spend the last ten minutes of the film cramming for a cornucopia of classes that he will invariably pass by the slimmest of margins. This isn't quite how it worked in my case.

My own Judicial Action Committee sat on the opposite end of a long oak table facing me; little paper nameplates in front of unfamiliar faces identified two professors (History and French), an admissions officer, and the head of judicial affairs, who wouldn't be voting but functioned as an independent moderator for the appeal. Once I had greeted the faculty and taken my seat next to Dean Cunningham, the head of Judicial Affairs said, "The members of this committee have already read your written statement. Now, before we go into the question and answer portion of the interview, you are permitted to deliver an opening statement if you feel so inclined."

I had prepared some notes highlighting what I saw as the key issues in my defense and produced these folded, handwritten notes from a back pocket to deliver to the room: "I want to tell you a little about my time at Dartmouth to shed some light on the situation I now find myself in. Dartmouth was always first on my list of potential colleges, and as soon as I received word that I had been accepted, I knew I would be spending the next four years of my life in Hanover. My transition to college student was much more tumultuous than I had anticipated. When I arrived on campus, I struggled to fit in and finally found acceptance in one of the major fraternities on campus. It is difficult to gauge when I began to slip into the chronic depression that was to stay with me for over three years, but by junior year the symptoms were impossible to ignore. I slept for the majority of the day, stopped attending classes, had a severe loss of appetite and combated my feelings of depression with alcohol. It was easy to slip into this lifestyle without setting off any warning signs, and no one seemed to notice the funk that I had fallen into. This eventually resulted in my suspension from the school. When I was readmitted to the college I was suddenly doing better in my classes than I had in years, and the anti-depressants I was prescribed reversed many of my previously destructive behaviors. This is apparent in my transcript. However, I soon had what I eventually learned was a relapse. I didn't want to be seen as weak for taking medication so I promptly stopped the treatment. This was at the end of the '03 summer, for which I had received some of my highest marks at the school. That fall was nearly identical to the term that had resulted in my suspension. My academic performance was enough to merit me a second judicial action. As you know, when this happens a second time, a student is automatically expelled. My poor marks that term can be attributed almost entirely to lack of attendance and participation. The work I turned in for the two classes I failed was in the C range; however, when participation was factored in, the professors decided to give me failing marks. I didn't complain or argue at the time, though I could have, and was anxious to plead my case before Dartmouth's deans whom I thought would surely understand the slump I had once again fallen into. Looking back I should have taken a medical leave at the end of the term, erasing those classes from my transcript and focused on mentally preparing myself for the next term. I am a student who has always been genuinely interested in learning. I made some poor decisions and got caught up in an unfamiliar lifestyle that was not compatible with academic success. For the last four years I have lived, breathed and slept Dartmouth, and it would be crushing to be expelled so close to my graduation. This would not have happened to the Chris Knight you accepted into the college five years ago. Dartmouth has made me into who I am today and to kick me out now would go against the principles Dartmouth was originally founded on. The final decision lies with this committee."

Having finished this speech I sat back in my chair and studied each of the faces before me to try to decipher some hint as to how my words had been received. This is what a real lack of control looks like. It's not getting blacked out drunk and acting the fool or embarrassing yourself in front of women on a regular basis. It was having your fate suddenly thrust into the hands of total strangers who don't know anything about you except for what's written on a piece of paper in front of them. If Wheelock's goal had truly been to tame the savage, then with me he seems to have succeeded.

"Why do you think you were unable to go to class?" the admissions officer asked.

"Chronic depression," I replied with zero hesitation. "I would wake up some mornings and just lie in bed, rationalizing that I could miss one more class, that the fact that I had woken up on time was the important issue. I honestly felt that shutting myself up in my room and reviewing the material was a far more effective learning device... for me at least, and so I stayed in bed."

"Didn't you realize that you were in danger of failing by missing so many classes?" the French professor inquired.

"At no point," I told her firmly, "did I consider the possibility that I wouldn't pass these classes as long as I turned in the work and didn't fail the tests. I couldn't bring myself to attend lectures, I don't know why but I gradually just... stopped going again. I attended some classes—maybe a third, but still got zero credit for participation."

"Do you honestly believe that attending a third of your classes constitutes participation?" the historian asked. "As a professor, I find that offensive."

"How can you guarantee that you'll go to class in the future?"

"Well, obviously I can't. The best I can do is promise you. I can pledge that I will show up for every class until I graduate. I was averaging all Cs on graded work without going to class; think of how much better I would do if I actually went."

"So you understand the importance of class?" the French professor asked.

"Absolutely."

Dean Cunningham nudged me. "*The medication...tell them you're back on your medication*," she whispered at a volume I perceived would certainly be audible to the committee.

"Oh yeah, and I started taking my medication again. I stopped during the summer because I didn't feel nearly as crummy anymore. I think I relapsed this fall," I stammered out, embarrassed for having resorted to such a tactic. Could I really use depression as an excuse? Wasn't Satchel right that everyone was depressed at heart? I had to accept that the depression wasn't a factor in what happened. I was. It was I who was different, and who was socially and intellectually deviant and who had now been unmasked to the gatekeepers of higher education. Dartmouth turned out to be the true proving ground for my worth as a person and in the opinion of those present, I had failed this test miserably.

That night of sheer hell waiting for the verdict the following morning was spent up all night in bed, staring at the blank apartment walls around me. What did Kouge ever see in me to begin with? Where were Beetle and Rats and Winston? They were somewhere out in the real world while I was stuck in a past they had all left behind. I was at once reminded of that torturous first night I tried to rush Chi-Gam.

The dean's office has these really comfortable leather chairs in the waiting room that are surrounded by academic magazines and journals of all kinds. I flipped through the latest copy of *Foreign Affairs* as I waited for Cunningham to call me in. Eventually she appeared at the door to her office, made eye contact with me, and then gestured for me to enter. Her body language gave nothing away; she merely smiled and offered me a seat.

"How are you this morning?" she asked, taking a place at her desk facing me.

"Okay," I answered. "A little nervous, but I suppose that's natural."

"Well, I wish I had good news for you." There was no pause, no suspenseful moment. "The committee has decided to uphold your separation." She sighed deeply as if a huge load had been lifted off her shoulders. I sank back defeated.

I always knew I was going to leave Dartmouth eventually, but I never thought it would be empty handed. I was soon to be on the outside, in my twenties, and with no college degree. I suddenly wasn't a student anymore as difficult as that was to believe and soon I wouldn't be a Ship Professional either. A *townie* is what I had become; I was now a fucking *townie*.

She talked for a long time while I thought of nothing but hate. Hatred for everything I had ever come across. Hatred for the school, for my country, for my friends, hatred for Ship. I hated myself at that moment more than I have ever hated anything in my life, and I hated that damn woman sitting in front of me.

She saw none of this, only my blank stare. This was taken for shock I imagine.

"...I know you probably aren't hearing any of this right now..."

And then nothing again. The loud brain buzzing takes over and suddenly I'm sitting on a bench in front of Parkhurst crying my eyes out and smoking a cigarette.

❄

My one-room single at the senior apartments was a prison for a day and a half. It had finally hit me. I was expelled. The majority of this time was spent rolling around awake in bed—allowing for the production and distribution of a substantial amount of sweat.

Where could I go? Home was out of the question. I couldn't show my face to my family or even consider telling them what had happened. With no money, no car and stuck in the middle of New Hampshire, my options were limited. I fantasized about joining the military or the Peace Corps; traveling overseas and dying a mysterious death, the only clue I would leave behind would be a handwritten note pinned to my corpse with the word "Cunningham" written on it. Not a newspaper mogul, nobody would spend any time investigating my last words... especially since I never learned what a dangling participle was. My story would disappear, erased from the memories of those who lived through it. Eventually I suspected there would be no record of me even attending the institution. The house will survive… for a time anyway, but in two or three years the word "Balls" would have no meaning. They may dismantle the ASP in its entirety and stop playing Ship, opting for the more social Shrub. Even worse I could return in four years and find the house playing Beirut. This thought terrified me. I played the guessing game. Where would I be right now if I had gone to say… NYU? The question drove me mad and all I could think about was collecting the shrunken heads of Dartmouth's deans on my mantle, and throwing darts at the stitching surrounding their eyes. How pointless it is to be angry at someone unaware of the pain they have caused you! I kept thinking back to what I told the Academic Committee, "Dartmouth has made me into who I am today." Suicide was beginning to look like a viable option.

This sort of dangerous thinking might have continued indefinitely had I not received a persistent knocking on my door the evening after the appeals hearing.

"Balls! Open up. I know you're in there. *I will break down this door.*"

I already knew my visitor's identity but feigned surprise when I unlocked the door and Halifax strolled past me smoking a cigarette. He sat himself down in front of my computer and began checking blitzmail.

"Where the fuck have you been?" he asked while simultaneously tapping out a series of terse emails.

I sat silent on the bed rocking back and forth with my legs folded in my arms.

He looked at me and frowned. "You don't want to talk about it?" Shaking his head disapprovingly he turned back to my computer. Then as if something came over him he spun back around and from underneath his baseball cap produced a rolled up bag of weed.

"I have some shit to unload, too. Let's get high, dude."

I nodded and he began rolling a blunt on my desk. We smoked and the whole story flowed out. He consoled me as best he could and lavished numerous attacks against the college in my defense, making me feel somewhat like a person again. How thankful I was at that instant to have someone there who could completely understand me.

"Dude…Balls. They're not going to get rid of you that easily."

I knew right then that Halifax would always have my back.

"I'm pretty sure that I've already been expelled."

"Not so fast. You can sue them."

"For what? Failing to provide classes that I felt compelled to attend?"

"You have a disability, dude. Oh yes, you do; don't look at me like that. Depression is recognized as a disability; the school ignored this and shat on you because of it. There are plenty of kids up here like you and me, Balls. The college doesn't even begin to understand the problem."

"I just can't help feeling that maybe this depression has nothing to do with it. I'm sure it didn't help but maybe this is what I really wanted all along."

"That's horseshit dude. The depression has everything to do with it. You can't think clearly up here. Wait until you get home. You will figure this out."

❄

I make no excuses, nor can I adequately explain what happened. The truth of the matter is that I failed out of college. I ask myself how and why this happened over and over. The question still keeps me up at night. A young man who scored in the 98th percentile on his college entrance examination boards with no Kaplan classes or even serious prep work beyond a few home administered practice tests. A student enrolled in all honors and AP classes who finished with near a 100% weighted average. A national merit scholar and AP artist who had never been drunk or done drugs of any sort right up through his senior year of high school. This is your college flunk-out protagonist.

While my experience was not at all typical of students at Dartmouth, the lifestyle I describe is common enough on campus. Not everyone was a Ship Professional, but there were plenty of panarchists, shitbergs, gatesmen, hard-guys and other disaffected students who adopted lifestyles that led them to flirt or fuck with failure. Perhaps mine is an extreme case, I'm willing to admit that.

Not everyone feels compelled to write a Beer Pong themed memoir. Perhaps we should say that despite honest efforts by smart minds, some students will unavoidably fall through the cracks and that I am an example of that and nothing more.

The fraternity is the obvious scapegoat in my story, and certainly the person I became was largely influenced by my environment and the people I surrounded myself with. Balls was the product of the Dartmouth fraternity system but it remains unclear how much responsibility my fraternity specifically has for the emergence of this usurper. Would this have been my fate if I pledged another organization? I have to say I think so. The truth is that I *allowed* this to happen to me and it could have been anywhere. For this reason I can't place one iota of blame on my fraternity or the brothers in the house while I was enrolled or the Greek culture in general that was so pervasive at the school. I just wasn't ready for it and as a result, I abused the house—the house didn't abuse me. My story was sad, yes. Sad and clearly my fault.

The hardcore drinking and games that went along with it that eventually did me in were an inevitable conclusion given Dartmouth's isolation, history, and almost complete lack of other social outlets. With the existence of the CFS houses there was a well-developed delivery system in place that could supply an unlimited amount of beer to the campus in a setting perfectly conducive to social interaction. With Beer Pong we had a highly accessible, campus wide game that was competitive, social and athletic but which invariably lent itself naturally to binge drinking. Then there was the pride of our drinking tradition—a sense that we all had to faithfully carry this torch to earn the distinction of becoming a "real Dartmouth student"—an accession to adulthood by way of a specific brand of debauchery we called "raging". These factors combined in such a way that Dartmouth without Greek organizations and excessive drinking seems unfathomable. We were smart kids, smart kids forced to learn to love to drink. And the vast majority went on to successful lives. Were they the ones who let me down? No, at various points my friends as well as the organization had all tried to help me. But a clown continues to paint his own face, even when all the other freaks think his act has gotten out of hand

The CFS system at Dartmouth will not vanish for a good many years, if ever. Alumni support is strong, and the frats themselves hold too many bargaining chips for the system to be dissolved outright. Ask the average student, male or female, and a healthy majority will tell you that they support the idea of a CFS system at Dartmouth. The alumni will tell you the same, though the specifics of what that idea entails may vary. We want the CFS system to be better but we don't want it to disappear.

I do think there is a mental health issue on college campuses that needs to be addressed. Why are so many students seemingly so willing to suddenly disengage from the larger world around them? You will find a Balls or two in almost every class of pledges in every fraternity on campus. Some made it through, others such as myself didn't. Is it okay to ignore these often troubled kids? Perhaps these Greek Organizations are a unique portal to access this at-risk student population on campus. Administrations and student leaders can and should do more to provide support to these students. Often these dangerous behaviors are hidden within the context of a general sense of group chaos and can be difficult to identify but would exist on campus, fraternities or not. A specially appointed Greek mental health counselor is one idea I've tossed around in my head whereby the administration could help fraternities identify kids who may be suffering from mental illness to provide resources for that student. Parents, usually footing the bill for this whole operation, can and should be involved if necessary. What I think I personally needed most of all was a sign, any sign really, that somebody out there cared enough about me and what I was doing to myself to talk to me about it with a real understanding of the complexities I faced in my everyday life.

At the end of the day the decisions I made were mine alone. The result of my continued infatuation with a fucking drinking game. There was a fire burning deep inside me, a very real feeling that Ship itself was a sacred ritual and that my thirst to be *running table* was not only natural but something that should be continuously cultivated. Nothing purer has ever existed for me. Even ten years later, as I sit here putting the final touches on this swan song to Beer-Pong, my nostalgia for Ship has not abated in the slightest.

The Chi-Gam legend of Balls existed for years after my departure and I think this has something to do with the fact that some part of everyone wanted to be Balls, and there was a sense that what I was doing was foolish and courageous at the same time. Sometimes it seemed that the only thing keeping my peers from sinking to my level was an evolutionary survival instinct. Both an internal and external expectation that you could and would at all costs maintain the persona of someone who had his shit together. I seem to lack this predisposition and suspect that I am not at all alone in this. Balls created himself using the raw materials of Hanover and nobody, especially not me, saw the transformation in time to save him.

My story resembles that of a Stockholm victim. The Pong lifestyle came naturally to me, and I mean the whole wonderful idea of it—the aesthetic principles of the game, its sacred rituals, and intense drinking requirements; the late night binges, missed classes, punishing drunken aftermath and obligatory hangovers—all set against an outlandish academic backdrop. It made sense in some twisted way that by assuming this character of "Balls" in the basement of a Dartmouth fraternity each evening, I was accomplishing something much more meaningful than was perceptible, some substantive life-value that few others could ever pursue. I had an opportunity to try to become the very best at something. A truly elite Pong warrior and the most degenerate kid you've ever met. And all I had to give up in the process was the thing in life which I should have held most dear, my bright future. Balls I now know has always been inside of me and this has been our goal from the beginning. To out-best the Dartmouth kids at what they did worst. This was my fantasy and it had to be believed in totality to continue to perpetrate what amounts to an ongoing charade. A travesty unfolding on a Pong table, hidden from view behind a vainglorious curtain, which had been lifted to reveal nothing more than a scared little boy who had lost the ability and will to engage the outside world in any meaningful way.

As I prepared to leave Dartmouth, I was a broken man.

Epilogue

Nobody responded to that desperate cry of *Three for Ship* that I shrieked from the foyer of the Chi Gamma Epsilon fraternity house in the days following my expulsion. I heard nothing but the pulsating bass of the basement; the house appeared to be deserted. So I shrugged and ventured upstairs to see if anyone shut up in their room might be persuaded to play Ship.

Footsteps could be heard above me on the second floor landing and as I peered over the railing and gazed upwards to see who was stomping about above me, I could see Halifax in a statuesque pose at the top of the third floor landing staring down at me. We locked eyes for a few seconds. He no longer looked stoned.

"I fucked up," I mumbled.

"You sure did," Halifax said, slowly descending the stairs from third to second floor, the specially groomed tourney paddle he practically always carried with him in one hand.

"Why did I do this? Can you explain that to me, James?"

"Look around you, Balls," Halifax said. "This is not real life—it never has been. It's a fucking amusement park. Kids come here to play their pathetic little games, they get their degree and then they piss off. Real life? That's the shit that comes next. Simple as that. This here is just a pit stop to them. But you and I? We're different somehow. We take this shit far too seriously. This is more than a game to us, Balls; it's a way of life. Always fucking remember that."

I thought seriously about his words for a few seconds. This might be as good an explanation as I might ever get out of another human being. We heard the front door to the house open and then close but ignored it.

"Ship on Varsity?"

"Shit yeah. Let's set up."

Whoever had just come in was now making their way upstairs and we were intercepted before reaching the ground floor.

"Balls, Halifax!" a junior nicknamed Queso blurted out while running up the stairs two at a time. "I've been looking for you two everywhere."

"What has your panties in a bunch?" Halifax asked, stopping immediately in his tracks.

"It's the basement," Queso said. "Follow me."

The first thing that struck me as we entered the basement was that the place had not been cleaned since the first party of the term the previous weekend. All eight garbage cans were overflowing with refuse, leaving one with little choice but to throw empty cups and cans to the ground. The basement floor showed this—you could hardly see the tile through the trash. What little floor did peek its way through was caked thick with grime, dirt and other far worse substances. Little clusters of food boxes and dirtied wrappers were also scattered along the lengthy back side bench, the tell tale sign of late night snacking orgies. Every available flat surface was populated by half drunken cups rife with stagnated beer.

And then the unthinkable.

Our premium Pong table, Varsity, had been stripped to its base. The Keystone Light table Halifax and I had spent so much time and energy constructing two terms before was simply gone. We had been playing an extended one-on-one Ship series on the Keystone Table that had begun with the first game ever played on it and continued until that very day. What began as a best of three ballooned into a best of seven, then eleven, then first to sixteen, and so on. The count currently stood at twenty-three wins each. I had never led during the series but had frequently tied.

We circled Varsity's bare base in unison, fingering and stroking the spots where the Keystone table should have been screwed into its wooden fixture.

"This was our baby," Halifax remarked in a barely audible tone.

"Last night…didn't Growler kick the table off the frame? I seem to remember him being really fucking angry about something and kicking the table and it bounced and I guess came loose," I rubbed my forehead in a vain struggle to muster some recollection of the previous night.

Halifax couldn't take his eyes off the spot where our table once rested. "He did. Fucking asshole. He was blacked out… probably doesn't even remember it." His words were staccato. "We're going to find out who took it, Balls."

I thought back on all the epic battles we'd had on that table, imagined the hundreds of games that must have been played during its short life and the painstaking effort Halifax and I had put into its construction. It really did feel like the culminating achievement of our college careers.

Another junior, T-Duct, joined us in basement but before we could prompt him he opened his mouth with information that from his wide eyed expression seemed would trump even ours.

"I have moderately good news and really awful depressing news," he said from the basement entrance and beckoning us with one hand. "Follow me."

T-Duct led us not back upstairs to the foyer but towards the Mud Room and back door to the house. As we passed by the door to our trough I couldn't resist taking a peek inside. Shuddering, I saw that urine and boot had already reached the top of the trough, now in a continuous state of overflow. Our Houseman had put up two strips of duct tape to ward off potentially brave users but apparently someone had already been inebriated enough to take on the challenge as now both strips hung limply from the door-frame. Wondering how long it would be before someone used this contraption again, I turned and trotted after my friends.

The back door to our parking lot was open and my eyes immediately caught sight of the missing table lying in the snow just outside the back entrance. I rushed over happily, not noticing how glum my friends looked, and came upon our wounded Pong-child. Chips of paint and polyurethane were everywhere. The table itself was in fine condition but the wood was completely bare in some parts, mostly on the upper silver portion that we had used spray paint to color.

"Fucking assholes."

This was a devastating blow and I sunk to my knees.

"Who do you think is responsible?" asked Queso. "Bones Gate, maybe?"

"This isn't the work of Bones Gate," said Halifax.

"Most of the chips and shit were on the table when we found it. They're only on the ground because we lifted the table." T-Duct observed.

"I can tell you exactly what happened," Halifax said, stooping down next to me and inspecting the remains of Varsity. "It's the beginning of the term right? Somebody was in the basement late last night when nobody was around. This was probably after two and they most likely were playing alone with the leftovers of our beer…Shrub on Varsity no doubt. Something inspires them to steal a table and to their luck Varsity lifts right off. In all probability if Varsity had actually been screwed down they surely would have moved on to an easier target but as we know, Growler unhinged it last night. So they get it out the back door and are ready to escape when something spooks them. A security van or someone in the parking lot or…whatever."

"Right," I said, continuing his thought. "Then the douchebags take off leaving the table sitting just like this in the snow. We still have seven or so hours until the table is discovered…depending on when these fucks pull this stunt. It was fucking freezing last night. The poly froze and broke off, stripping the paint underneath with it." I shook my head in disgust. "A senseless crime indeed!"

"Let's get this little guy inside." Halifax said after a moment's thought. He knelt down beside me and put his hand on my shoulder.

With deliberate care, Halifax and I solemnly returned our table to its home atop the four wooden support beams geometrically spread out across our basement's floor and under the watchful gaze of Varsity's lights. Minus the mangling of the paint (which had reduced the original design to a garbled mosaic mess) I noted that the table itself wasn't warped in any way and could still be used for Pong—that very instant even. Halifax had apparently come to the same conclusion.

"Might as well go out swinging," he said to me but I was already halfway across the basement, closing in on the keg cave and planning to nab a cold case. There was a brief moment of anxiety as I lifted the lid of our cooler and a wave of relief as I saw a single full thirty pack—ice cold. After pulling this case out of the cooler, I turned to the sound system and clicked off the receiver. The music had started to give me a headache.

When I returned to Varsity I said, "I assumed you meant 'swinging a Pong paddle.'"

"I did," Halifax confirmed.

"What are teams?" asked T-Duct.

"The teams are me versus Balls," Halifax sneered. "One on one, which means you get to sit your ass on the side bench and watch or better yet you can go to your room and jerk off or something."

"Sweet dude," T-Duct said to me cheerfully while nodding towards Halifax.

I removed the stolen Thayer Hall eight ball, shredded my pea coat, and dumped the eight ball in a nearby garbage can.

"Tell me about it." I said. The two juniors said their goodbyes and departed. It was now just Halifax and I in the basement.

We filled our game of Ship and played. At times Halifax seemed in complete control and at other times I couldn't miss his boats if I tried. Seesawing action. Epic Pong play. We were about as evenly matched as Ship opponents get. Boats were mortally wounded and promptly sank. I vomited after my fifth beer. Halifax urinated in the overflowing trough. Before long only a sinkable four boat remained on each side. We rallied back and forth a few more times—each aware that every shot could very well be the last. And then it happened.

Halifax hit an absurdly high return shot, completely off balance and giggling the entire way, but still, miraculously an outside observer might think, connected beautifully, and we both watched breathlessly as the ball tore through the air toward my last vulnerable boat. The ball's deadly trajectory reinforcing for me, one last time, the absolute truth of it all—that in Pong as in life, loss and gain were not mutually exclusive. I saw that it had hit that fateful line above Varsity that faithfully guided balls so consistently and always gracefully into boats.

"Good game, dude," Halifax said, tossing his paddle onto the table as the ball splashed into my deepest cup.

But I wasn't paying attention anymore. I ignored his sardonic grin and hardly noticed as I involuntarily shook his hand when he walked over to greet me. The outcome of a game of Ship seemed to have lost its meaning. I had to stop feeling sorry for myself. Nobody cared about this perpetual and paralyzing self-loathing except for me. I realized that I could get readmitted into Dartmouth. I could graduate, no, I *would* graduate. Nobody had the power to prevent me from doing that—nobody except myself. A beam of light momentarily blinded me, parting the dense gray clouds that obstructed the future and I marveled at my life and my friend and our simple but beautiful game. I smiled and pulled our Ping Pong ball out of its cup, shaking the beer off like a wet dog.

Halifax nodded, and although it didn't need to be said, confirmed the inevitable.

"Best two out of three?"

About the Author

Six months after being separated from Dartmouth, Chris Knight appealed his expulsion directly to the Dean of the College, citing the "extenuating circumstances" that he had failed to present to the academic committee who had overseen his first appeal. The decision was reversed and Knight was cleared to enroll in classes the following term. Following the winter of 2005, seven years after first being accepted into the school, Chris Knight left Dartmouth College for good—a degree in hand.

Acknowledgments

There are many people who have helped me get to this point, but none more so than my mother, Valerie, who has always been my biggest unconditional supporter. I would like to acknowledge my two editors, David Hornbuckle and Meghan McDevitt, for spending long hours whipping the manuscript into shape over the past six months and for providing great feedback and advice as I prepared to self-publish. I'd also like to thank Sarah, my spectacular cover artist and one of my oldest friends. Sarah has been a rock of constant and much needed encouragement from the earliest days to the last few weeks.

Dartmouth College never truly gave up on me the way I gave up on it, and I owe the school a massive debt for allowing me to finish my degree. The Chi Gamma Epsilon brothers deserve some recognition too for never offering anything but positive thoughts. Thank you also to the Dartmouth community at large for giving this story a chance to breathe and for hopefully not being too upset that I decided to put myself and our beloved school "out there" in this fashion; in some way this story belongs to all of us.

My final thanks are reserved for the Pong Gods.

—Crispus Knight

13870995R00129

Made in the USA
San Bernardino, CA
07 August 2014